USIA

USIA

Public Diplomacy in the Computer Age

Allen C. Hansen

PRAEGER SPECIAL STUDIES • PRAEGER SCIENTIFIC

New York • Philadelphia • Eastbourne, UK
Toronto • Hong Kong • Tokyo • Sydney

Library of Congress Cataloging in Publication Data

Hansen, Allen C.
  USIA, public diplomacy in the computer age.

  Bibliography: p.
  Includes index.
  1. United States. International Communication Agency.
2. United States—Relations—Foreign countries. 3. United
States—Foreign relations administration. I. Title.
II. Title: U.S.I.A., public diplomacy in the computer age.
E840.2.H36 1984   327.73   83-24515
ISBN 0-03-063286-2 (alk. paper)

Published in 1984 by Praeger Publishers
CBS Educational and Professional Publishing
a Division of CBS Inc.
521 Fifth Avenue, New York, NY 10175 USA

456789 052 987654321

Printed in the United States of America
on acid-free paper

To Charmaine

Titus Hoyt said, "No, man. We just can't have all you boys talking about pictures all the time. I will have to get some propaganda for you boys."

Boyee said, "Mr. Titus Hoyt, what we want with propaganda? Is a German thing."

Titus Hoyt smiled. "That is not the proper meaning of the word, boy. I am using the word in its proper meaning. Is education, boy, that makes me know things like that."

from *Miguel Street*
by V. A. Naipaul

"Talk my talk, man
And jump my way,
Else I ain't listen,
To nothing you say."
　　—Trinidadian calypso.

PREFACE

The mission of U.S. public diplomacy has often been debated, but any review of the legislation that created the U.S. Information Agency (USIA) and, later, the International Communication Agency (ICA), as well as presidential directives and memoranda, clearly shows that the prime objective of U.S. public diplomacy has always been support of U.S. foreign policy, or, in other words, political advocacy.

USIA, which was created in 1953, became the "International Communication Agency" on April 1, 1978. That this was April Fools' Day caused some comment, but more serious criticism ensued. The new organization merged the informational and cultural exchange activities of USIA and the educational and cultural exchange programs of the U.S. Department of State. From its inception the acronym "ICA" was criticized because of possible confusion with the letters "CIA," as was the name of the new organization because it did not clearly signify that the "International Communication Agency" was a U.S. government entity. Use of the acronym "USICA" to identify ICA with the United States was only partially successful.

As part of the Fiscal Year 1982 authorization bill signed by President Ronald Reagan August 24, 1982, the name of America's public diplomacy agency again became USIA. At the same time, USIA's 202 overseas posts in 124 countries also became known once again as offices of the United States Information Service, or USIS. "USIS," used for nearly 25 years prior to the creation of ICA in 1978, had become a well-known and highly respected acronym throughout many parts of the world. Thus, many public diplomats, and many individuals of differing nationalities who had long utilized the cultural, educational, and informational services of USIA, welcomed back those familiar letters. A minority would have preferred to stay with "USICA," changing the name of ICA to "U.S. Information and Cultural Agency," a more accurate description of the range of public diplomacy activities in which USIA engages. It appears, however, that USIA and USIS are now here to stay.

When the Department of State's educational and cultural exchange activities came under the administration of the new ICA, there was a great deal of hand-wringing and soul-searching in government circles and academia as to whether tendentious information programs and "pure culture" could exist together in the same organization. The fact is, however, that they had coexisted for many years. USIA officials in American embassies and consulates, in their roles as public affairs officers and cultural affairs officers, were the ones who, since USIA was born in 1953, had always administered the U.S. government's major educational and cultural exchange programs abroad. In many instances the cultural affairs officer, also known as the cultural attaché, is the chairman of the binational Fulbright Commission in his country of assignment. The Fulbright Commissions supervise academic programs that to an admirable degree maintain their independence from political influences, as the founders of the Fulbright Program intended.

For an organization whose primary goal is political advocacy to conduct nonpolitical educational and cultural exchange programs may seem inconsistent. The explanation lies in the fact that, while USIA's *major mission* is support for U.S. foreign policy, this is not its *only mission*. Furthermore, it is well recognized that the indirect benefits of exposing key foreign leaders and potential leaders to U.S. education and culture can, in the long term, end up being politically significant (as well as being significant in other ways), even though a particular grant or program was not specifically designed for political purposes.

There will always be differing views as to how the foreign policy goals of the U.S. government can best be advanced by public diplomacy, as well as questions about USIA's tactics, strategy, and organization. In addressing these questions, the comments and ideas presented in the pages that follow are based on more than 25 years of experience in public diplomacy, including 18 years in a variety of jobs in eight countries. In addition, three Washington assignments provided me with an intimate view of USIA's headquarters bureaucracy Although more than a quarter of a century can be considered a rather lengthy period of time, public diplomacy is a relatively new profession, the term itself having been invented in the mid-1960s and still not commonly used. It is my contention, therefore, that public diplomats are pioneers in a new field. And in a world that continues to shrink in time and space as communications and space technology gallop ahead, public diplomacy is of growing importance.

While political advocacy remains the major goal of U.S. public diplomacy today's rapid technological changes in communications systems, particularly with respect to satellites and computers, require the creation of new public diplomacy techniques that can meet the conditions created by these changes, and can utilize the new technologies for more efficient global communications.

The developed world today is experiencing a new phenomenon—the computer culture. Computers are increasingly involved in almost all human activity in the developed countries, while satellite systems have made distances irrelevant in terms of communication both within and between these countries. This development is seen by some as being as historically important as the development of printing in its effect on human thought and actions. But while the *developed* countries have become permeated with these new technologies, and while these new inventions have the potential to propel *developing* societies forward at an accelerated pace, this potential has not yet been realized. On the contrary, the computer culture of the developed world has widened even further the gap between the developed countries and developing societies.

The dramatic, historically significant development of communication satellites and computers opens tremendous new opportunities for those who are engaged in global, cross-cultural communications. To take advantage of the new communications technology, however, today's public diplomats must adopt new patterns of thought and action a challenge difficult enough for individuals, and even more difficult for government bureaucracies, which tend to be conservative—even bureaucracies as communications conscious and globally oriented as USIA. However, it is in this context that I and others, with very limited success to date, advocate greater use by USIA of the new technologies in order to support the prime U.S. foreign policy goals of a more peaceful, productive, and stable world. Why this should be done, and how this can be done, is a major thesis of this book. A brief glance is also given to the public diplomacy efforts of other nations, with particular emphasis on the Soviet Union, the chief political, ideological, and economic competitor of the United States, and one whose goals and tactics differ so greatly from our own.

In discussing the internal operations of USIA, such topics are covered as the need for more efficient internal administration, greater attention to personnel matters, the value of good labor-management relations, and the need to recognize the contribution and special needs of women and minorities, for, no matter how sophisticated communications technology becomes, the professionalism and personalities of the public diplomats who direct American public diplomacy abroad determines more than anything else the success or failure of USIA programs. Other subjects discussed range from the advantages of consolidating USIA Washington operations to the role of the Voice of America, an entity of USIA better known at home and overseas than its parent organization.

It is my hope that this book will provide timely information on USIA that has not been available in any single, convenient form in recent years. It is intended to serve students and scholars, as well as those among the general public, interested in the work of America's public diplomacy agency. If it brings to the attention of U.S. government leaders not directly involved in public diplomacy the importance of this type of activity in achieving U.S. foreign policy objectives, as well as some of its strengths and weaknesses, it will have achieved one of its major purposes. Hopefully, USIA's current leaders, who are in a position to remedy some of the administrative and program defects that I believe need remedying, will consider at least some of the recommendations that are made.

The time is propitious for a thorough analysis of American public diplomacy. No such analysis has been undertaken, except in the context of congressional hearings or governmental reports, for more than a decade. In 1970, *The Case for Reappraisal of U.S. Overseas Information Programs* was published by Praeger in its Special Studies in International Politics and Special Affairs. Edited by Edward L. Bernays and Burnet Hershey, it incorporated Congressman Dante Fascell's hearings report, "The Future of U.S. Public Diplomacy." Praeger's 1973 volume, *Public Diplomacy and Political Change*, by Gregory Henderson, was a different type of book. The last major attempt by a single, authoritative individual to examine USIA was Thomas C. Sorensen's book, *THE WORD WAR, The Story of American Propaganda*, published in 1968.

I would like to thank Dr. Arlene Jaquette, a former professor of expository writing who has begun a new career as a public diplomat and was kind enough to read the first draft of my manuscript, offering many valuable suggestions; my editor at Praeger, Betsy N. Brown, whose patience, understanding and good advice were also exceedingly helpful in completing this project; the Office of Research of USIA whose reports were so useful to me, particularly those of Social Science Analyst Hugh W. Olds, Jr., and *Problems of Communism* editor Paul A. Smith, who agreed to read the final manuscript.

Work on the manuscript was begun during a Washington assignment in 1981. It was completed in Islamabad early in 1983.

Allen C. Hansen

CONTENTS

USIA

1

PUBLIC DIPLOMACY
AND
PROPAGANDA

When, early in their careers, Anwar Sadat, Valery Giscard d'Estaing, and Helmut Schmidt, among many other world leaders, visited the United States under the educational exchange programs of the United States government, U.S. public diplomacy was at work. When Latin Americans viewed a film called *The Trip* on their local television stations depicting the dangers to all societies, including their own, of illegal narcotics trafficking, they were watching a product made by USIA and distributed by U.S. public diplomats. When American astronauts landed on the moon for the first time, it was the Voice of America, the radio service of USIA, that carried Neil Armstrong's words to millions here on earth.

When a student or a scholar in a developing country conducts research in an American center in his capital city, he is utilizing one of the popular services provided by U.S. public diplomats in his country. When a newspaper correspondent asks for clarification of a statement allegedly made by a high-ranking U.S. official, he contacts the U.S. embassy's press attaché – a U.S. public diplomat. When a student or an educator in a country where USIS operates wants to know more about U.S. education in general or a specific college or university program in the United States, it may be a U.S. public diplomat, or someone on his staff, to whom such a query can best be directed.

When a U.S. performing artist is on a foreign tour sponsored by the U.S. government, U.S. public diplomats in the cities he visits will publicize the tour and make the arrangements for his performances. When a need is perceived to publish a pamphlet in a particular country or group of countries on a subject of binational interest, U.S. public diplomats may be the ones who plan such a pamphlet, and arrange its publication and distribution. These are but a few of the various activities with which the practitioners of public diplomacy become involved, but they demonstrate the scope and variety of modern public diplomacy.

Elmer Staats, former comptroller general of the United States, once described public diplomacy as being "made up of international information, education, and cultural relations." His report to the Congress of July 23, 1979, entitled *The Public Diplomacy of Other Countries: Implications for the United States*, went slightly further: "Public diplomacy (is) international communication, cultural and educational activities in which 'the public' is involved," and he added, "public diplomacy has become the principal instrument of foreign policy for the U.S. and other nations."

According to a Library of Congress study of U.S. international and cultural programs and activities prepared for the Committee on Foreign Relations of the U.S. Senate, the term "public diplomacy" was first used in 1965 by Dean Edmund Gullion of the Fletcher School of Law and Diplomacy at Tufts University. It was created with the establishment at Fletcher of the Edward R. Murrow Center of Public Diplomacy. In the Fletcher School catalog of Tufts University, public diplomacy is defined as the "cause and effect of public attitudes and opinions which influence the formulation and execution of foreign policy."

Pollster Daniel Yankelovich, in *Making Public Diplomacy Work Through Social Science*, noted that for him public diplomacy is essentially the creation of dialogue, writing:

> As contrasted with traditional diplomacy, which develops relations between governments, public diplomacy establishes between societies a dialogue on issues of mutual concern. Its goal is to improve perceptions and understanding between the people of the United States and the people of other countries.

Dialogue is certainly an essential element of public diplomacy. ICA's first director, John Reinhardt, once wrote that he defines public diplomacy as "those efforts through which the United States Government enters the international marketplace of ideas."

Former Deputy Secretary of State Warren Christopher demonstrated his recognition of the importance of public diplomacy during congressional hearings held prior to the establishment of ICA when he said that "public diplomacy complements and reenforces traditional diplomacy by seeking to communicate with peoples of other nations." While not defining public diplomacy per se, he said that it has four purposes:

> . . . first, to insure that other nations more accurately understand this country, its values, institutions, and policies.
>
> Second, to insure that our understanding of other nations and of our interrelationship with them is informed and accurate.
>
> Third, to insure that this mutual understanding is bolstered by collaborative individual and institutional relationships across cultural lines.
>
> Fourth, to insure that as the international policies of our Government are formed, we take into account the values, interests, and priorities of publics abroad.

He also commented on the importance of dialogue in public diplomacy, for he added that "in particular, it seeks to establish a dialogue with those who are importantly involved now or are likely to be involved in the formulation and discussion of the attitudes and ideas which affect the U.S."

The fact that public diplomacy is a relatively new term results in its exact meaning being somewhat elusive. Now that the Murrow Center has been in business for a number of years, it has tackled the job of defining public diplomacy in a more detailed fashion, as seen in these excerpts from the center's brochure:

> Public diplomacy . . . deals with the influence of public attitudes on the formation and execution of foreign policies. It encompasses dimensions of international relations beyond traditional diplomacy; the cultivation by governments of public opinion in other countries; the interaction of private groups and interests in one country with those in another; the reporting of foreign affairs and its impact on policy; communication between those whose job is communication, as between diplomats and foreign correspondents; and the processes of intercultural communications.
>
> Central to public diplomacy is the transnational flow of information and ideas.

The Murrow Center also helps explain what public diplomacy entails by mentioning that the courses it offers on this subject include the effects of technological developments in television, satellite communications, data and image storage and transmission, and publishing methods. Special attention is given in Murrow Center studies to "government information programs, educational and cultural exchange, and the communications aspects of travel, international business, and the foreign programs of labor unions, churches, universities, foundations, and international organizations."

When veteran congressman Dante Fascell, long a student of public diplomacy and one who knows better than most the meaning and importance of this twentieth-century term, was chairman of a congressional subcommittee that held hearings a few years ago on "Public Diplomacy and the Future," he commented that a better understanding was needed *in the Congress* as to what "the mission of public diplomacy is." If U.S. lawmakers, whose activities interact daily with foreign relations, need a better understanding of public diplomacy, how much greater is the ignorance of public diplomacy and its importance beyond the halls of Congress!

That public diplomacy, however one defines it, is of growing importance appears to be a generally accepted truth among those who have followed its development. Recognition of its importance has not, however, spread beyond its actual practitioners and those relatively few in government and academia who have watched its growth with interest. This may be due to the normal lag in attitudinal changes. Nor have restrictions on distribution of USIA products within the United States helped to educate the American public on the value of public diplomacy in defending and furthering U.S. interests.

"Public diplomacy" as a conceptual phrase is not yet two decades old, assuming it was originated by Dean Gullion as recently as 1965. Certainly it is only now beginning to be popularized. If proof is needed, this can easily be ascertained by looking in almost any library card catalog for the term "public diplomacy." In July, 1982, a search of the Library of Congress computerized card catalog brought forth only four titles containing the term "public diplomacy."

It could be argued, of course, with considerable justification that "public diplomacy" is simply old wine in a new bottle. After all, there is nothing new about "psychological warfare," a phenomenon as closely related to peacetime public diplomacy as warfare is to traditional diplomacy. Government information programs have been in existence for a long time. However, what make public diplomacy today distinct and more important than ever before are the explosion of communications technology and the recent dramatic growth of international economic interdependency.

Although recognition of the importance of public diplomacy has not grown dramatically, it has grown steadily. For example, when President Eisenhower was in the White House, he called what is today encompassed by "public diplomacy" the "P" factor—the psychological factor—and he indicated that it warranted consideration along with the military, political, and economic factors.

Some years ago, the Brookings Institution issued a report that recommended the creation of a Department of Foreign Affairs in which there would be three divisions: one for political diplomacy, one for economic diplomacy, and one for public diplomacy. More recently, the controversial Stanton Commission report suggested, in so many words, that public diplomacy deserves near-equal billing with traditional diplomacy. And finally, in the 1980 report of the United States Advisory Commission on Public Diplomacy, the chairman of the commission at the time, Professor Olin Robison, president of Middlebury College, stated: "USICA, as the government's principal resource in public diplomacy, is not a luxury item in the federal budget. It is indispensable to our national security and warrants far more than existing inadequate levels of support. Public diplomacy is as important to the national interest as is military preparedness."

At one time the guiding phrase of USIA was, "Truth is our greatest weapon." This phrase inspired Wilson Dizard, who wrote the first of the relatively few books that have been written about the U.S. government's public diplomacy machinery, to entitle his book, "The Strategy of Truth." Somewhat the same idea was expressed when former USIA Director Edward R. Murrow said of USIA, "Our aim is not to close men's minds, but to open them." In the same vein is the thought, expressed years ago, that for USIA to be truthful and accurate when discussing the United States the agency must show "warts and all."

In 1982 USIA Director Charles Z. Wick initiated "Project Truth"— though this was not on the grand scale of the broad, philosophical approach that shaped the agency's earlier operations and that continues to this day. The new "Project Truth" has the narrower goal of countering and exposing Soviet propaganda themes and techniques. The Soviet Union has been caught not infrequently utilizing forged documents, rumors, and insinuations as well as altered facts and outright lies in its propaganda efforts. Still, the adherence on the part of U.S. public diplomats to the Murrow ideal of depicting U.S. society as truthfully as possible, thus as realistically as possible, prevails within USIA today. No one is more conscious of this than the managers of the Voice of America who, despite the controversies that periodically develop about VOA broadcasts, know full well that without accuracy in their reporting of the news their reliability will diminish, along with their audiences.

So determined to follow the straight and narrow path have been U.S. practitioners of public diplomacy that they have always expressed a certain amount of concern with the attribution of information materials they create and/or distribute. At one time the policy was to produce and distribute only material that, if not attributed, was "attributable." This was changed later to a virtual decree that everything produced by USIA had to be attributed—although in practice this is not always possible since once an item of information is used by someone else, as often happens, there is no longer any means for assuring that it will be acknowledged as originally emanating from U.S. public diplomacy sources. The fact is that today USIA conducts all of its activities in as open a fashion as possible. There are no secrets, and no reason for any, with regard to USIA programs.

Propaganda is sometimes described as being of three kinds—black, grey, and white. Black propaganda is the attribution of allegations, which may or may not be true, to a third party. The validity and accuracy of the allegations are immaterial. Grey propaganda consists of allegations of questionable validity and where attribution to the source is consciously avoided. White propaganda, or what one might call "legitimate propaganda," can be described as "the spreading of true or accurate information for what one considers a worthy cause." USIA officials would argue that only by this last definition can USIA be considered "a propaganda agency."

In addressing the Boston World Affairs Council in 1979, ICA Director John Reinhardt said that "attempting to 'sway' public opinion in other countries . . . not a new idea in itself . . . has come to be known as 'propaganda' . . . in the unfortunately pejorative connotation which the word acquired through the devious Dr. Goebbels, and others, like Tokyo Rose." He added that, in any case, the connotation of the word propaganda "hardly fits any definition of diplomacy with which most Americans could live."

He went on to say, "In a purely dictionary sense, public diplomacy embraces some of the aspects of propaganda—the spreading of ideas and information for the purpose of helping an institution or a cause. Certainly this is one part of the process of international communication as we know it today; obviously, we must convey ideas to others—in our case ideas meant to create true, not false, images."

When John F. Kennedy was in the White House, he sent a memo to the director of the USIA on January 25, 1963, which stated that USIA staffs abroad would be responsible "for the conduct of overt public information, public relations, and cultural activities" that were intended "to inform or influence foreign public opinion." Some 15 years later, President Jimmy Carter directed the new public diplomacy agency, ICA, to give foreign peoples "the best possible understanding of our policies and intentions, and sufficient information about American society and culture to comprehend why we have chosen certain policies over others." He also directed that "the Agency will undertake no activities which are covert, manipulative, or propagandistic."

In President Carter's view, judging from the above, propaganda is verboten. This will not, of course, end the discussion of whether USIA fits the description of a propaganda agency. The U.S. taxpayer must get some return on his investment in U.S. public diplomacy activities, and that return will continue to be described by many persons as being the result of "propaganda." To influence foreign public opinion has always been, and will always be, a major goal of the U.S. public diplomat, as spelled out in President Kennedy's memo to the USIA director and elsewhere. The return on the taxpayer's investment accrues in better understanding by other nations of U.S. policies and actions, and of the culture out of which those policies and actions spring.

Among the things U.S. public diplomacy leaders have learned over the years is that their programs and activities must be honest to be credible—there are times when they must show "warts and all" if their all-important believability is to be maintained.

U.S. public diplomats may not be "propagandists" by Webster's strict definition of that term, which must have been what President Carter had in mind, but in an historic context, and graded "black, grey, and white," with the latter applicable to U.S. public diplomacy, the propaganda label is not completely inappropriate. In many aspects of public diplomacy, however, whether U.S. officials are acting as "propagandists" or not depends on one's point of view.

2

ORGANIZATION
AND
GEOGRAPHY

It may seem strange to discuss how an agency should be organized before discussing in greater depth its special mission (which is left for the next chapter), particularly since organizational structure is only one element, albeit a major one, that helps determine effectiveness. But given the global reach of U.S. public diplomacy and its attempts to communicate with so many different cultures, the relationship between the internal organization of USIA and world geography is vitally important.

In a world of rapid technological change, frequent changes in the interests and priorities of the United States and other nations, and somewhat slower changes in social and economic events, cultural geography is a constant. It is also a constant in a communications effort that deals with social, economic, political, military, educational, and cultural affairs in varying degrees, at varying times. But, most important, in relaying messages from one person to another and particularly, from one culture to another, if the proposed recipient of your message isn't tuned in, isn't listening or is listening to someone else at the time, can't understand your lingo or is simply not interested in what you have to say, then your message falls on deaf ears—regardless of how loud you scream.

"It is the last three feet that count," as Ed Murrow once said. A message sent to another culture will not cross those last three feet, however, unless the sender understands the intended receiver well enough to know what tunes him in, an understanding that comes only with knowledge about a particular culture. Thus, to be most effective, USIA must be organized in a manner that provides ready access to such knowledge and enables decisions to be based on that knowledge.

Another reason for giving prominence to USIA's internal organization is that U.S. public diplomats are still "digesting" some of the major changes brought about, first, with the establishment of ICA in 1978, and, secondly, with the changes initiated under the Reagan administration when President Reagan's long-time friend and fellow Californian, Charles Z. Wick, took over the directorship of USIA. Wick proved to be highly controversial in his dynamic, some would say "novel," approach to public diplomacy. At the same time he made the agency much more visible to the American public than did most of his predecessors and ably defended its importance at congressional hearings, successfully fending off what could have been far more drastic budget cuts in the early Reagan years.

In the mid-1970s there was a great deal of discussion about how the U.S. public diplomacy effort should be organized, which led to the Stanton Commission report and others, and finally, the establishment of the new public diplomacy agency, ICA. The main decision of the president and the U.S. Congress at that time was to put all major public diplomacy programs of the U.S. government into one organization. How that one organization organized itself internally was left, apparently, to its first director, John Reinhardt. Thus, the first few years of ICA's existence became a period of experimentation—a "shake-down cruise" in naval parlance. In a way, U.S. public diplomats are still on that cruise.

One of the first things John Reinhardt did, intentionally or not, was to downgrade the role of the geographic area directors. For years USIA had operated through more than a dozen "assistant directors." There were, in the 1960s, six assistant directors in charge of agency programs in six geographic areas (later reduced to five); four assistant directors responsible for each of the four media services—broadcasting (the Voice of America); Press and Publications; the Motion Picture and Television Service; and the Information Center Service (responsible for book translations and publication, English teaching programs, libraries, binational centers and exhibits). A number of others in the USIA hierarchy, some of whom had far smaller staffs and responsibilities, were also "assistant directors" of the agency. There were assistant directors for administration, personnel, the Office of Equal Employment Opportunity, research, and public information about the agency's operations.

The large number of assistant directors was administratively impractical and hardly logical, especially when one compares, for example, the responsibilities of an assistant director in charge of all of the agency's programs in a large geographic area with those of an assistant director responsible solely for providing personnel services within the agency. With the exception of the head of the Voice of America, all other media assistant directors headed primarily servicing units—units that processed and filled the information requests of the overseas posts under the jurisdiction of the area assistant directors.

There was good reason, then to abolish this phalanx of assistant directors. In the new organization, in addition to a deputy director for the agency, four "associate directors" were established, all of whom reported directly to the head of the agency; one for broadcasting (the VOA director); one for "programs," to whom the various other media directors now reported; an associate director for educational and cultural affairs, considered to be a requisite since educational and cultural exchange programs were, for the first time, removed from the Department of State and placed within ICA; and an associate director for management, who, in addition to being responsible for the administration of the agency, became the administrative superior of the director of personnel, a logical chain of command though in practice the politics of personnel administration often overrules logic. Unfortunately, while this system had some advantageous results, such as the elimination of the unwieldy and impractical phalanx of assistant directors, from one point of view the baby was thrown out with the bathwater.[1]

The nature of international broadcasting, which, unlike other media services, delivers a worldwide product across national boundaries directly from Washington, the size and importance of the Voice of America, and the fact that the VOA is much better known both within and without the United States than its parent agency all suggest that this important and unique unit deserves to be headed by a person who reports directly to the director of USIA. A similar case can be made for the associate director for educational and cultural affairs, though for different reasons. The programs under the jurisdiction of his office are closely related to American academic institutions, involve relationships with U.S. and foreign entities built up over the many years when they were supervised by the Department of State, and have a formidable constituency in Congress and academia concerned about how these programs fare. Thus it can easily be argued that the official responsible for the Office of Educational and Cultural Affairs should occupy a position equal to that of other associate directors and, like them, should enjoy direct and immediate access to USIA's overall director.

The associate director for programs, whose various offices, for the most part, fill field requests for information and cultural services, and the associate director for management, who, it is presumed, carries out the management instructions of the head of the agency and provides the internal logistical support to keep the agency functioning efficiently, need not necessarily be on a par with those responsible for planning and executing the agency's mission.

The downgrading of the influence and responsibility of the various geographic area offices, as occurred in the early days of ICA, was unfortunate. While lip service was often paid under the Reinhardt administration to the importance of the area offices, and while they were held responsible for the agency's field programs under both the Reinhardt and Wick administrations, the fact is that USIA's organization chart puts them where they fell in practice—at the bottom—or at least below the associate directors.

When James Mosel, professor of psychology at George Washington University, addressed a seminar of USIA Officers at American University February 23, 1976, he noted that, unless messages are tuned to local interests, audiences are apt to evade, distort, or simply forget many of them, especially those emanating from outside their own culture. One must understand local cultures in order to tailor incoming messages to local needs and interests. One of the most important roles of geographic area offices in Washington and individual USIS offices overseas is to understand, and interpret, local cultures. No matter how technologically efficient our communications become, the results depend, in the final analysis, on knowledge of the local culture.

This essential requirement of knowing your audience if your message is to be received makes geographic area directors the key Washington-based USIA officials in assuring that public diplomacy programs are effective. They are recognized experts on their geographic areas, having studied, lived, and worked in those areas before becoming area directors. They are, or should be, the alter egos of the agency's director—his "eyes and ears" when they travel in their areas, as they frequently do, and this is exactly how USIA's first director, Theodore C. Streibert, is said to have described his geographic area directors. For these reasons, they should be at the top of the hierarchy in the internal organization of USIA.

The importance of the geographical approach is also seen in recent agency history involving the Office of Educational and Cultural Exchanges (designated "E" in 1982) and USIA's Office of Research (designated "P/R"). When the former was in the Department of State and joined USIA to become ICA in 1978, it was originally believed that those who supervised these programs could be attached to the geographic area offices, or at least be represented in those offices. (When these activities were conducted by the State Department prior to the creation of ICA, geographical divisions existed among the offices responsible for educational and cultural exchanges.) It soon became apparent, however, that the exchanges representatives could not serve both the Exchanges Office and the Area Office, so they were later placed in the Exchanges Office, though primarily with a functional rather than a geographical breakdown in responsibilities. Ironically, at the same time that the Exchanges Office was giving up its geographical divisions in favor of functional divisions, the research office of the agency had had enough of operating under functional divisions and returned to the type of organization it had operated with years earlier—using geographic divisions of responsibility.

Even if USIA were to maintain its four associate directors as currently organized, but changed the five area directors into associate directors of equal or near-equal rank, providing them with their old powers and responsibilities, this would be a move welcomed by many senior Foreign Service officers of the agency, based on past experience, and particularly the experience since 1978.

An example of an incident that might not have occurred if area directors had more authority and responsibility occurred in the latter days of John Reinhardt's administration of ICA. The decision was made in Washington that certain ICA overseas posts would make a special effort in the field of disarmament, a subject that has long interested the U.S. government and that periodically receives special attention. The ICA leadership began to arrange for this theme to be given priority public diplomacy treatment in selected countries. The opinions of the area directors were apparently not solicited, nor were field officers queried as to the feasibility of pursuing this subject in their respective countries in a new, intensive manner. This was a gross tactical error. Where local interest was lacking, and the probability of creating interest was poor, it would be a waste of time and effort to pursue this theme, while in some instances to do so could be counterproductive. Fortunately, the whole project was aborted when it became clear that the approach was wrong, but not before a number of USICA posts had spent considerable time in formulating plans as they had been directed to do by Washington headquarters. Had the area directors been involved from the start, and had they been listened to as they should have been, much wasted effort might have been avoided, for they were in a position to know in which of their countries this type of program was feasible, and in which countries it would be a waste of time.

The way USIA was organized in the early 1980s, those most responsible for the effectiveness of the U.S. government's public diplomacy programs, the area directors, remained stripped of much of the authority needed to carry out their responsibilities most effectively. Their voices in such important matters as policy, program, and personnel decisions, while not stilled, are today but echos of what they were in earlier days of U.S. public diplomacy. Just as "USIA" and "USIS" have been reinstated, the full authority of the most knowledgeable about the ambience and cultures in which USIA operates overseas—the area directors—should also be reinstated.

NOTE

1. When Charles Z. Wick became director of ICA in 1980, a new position was created, that of counselor of the agency. This position was filled by John W. Shirley, a highly knowledgeable career Foreign Service information officer with broad experience who had been serving as acting director of the agency during the interim between the departure of ICA Director John Reinhardt, and the arrival of Charles Z. Wick as director. It soon developed that the counselor of the agency was charged with running the day-to-day operations of ICA and later, USIA, while Director Wick focussed on broad policies and was the agency's spokesman to the Congress, the American public, and overseas audiences.

3

USIA'S MISSION
CLEAR FOR SOME
CONFUSING FOR OTHERS

Some 65 major studies on reorganization of the foreign affairs agencies of the federal government, made during the past three decades, were examined by Lois Roth, a senior USIA officer with years of experience in public diplomacy. In April, 1981, in an essay that presented her conclusions following her review of these 65 studies, she wrote: "They add up to a 30-year attempt to understand the proper role of official 'information' and 'cultural' programs in a democratic society, where their activities are multi-faceted and constantly open to scrutiny, and in which consensus as to their objectives and their value has never been achieved"[1]

Some of the confusion surrounding the mission of USIA, as interpreted by various individuals, committees and organizations over the years, comes from the American abhorrence of "propaganda" and the idealistic views of those who believe education for education's sake is sufficient reason for the U.S. government to fund exchange programs. Nevertheless, seasoned public diplomats know that, through the history of USIA and ICA, the basic mission of U.S. public diplomacy has been the fostering of U.S. foreign policy. Whatever else USIA may do, without this objective the rationale for the U.S. government to maintain some 200 USIA posts overseas in about 125 countries would be difficult to defend.

When the United States Information and Educational Exchange Act of 1948 (known as the Smith-Mundt Act) became law, the Congress declared that its objectives were "to enable the Government

15

of the United States to promote a better understanding of the United States in other countries, and to increase mutual understanding between the people of the United States and the people of other countries." The Smith-Mundt Act's goal of "mutual understanding," which was also a goal of the Fulbright amendment to the Surplus Property Act of 1946, was so vague as to be subject to personal interpretation.

Among the means to be used in achieving "better" and "mutual understanding," however, were:

(1) *an information service to disseminate information about the United States, its people, and policies* promulgated by the Congress, the President, the Secretary of State and other responsible officials of Government having to do with matters affecting foreign affairs. (Italics mine.)

On January 29, 1953, acting on a campaign promise, President Dwight Eisenhower established the President's Advisory Committee on Government Organization. Appointed to the committee were Nelson Rockefeller as chairman, Arthur S. Fleming, and Milton Eisenhower, among others. With the full concurrence of Secretary of State John Foster Dulles, the committee recommended that, through either legislation or reorganization, the president should:

Establish a new foreign information agency in which would be consolidated the most important information programs and cultural and educational programs now carried on by the U.S. International Information Administration, by the Technical Cooperation Administration, by the Mutual Security Agency, and by the Department of State in connection with the Government of Occupied Areas.

President Eisenhower's Reorganization Plan No. 8, based on the Committee's recommendations, was transmitted to the Senate and House of Representatives. It sought the creation of the United States Information Agency (USIA). When passed by the Congress it transferred to the director of the new agency the functions vested in the secretary of state under Title V of the Smith-Mundt Act of 1948, which had authorized "*the preparation, and dissemination abroad, of information about the United States, its people, and its policies*, through press, publications, radio, motion pictures, and other information media, and through information centers and instructors abroad." (Italics mine.)

President Eisenhower also asked eight distinguished citizens under William H. Jackson, to serve on the President's Committee on International Information Activities. In its assessment of the U.S. foreign information program, the committee recognized that the program "suffered greatly from confusion regarding its mission."[2] Ms. Roth speculates that this stimulated President Eisenhower's October 1953 Statement of Mission for USIA. That statement, adopted by the president and the National Security Council on October 22, 1953, reads in part:

1. The purpose of the U.S. information Agency shall be to submit evidence to peoples of other nations by means of communication techniques that the objectives and policies of the United States are in harmony with and will advance their legitimate aspirations for freedom, progress, and peace.

2. The purpose of paragraph 1 above is to be carried out primarily:

a. By explaining and interpreting to foreign peoples the objectives and policies of the United States Government.

b. By depicting imaginatively the correlation between U.S. policies and the legitimate aspirations of other peoples of the world.

c. By unmasking and countering hostile attempts to distort or to frustrate the objectives and policies of the United States.

d. By delineating those important aspects of the life and culture of the people of the United States which facilitate understanding of the policies and objectives of the Government of the United States.

This was a major attempt to clarify the mission of the U.S. government's new information and cultural affairs agency. That mission, as seen by President Eisenhower in 1953, was to "submit evidence . . . by means of communication techniques", that U.S. objectives and policies support "freedom, progress, and peace," all of which, in the U.S. view, are "legitimate aspirations" of all peoples. This was to be done by "explaining and interpreting" U.S. objectives and policies, demonstrating that these policies are consistent with the "legitimate aspirations" of other nations, countering anti-U.S. policies and actions, and presenting ("delineating") U.S. life and culture that should "facilitate" the understanding of U. S. policies. In other words, seek support for U.S. foreign policy.

In the thirty years since President Eisenhower's statement of mission was enunciated, and despite much discussion on the goals and objectives of USIA and ICA, support for U.S. foreign policy has continued to be the basic mission of American public diplomacy.

Confusion concerning the mission of USIA and ICA has continued through the years, perhaps, because while support of U.S. foreign policy objectives has always been the basic mission of American public diplomacy, this is not its sole mission. Two elements, perhaps more than any others, that have added to the confusion are, on one hand, the Voice of America and the way in which it carries out its programs, and on the other the U.S. government's cultural and educational exchange programs.

In 1976, the broadcasting service of USIA received a special "charter" from the U.S. Congress in recognition of its unique position as the only element of the U.S. public diplomacy effort that goes directly from Washington to individual recipients of its programs—VOA listeners. The Voice of America charter reads as follows:

> The long range interests of the United States are served by communicating directly with the peoples of the world by radio. To be effective, the Voice of America must win the attention and respect of listeners. These principals will govern VOA broadcasts:
>
> 1. VOA will establish itself as a consistently reliable and authoritative source of news. VOA will be accurate, objective and comprehensive.
>
> 2. VOA will represent America, not any single segment of American society. It will therefore present a balanced and comprehensive projection of significant American thought and institutions.
>
> 3. *As an official radio, VOA will present the policies of the United States clearly and effectively.* VOA will also present responsible discussion and opinion on these policies. (Italics mine.)

As noted above, while the VOA helps USIA to achieve its basic mission of supporting U.S. foreign policy, it has, at the same time, established itself as a "reliable and authoritative sources of news," a prerogative that it has maintained to this day and that it jealously guards. The pursuit of these two separate goals by the VOA has been the cause of some of the confusion Lois Roth documents in her study. However, it is argued by the current USIA leadership, as well as its predecessors, that these two objectives are not mutually exclusive—that for the VOA to do both is neither contradictory nor confusing, as long as each VOA program is clearly identified for what it is—news, opinion, or U.S. policy.

Another cause for confusion as to USIA's mission developed with respect to the agency's educational and cultural exchange goals. At one extreme are those who believe these programs should be devoid of politics while at the other extreme are those who believe they should serve U.S. foreign policy objectives just as USIA information programs are generally designed to do.

In 1961, the Mutual Educational and Cultural Exchange Act was passed. Known as the Fulbright-Hays Act, it consolidated the various educational and cultural exchange programs of earlier legislation. "Mutual understanding" was still described as the main goal. The preamble of the Fulbright-Hays Act states that it is "an act to provide for the improvement and strengthening of the international relations of the United States by promoting better mutual understanding among the peoples of the world through educational and cultural exchanges."

Educational and cultural exchange programs were never designed to support specific U.S. foreign policy objectives. The return on the U.S. investment in these programs is expected to come from increased understanding and the promotion of peaceful pursuits on a cooperative basis among nations. The 1961 Act further states that its purpose is:

> to strengthen the ties which unite us with other nations by demonstrating the educational and cultural interests, developments, and achievements of the people of the United States and other nations, and the contributions being made toward a peaceful and more fruitful life for people throughout the world; to promote international cooperation for educational and cultural advancement; and thus to assist in the development of friendly, sympathetic, and peaceful relations between the United States and the other countries of the world.

The Fulbright-Hays Act authorized the president, "when he considers that it would strengthen international cooperative relations" to provide, through grants, contracts, or otherwise, educational and cultural exchanges and enable U.S. participation in international fairs and expositions abroad. The language in this act comes closest to supporting U.S. policies when noting that certain programs can be initiated under this legislation when the president determines that they are in the "national interest" or when he deems them to be "in the public interest."

Senator William J. Fulbright, cosponsor of the 1981 Act, held strong views regarding the purpose of U.S. educational and cultural exchange programs. In a statement before the Senate in June, 1961, he noted: "I utterly reject any suggestion that our educational and cultural exchange programs are weapons or instruments with which to do combat. . . . there is no room and there must not be any room, for an interpretation of these programs as propaganda, even recognizing that the term covers some very worthwhile and respectable activities."[3]

A decade after USIA was created, the need to clarify the agency's mission was still so strongly felt that on January 25, 1963, President John F. Kennedy sent a memorandum to the director of USIA in which he expressed his views on this subject.

"The mission of the U.S. Information agency," the memo began, *"is to help achieve U.S. foreign policy objectives* by (a) influencing public attitudes in other nations, and (b) advising the President, his representatives abroad, and the various departments and agencies on the implications of foreign opinion for present and contemplated U.S. policies, programs and official statements." (Italics mine.) It went on to say that "the influencing of attitudes" was to be carried out "by the overt use of the various techniques of communication—personal contact, radio broadcasting, libraries, book publication and distribution, press, motion pictures, television, exhibits, English-language instruction, and others."

Ten years later, in 1973, two U.S.-supported radio stations that had been operating for years in Western Europe with programs aimed at Eastern Europe and the Soviet Union, came in out of the cold. Though involved in public diplomacy and supported by U.S. government funding, these two stations, known as *Radio Free Europe* and *Radio Liberty*, were not then, and are not now, a part of the agency within the U.S. government charged with the primary responsibility for U.S. public diplomacy. This situation, along with other factors, contributed in 1973 to considerable public discussion as to whether or not these stations should continue to operate under U.S. government auspices. The U.S. Congress resolved the issue by passing the "Board for International Broadcasting Act of 1973." This law established a "Board for International Broadcasting" and authorized "the continuation of (U.S. government) assistance to Radio Free Europe and Radio Liberty." The declaration of purposes of the act reads, in part:

The Congress hereby finds and declares—

(1) that it is the policy of the United States to promote the right of freedom of opinion and expression, including the freedom "to seek, receive, and impart information and ideas through any media and regardless of frontiers," in accordance with article 19 of the Universal Declaration of Human Rights;

(2) that open communication of information and ideas among the peoples of the world contributes to international peace and stability, and that the promotion of such communication is in the interests of the United States.

In establishing the Board for International Broadcasting, which enabled Radio Free Europe and Radio Liberty to continue their broadcasts to Eastern Europe and the Soviet Union, the Congress also noted that the two stations "have demonstrated their effectiveness in furthering the open communication of information and ideas" in the communist bloc; that the operation of these two radio stations "is in the national interest," and that they encouraged "dialog" with the peoples of the Soviet Union and Eastern Europe.

The Board, consisting of seven members, five of whom are appointed by the president with the advice and consent of the Senate, reviews and evaluates the mission and operation of the two stations and makes grants to them. Members are charged to "bear in mind the necessity of maintaining the professional independence and integrity of Radio Free Europe and Radio Liberty."

Five years later, in 1978, after much discussion about USIA and its mission, which again had captured the attention of the Congress and the press, the decision to combine the educational and cultural exchange programs of the Department of State and the information programs of USIA was made. The International Communication Agency (ICA), an agency of the executive branch of the U.S. government, was established April 1, 1978. Radio Free Europe and Radio Liberty remained as they had always been, apart.

President Jimmy Carter's memorandum of March 13, 1978, to the director of the new International Communication Agency described his view of the mission of ICA. It reiterated what the president had said in transmitting Reorganization Plan No. 2 of 1977 to the Congress, that "the principal function of the Agency should be to reduce the degree to which misperceptions and misunderstandings complicate relations between the United States and other nations." He then listed five main tasks for U.S. public diplomats:

1. To encourage, aid and sponsor the broadest possible exchange of people and ideas between our country and other nations.

2. *To give foreign peoples the best possible understanding of our policies* and intentions, and sufficient information about American society and culture to comprehend why we have chosen certain policies over others.

3. To help insure that our government adequately understands foreign public opinion and culture for policymaking purposes, and to assist individual Americans and institutions in learning about other nations and their cultures.

4. To assist in the development and execution of a comprehensive national policy on international communications, designed to allow and encourage the maximum flow of information and ideas among the peoples of the world.

5. To prepare for and conduct negotiations on cultural exchanges with other governments . . . . (Italics mine.)

From this quick review of the post-World War II development of U.S. public diplomacy, it is clear that support of U.S. foreign policy has been, and continues to be, its basic objective, as spelled out in congressional and presidential documents. At the same time, the educational and cultural exchange programs are generally viewed not as vehicles to directly support specific foreign policy objectives, as is the case with many of USIA's information activities, but are intended to provide a framework that can demonstrate, and thus help foreigners to understand, the culture out of which U.S. policies and actions spring. At most, the educational and cultural exchange programs are designed to promote "the national interest" or "the public interest" by "strengthening international cooperation."

With the creation of ICA, U.S. public diplomats received a broad, new order. While they were to continue to explain U.S. foreign policy and portray U.S. culture to foreign audiences, they were charged with a new mission—often referred to as a "Second Mandate"—which was "to assist individual Americans and institutions in learning about other nations and their cultures." This new mandate initially caused considerable consternation among ICA's Foreign

Service officers and others who were expected to carry out this new objective, since the agency was given neither additional funds nor additional staff to do so. In this situation the most that many knowledgeable observers expected was an increased emphasis on exchanges of American and foreign teachers, scholars, students, and leaders, such exchanges being excellent vehicles for learning about other cultures.

Aside from the exchange programs, only one small unit of the agency became the entity specifically charged with attempting to fulfill the Second Mandate. This was the Office of Private Sector Programs, which had a budget in Fiscal Year 1981 of about $10 million. But given the lack of detailed guidelines, the limited funds designated for this purpose, and the limited number of personnel specifically assigned to this task, how much ICA could and should have done remained unresolved questions. Furthermore, difficult as it is to measure the successes and failures of overseas information programs with specific objectives, measuring the success or failure of the "reverse flow," with its nebulous goal of "learning about other nations and their cultures," would be even more difficult. In short, the Second Mandate never really got off the ground.

Prior to the arrival in Washington of the new Republican administration of President Ronald Reagan, the mission of ICA could be described as threefold: to support U.S. foreign policy, to depict U.S. culture in its broadest sense, and to foster greater knowledge in the United States of the peoples of other cultures with whom we share this planet. Despite the limited resources provided ICA and, in particular, the limited resources allotted for the new mandate, U.S. public diplomats carried out ICA programs and activities in much the same way as they did when USIA was in business. Despite lengthy, philosophically oriented instructions to field posts from Washington headquarters, the substance of most ICA programs and activities were, for the most part, unchanged from what they were under USIA. This was one of several factors that made it easy in 1982 to return to "USIA" and "USIS."

For many years prior to the Reagan administration, the trend had been toward continuing reductions in the number of agency employees and in the agency's annual budgets in terms of constant dollars. From a peak of 12,358 employees in USIA alone in the mid-1960s, the number of personnel dropped to 8,671 in 1980 (4,489 American personnel—1,062 abroad and 3,427 in the United States, and 4,182 non-Americans hired locally in foreign countries).[4]

By 1983, due in part to having "a gifted professional communicator" in the White House, who recognized the value of public diplomacy, the number of personnel stabilized despite major budget cuts for the federal government in general (the Department of Defense excepted). USIA was encouraged to request $644 million for its Fiscal Year 1983 budget, an increase of $162 million over the amount approved earlier by the Office of Management and Budget.[5] Some $115 million of the increase being requested was for a substantial radio construction program. Also planned were increases in the exchanges program that would put its budget over $100 million for the first time, and increases in the number of satellite television transmissions.

Despite budgetary and manpower limitations that can only be overcome by greater awareness on the part of governmental and public leaders as to the value and importance of public diplomacy, there appears to be a growing body of opinion that believes the USIA's traditional mission should be further expanded to yet another objective. As Professor Wilbur Blume, in a highly perceptive paper developed for USIA a few years ago, wrote: "What is needed is a bold new initiative which transcends the limits of past thinking about propaganda and considers the opportunity that the U.S. has to use its resources of information and technology in assisting the human race."[6]

The "bold new initiative" Blume advocates is not only consistent with U.S. ideals and U.S. national interests, but makes use of U.S. technology to make peace, not war. It would, if adapted, put U.S. public diplomacy fully into the Computer Age, utilizing computer technology for the social and economic benefit of friendly developing nations, and, in turn, for the benefit of the United States. Why this "bold new step" should become a new mission of USIA in the 1980s, and how, are discussed in later chapters.

NOTES

1. Roth, Lois, *PUBLIC DIPLOMACY AND THE PAST, The Studies of U.S. Information and Cultural Programs (1952-1975)*, Executive Seminar in National and International Affairs, U.S. Department of State, April, 1981, p. 1.

2. *Ibid.*, p. 9.

3. *Ibid., p. 18.*

4. In 1964 the Bureau of Educational and Cultural Affairs of the Dept. of State also had 420 employees working in activities later incorporated into ICA. It should also be recognized that the demands of Vietnam help account for the high number of USIA employees in the mid-1960s.

5. Adelman, Kenneth L, *"SPEAKING OF AMERICA: PUBLIC DIPLOMACY IN OUR TIME," FOREIGN AFFAIRS*, Vol. 59, No. 4, Spring 1981, pp. 913-36.

6. U.S. Congress, House. Committee on International Relations, Subcommittee on International Operations. *Public Diplomacy and the Future*, Washington, D.C.: Government Printing Office, 1977, p. 664.

4

THE COUNTRY PLAN

Because each country is different, with a different set of bilateral issues, problems, and priorities with respect to its dealings with the United States, almost every U.S. government agency that has relations with a foreign country develops individual annual plans concerning these relationships. This planning usually begins about eight months or so prior to the start of the fiscal year, which, for the U.S. government, runs from October 1st through September 30th.

The Department of State, for example, focuses attention in this way on those political and economic issues and problems which the Department, in conjunction with the U.S. ambassador in each country and his advisers (known as the "Country Team"), believe should be given priority in that country during the coming year. Likewise in those countries where there are U.S. economic assistance programs, USAID officials abroad must present their economic assistance plans for the forthcoming year, which must then be discussed and approved by Washington. The commercial attaché who makes the annual plan for stimulating U.S. exports to his country of assignment is another example.

President John F. Kennedy was the first U.S. president to specifically mention that he expected USIA to plan its programs and activities on an individual country basis. In his memorandum to the director of the U.S. Information Agency of January 25, 1963, the president noted that "Individual country programs should specifically and directly support country and regional objectives determined by the President and set forth in official pronouncements, both classified and unclassified." To provide such support, planning is, of course, essential.

The planning process for USIS posts abroad begins when USIA Washington provides basic guidelines, the format to be followed for that particular year, and U.S. global and regional priorities as seen from Washington, usually presented as themes. Only those global and regional themes that are applicable and which, it is believed, can be effectively treated in the post's programs, will be included in the planning document of any particular country. While the material in some of these documents may, by its very nature, be somewhat sensitive, USIA's annual plan for each country is normally unclassified and as open as all of USIA's activities, though exceptions occasionally occur in highly sensitive situations. This annual planning document of each USIS post is called the "Country Plan."

When ICA was established in 1978, a new system was devised to carry out this annual chore. For the first time, field officers were directed to initiate their annual plans with a written commentary entitled, "The Bilateral Communication Relationship," an innocuous-sounding title that could logically be expected to set the scene for detailed information concerning ICA's projected programs for the coming year. This commentary, or essay, consisted of two parts: (a) a narrative discussion of the so-called bilateral communication relationship and (b) a list of major issues, in priority order, which were to be addressed by ICA programs.

This "bilateral essay" was based on the idea that underlying the normal relationships between Americans and the nationals of other countries were certain problems, issues, concerns, and blind spots. Given the field officers' knowledge of the local culture, guided by ICA's highly professional national staff members, who are thoroughly familiar with their own culture, such problems, issues, and concerns were to be extracted from the social, political, cultural, economic, educational, military, and familial relationships that existed between the people of the United States and the people of Country "X." This was to be explained in the essay, thus providing the rationale for ICA programs in each country.

A major difficulty in adapting to the new system of country plans when first initiated by the ICA leadership occurred because the field officers who had to write these plans were instructed to identify "communications tensions" which, it was alleged existed between the United States and most societies. Unfortunately, no one ever adequately explained the term "communications tensions." Without a clear definition of this phrase, field officers were left to use their own imaginations as to what was meant by this innovative term. The frustration that resulted is not difficult to imagine. Many enterprising ICA field officers, however, nevertheless managed to "pull rabbits out of hats." Despite the vagueness of the term "communications tensions," some brilliant essays were written about bilateral relations. Whether anyone other than a few selected Washington bureaucrats ever read those essays is another matter.

An effort to explain "communications tensions" was made, but, since this term was based on questionable premises, the effort was hardly successful. For example, in September, 1978, ICA overseas posts were notified that the "rationale" presented in their written commentary on the bilateral relationship with the host country "can be expressed in terms of the tensions—the explicit or implicit communications tensions—between the host society and the United States. These tensions can be revealed by disdain for American cultural and aesthetic values; by ignorance of our efforts to erect a humane, libertarian society; by outright opposition to our nuclear nonproliferation policies; or in other, sometimes hidden ways." If this made sense to some, it was gobbledygook to many.

The formal instructions to U.S. public diplomats abroad also made an attempt to define these "communications tensions" but with limited success. The instructions read, in part:

> Your bilateral communications essay should have enduring validity and should not require more than limited amendment in the next few years. . . . Some concerns that you identify can support mission goals and objectives. Others will reflect a longer-term, societal, or cultural orientation.
>
> . . . Central to the analytical process is a succinct discussion of the important cultural, societal, political, and economic forces in your society, and how and which of these forces impinge importantly upon its relationship with the U.S.
>
> The essay should describe important communications tensions and/or assets within these forces: What are the underlying problems which stem from cultural differences, distortions, or the absence of a sustained dialogue between the people of the two countries?

When some posts asked for clarification as to what, exactly, are communications tensions, one Washington office repeated the above. Some examples were also given to at least one post which expressed befuddlement as to what these communications tensions were all about. These examples were given:

> A residual suspicion of U.S. intentions, motives and business motives (sic) would qualify as a communications tension if it were developed to include reasons for and the nature of the suspicion.

> An example from (Country "Y's") essay: "Deeply ingrained are those attitudes which reflect the opinion that the U.S. citizen is somehow too materialistic and certainly less spiritual than is ("Y's") neighbor.

> Some (people of Country "Y") are concerned because of what they perceive as too much U.S. influence on their way of life. The U.S. is a society of undesirable sexual mores, drugs, pollution, consumer avarice and crime. Those who view the U.S. in this negative light are, understandably, opposed to any increase in U.S. influence here and will resist what they view as cultural domination.

> Despite all the communications flow, real communication generating a sound understanding of American political and social realities seems ragged and occasional. On the slightest prompting (people of Country "Z") will in good faith praise American freedoms and scientific prowess. But if one enters the realm of values which underlie those freedoms, that process, that ability and power, he leaves the (national of Country "Z") behind. This superficial comprehension presents a serious problem.

Perhaps the above helped to clarify for some what ICA officials in Washington were seeking from their field officers, but it contributed little to convincing many senior public diplomats in the Foreign Service that this new approach was valid, let alone important. First, should it be a major objective of the slightly more than one thousand Americans serving ICA (now USIA) throughout the world to tackle deep-seated cultural beliefs held in one or more countries about the United States, regardless of the reason and the importance to the United States of such beliefs? Secondly, even if one were to agree that this should be a major concern of U.S. public diplomats, it is plausible, given USIA's limited resources, that the historic, ingrained cultural beliefs of a slew of countries, many of which are inconsequential in terms of U.S. interests, could be importantly affected by USIA's efforts at the same time that USIA officers pursue foreign policy and the other goals discussed earlier?

In May of 1979, a headquarters communication went out to the U.S. public diplomats abroad concerning the forthcoming Country Plan for the following year. It read:

> The one central document in your work and Washington's is the Country Plan. Writing it offers an opportunity to review the truly important, continuing, underlying communications problems and opportunities between your society and the United States . . . *it provides all of us with an opportunity to organize ourselves to deal with the important, persistent problems of communication.* (Italics mine.)

As foggy as the term "communications tensions" is, the above quote helps explain another difficulty encountered in the writing of country plans at the time ICA was created. Somewhere along the way, the idea apparently developed that the problems of the world are solely, or predominantly, communications problems. Thus the country plan became an instrument to provide "an opportunity to . . . deal with the important, persistent problems of communication." But many, if not most of the world's problems go far beyond communications, despite the ever-increasing importance communication plays in the modern world. Need it be said that political, economic, social, and military problems continue to plague the peoples of the world? Such problems as Soviet military intervention in Afghanistan, the taking of U.S. hostages in Iran, the search for greater freedom by the Polish people and others, and the search for peace in the Middle East are more than communications matters.

When the Reagan administration took office in Washington, and faces changed in the ICA hierarchy as in other government offices in the nation's capital, the term "communications tensions" mysteriously disappeared from the agency's lexicon. Although a written analysis of the local communications environment as well as the political, economic, social and, in some instances, military situation, with particular reference to U.S. interests, is still a part of the country plan at each overseas USIA post, "communications tensions" is no longer used in the agency's official documents.

A more positive innovation initiated with the birth of ICA was the development of a system, incorporated in a new Country plan format, which enabled the headquarters office in Washington to computerize the diverse informational and cultural support items needed by more than a hundred posts. With some exceptions, this support effort worked fairly well from the beginning and improved as more experience with it was gained. It helped simplify the country plan process, a continuing goal of agency administrators and one of the reasons why the format of country plan has changed periodically. Sometimes the changes did not achieve their intended purpose, since learning the new format became, at times, more time-consuming than the changes were worth.

Each post's country plan, after receiving the approval of the head of the U.S. Mission in that country, is then submitted to USIA Washington, where it is studied, edited, and refined. Approval by Washington superiors must be obtained before the plan becomes operational. This has, in the past, been the cause of some difficulties in the field-Washington relationships within USIA. While it is difficult enough to reach an agreement between two individuals on how a complex, or even a simple idea should be expressed in written form, the system in Washington for country plans requires at least three persons in the area geographic office alone to approve the essay and the "issues and concerns" as developed by USIA Officers abroad. (These three officers are the desk officer, who is the key contact and Washington's country specialist for the post; the area policy officer; and the area director.) The plan also has to have the approval of the Office of Planning and Guidance. Thus, individuals in both of these offices can edit, criticize, rewrite, or reject what the presumed experts in the field have written. Needless to say, much time and effort is expended throughout the world, and particularly in Washington, on this exercise.

In recent years the Department of State has developed its planning process for individual countries to the point where U.S. Mission objectives are presented with a minimum of words. This has been a real achievement, applauded by all concerned. The State Department's basic country planning document should be the base from which the USIA country plan is developed since the Department of State formulates the policies that should be supported by public diplomacy efforts. This has, admittedly, always been done to a certain extent. However, the State Department's succinctness in this instance (somewhat of a rarity for the State Department, some will say) should be matched by USIA.

Elimination of the term "communications tensions" was a great step forward in simplifying the country plan process. Efforts must continue in the direction of focusing the limited resources of U.S. public diplomats on those themes and issues considered most important to U.S. foreign policy. USIA should follow the lead of the Department of State and simplify even more the necessary but time-consuming country plan process. Some of the tremendous amount of time and effort that this annual USIA planning document has required in recent years might better be expended in carrying out the creative programs which the plan addresses. Computerization offers an avenue in that direction.

5

THE DEVELOPING WORLD
A SPECIAL CHALLENGE

On November 6, 1980, a story about the Republican election victory in the United States appeared on page five of Addis Ababa's English-language daily newspaper. It read, in its entirety, as follows:

Washington (Agencies)—Republican Ronald Reagan was elected president of the United States Tuesday.

Reagan advances the philosophy of militarism and is a staunch supporter of the preservation of exploitative capitalist production relations.

His vice president, George Bush, a former congressman and ex-director of the Central Intelligence Agency (CIA), is a millionaire.

Mr. Reagan will be the oldest man ever inaugurated as a U.S. president.

Republished in the November 21, 1980 issue of the *Washington Post* in a column concerning UNESCO's continuing debate about the role of the press, the *Post*'s "Ombudsman," columnist Bill Green, commented that "while it is patently unfair to use that story as a representative of Third World press coverage since Ethiopia is a Soviet ally, it does serve as a graphic reminder of the effects of a press that is under control by its government."

Government control of the press, common, of course, to Communist countries, is also widespread in most of the countries of the developing world. This is but one of the special challenges

U.S. public diplomats face in seeking to present the views and policies of the U.S. government in developing countries, though press control can work both ways. If a government friendly to the United States controls the press, placement of USIS materials in the local media is often not difficult, though such a situation runs counter to the basic U.S. philosophy that a free press is essential for political maturity. How frightened so many government leaders throughout the world are of a free press is clear from the relatively small number of countries, particularly in the developing world, where a free press exists.

The well-known and much-discussed gap between the developed and the developing worlds continues to widen. Significantly, however, as the decade of the 1980s marches on, that gap is widening at an accelerated pace because the developed world has now entered the Computer Age. The effect of this is to leave the developing world still farther behind. Though computerization is what contributes to that accelerated pace, it also offers developing countries a potential means for accelerating their own development if they have the opportunity and the will to make use of the benefits computers can bestow.

The type and style of public diplomacy that should be pursued in a *developed* nation where sophisticated communications technology is abundant, where the flow of information is torrential, where the standard of living is high for the majority rather than for the minority, and where the educational and literacy levels of the population are also high, are markedly different from those required in a *developing* country. While the above is obvious, USIA in its programs emanating from Washington has given neither the fact of these differences, nor the developing countries themselves, the degree of attention they merit.

In 1977, Peter Grose, in a column in the *New York Times* entitled "The Third World's Clamor Grows," wrote: "There are . . . a host of other issues in the world . . . but none detracts from the growing importance of the North-South dialogue. . . . This dialogue stands as a ticking time bomb for the Carter Administration." The time bomb went off in Iran and Afghanistan. The Middle East, hardly a developed area, remains a major concern. Recent U.S. administrations have been faced with problems in Vietnam, the Dominican Republic, Guatemala—all third world countries. Today there are El Salvador, Nicaragua, and Cuba. Large, major countries tend to be more stable, and it is doubtful that tomorrow will be much different in this respect than the past. Yet within USIA there has been a tendency, if not to treat all USIA posts alike, to fail to sufficiently credit third world countries with unique informational and cultural requirements and an importance to U.S. interests that merits special attention.

One quick way of determining the importance to the United States of numerous developing countries is to examine the list of nations that receive U.S. economic assistance. Regardless of other arguments that might be made, and except for truly emergency situations to which the U.S. government and the American people have generally been quick to respond for purely humanitarian reasons, AID programs normally serve U.S. interests as well as local interests in whatever country those programs exist. Thus, whereever there is an AID program it can be presumed to be justified in terms of U.S. interests. This generally being the case, the public diplomacy aspects of those interests should be represented by an adequate USIA staff with adequate resources.

In addition to the political concerns that the United States shares with many countries of the developing world, in many cases mutual economic interests are even greater. The oil-rich nations are the most obvious examples. In today's interdependent world, the high technological society of the United States relies ever-increasingly on other countries, mostly developing ones, for needed natural resources from minerals to natural gas. And as the health of the U.S. economy comes to depend more and more on export industries, it is worth noting that some of the best markets for U.S. products are found in countries with a rapid rate of development.

In an address at the National Press Club in Washington, D.C. May 18, 1982, U.S. Trade Representative to the General Agreement on Tariffs and Trade (GATT), William Breck, pointed out that today almost 20 percent of the goods produced in the United States are exported. "One acre out of three of our farmland is planted for export," he said, "and farm exports as a percentage of farm sales have doubled to 20% over the last ten years." Stressing the importance of developing nations as markets for U.S. products, he also noted:

—U.S. exports to developing countries have increased from 7,000 million dollars in 1961 to 89,000 million dollars in 1981.

—Currently we export more to developing countries than to all of Western Europe and Japan combined.

—In manufacturing trade . . . we have expanded our exports to developing countries seven-fold since 1970.

—Today nearly 40 percent of U.S. exports of manufactures are shipped to the Third World.

USIA posts in developing countries have a different role to play, and must play it differently, than in the developed world. In developed countries USIA officers must be able to quickly provide accurate information about U.S. policies, actions, and intentions. The flood of information that pours into a highly developed nation concerning the United States can sometimes result in a cacophonous swirl of competing ideas or statements from various U.S. sources, which can leave foreign audiences wondering which source speaks for Uncle Sam. Or a message received from a news agency source might be garbled, partially presented, biased, or interpreted wrongly.

While it is *the diplomat's job* to explain to the foreign office of the host country what the U.S. stand is on a particular issue of interest or concern to the local government, it is *the public diplomat's job* to make available such information to a much wider audience. It is doubtful, as a rule, however, that the local media— the press, radio, television, etc.—of a developed country will be readily accessible to USIA programs *per se*, except in a most unusual circumstance and one in which local concern is exceedingly high. This does not happen often. The best that U.S. public diplomats in the developed world can do most of the time is to keep lines open to local communicators—to communicate with the communicators. In a developing country, however, where local media are usually at the same stage of development as other aspects of the local society, the communications industry is probably anxious and willing, if political considerations allow, to utilize any number of USIA programs in its press, radio, and television outlets so long as the quality of these programs is high, and particularly if there is local interest or a local angle.

With respect to educational and cultural exchange programs in developed countries, public diplomats are generally more involved in encouraging and assisting on-going programs and stimulating new private exchanges than in conducting their own programs in this category. There are generally sufficient, privately generated funds from sources either in the host country or the United States available for these purposes. As for performing artists, commercially profitable markets generally exist, making it unnecessary for U.S.

government sponsorship of such artists. In many developing countries however, the government's financial support may be crucial. Without such support, far fewer educational and cultural exchanges would take place.

One of the most effective information vehicles available to public diplomats today is, of course, television. However, given the agency's emphasis on high-priority, developed countries, and the fact that the demand for television programming by USIA posts there is practically nonexistent as compared with that in developing countries—who are hungry for good quality materials— USIA's capability for producing its own TV programs has diminished in recent years. Thus, in early 1980, when global interest was focused on the U.S. hostage situation in Iran and the Soviet invasion of Afghanistan, USIA (then ICA) was unable, or unwilling, to be immediately responsive to requests from overseas posts in developing countries for television programs, or unedited TV materials, on these subjects. Had such materials been available, they could easily have been placed on leading news shows in many friendly countries, given their news value and importance at a time when the United States was seeking support from other nations regarding these two issues—support that could have been strengthened by such materials. Eventually some TV materials were put together in Washington and utilized overseas, but the agency's reaction time in fielding such requests during these two incidents of major importance to the United States was much slower than it should have been. If the needs of developing nations where television placement is generally feasible, had received a higher priority, the agency would have had the capability to respond much more quickly. However, so long as the Washington headquarters of American public diplomacy continues, apparently, to consider North-South relations of far less importance than East-West relations, this situation will prevail. Countries like Denmark, Sweden, and England, for example—with very few television channels (in the case of Denmark, only one!); with no lack of materials for their telecasts; and with the view among many individuals that "if it has a U.S. government label, it must be propaganda"—will seldom be interested in any kind of television programming USIA might provide. This is the exact opposite of the situation in the majority of developing countries.

One aspect of public diplomacy programming that has been discussed at various times in recent years is whether U.S. public diplomats and the communications specialists who occasionally travel abroad under agency auspices should be involved in training programs for communicators in developing countries. The position of the ICA leadership in the late 1970s was negative concerning such "training," Top ICA officials contended that training was *not* part of USICA's mission, that the Congress would object, and that it was up to AID to include in its programs any training activities of the U.S. government (other than military) in foreign countries. Despite this view, a certain amount of short-term training by American specialists sponsored by ICA under the "American Participants" program took place, and still does under USIA auspices.

It can be argued that an economist or political scientist who is an American Participant under USIA sponsorship and who conducts a seminar in his field of expertise is not involved in training per se, but often he is, even though it may not be called training. Thus it was difficult to understand why ICA officials objected to communications specialists being involved in teaching situations that could also be described as training programs. The argument that "training activities" should be left to AID is particularly invalid when it comes to communications expertise. Not only are public diplomats much more at home in this field than most AID officials, but AID has shown little interest in communications development compared with other interests. Aside from a few isolated, education-oriented satellite programs, the main concerns of AID in recent years have been to provide assistance in agriculture and rural development, public administration, population planning, health education, and human resources development. Fortunately, the early 1980s have seen the development of a more positive U.S. government outlook on assisting developing countries in communications training, which has at least removed the earlier taboo on training that ICA leaders dictated. However, there is much more that USIA could do in this field that would be beneficial both to the United States and the other countries concerned.

While not universally accepted, perhaps, it is generally believed that the interests of the United States and world peace are served if countries of the third world are aided and encouraged to develop their economic potential to the greatest extent possible. Even if viewed from the interests of the United States alone, the case for U.S. economic assistance to developing countries can easily be made. A Department of State document entitled "US Development in an Interdependent World," commenting on the political and economic impact of developing countries on the United States, suggests that while U.S. economic assistance benefits the recipient countries, it also benefits the United States. It notes that "from them we (in the United States) seek:

—cooperation in finding international solutions to complex world problems—food, energy, population, environment, etc.

—opportunities for mutually productive and profitable investment of capital and technology.

—markets for the products of U.S. enterprises—the developing countries now buy nearly a third of U.S. exports and supply two-fifths of U.S. imports—which create jobs for workers on both ends of the trade pattern.

—raw material imports to meet the needs of American industry and American consumers. In terms of essential minerals—e.g., tin, nickel, bauxite, and manganese—from 50 to 100% of U.S. domestic requirements are imported from the less developed world.[1]

With the above in mind, it would seem that the public diplomacy arm of the U.S. government should support U.S. policies in economic and social development in those countries where we have AID missions. This is, in fact, generally done, but the past reluctance, especially by ICA, to become involved in training in the communications field when the U.S. public diplomacy agency has a great deal to offer in the way of experience, and access to experience, is unfortunate.

Communication plays a vital role in all societies, traditional as well as modern, and it is a vital element for development, though the more developed (complicated) a society becomes, the more important its communications system becomes. Most developing countries, understandably, are seldom any more developed in their communications systems than they are in other aspects of their societies, i.e., transportation, industrialization, educational facilities, etc. The role communication plays, however, in expediting development in all fields gives it its special importance.

If one assumes that: (1) economically viable countries generally serve U.S. interests better than those with serious social and economic problems and (2) that communications systems are of major importance to social/economic/political development, then it seems logical that since USIA has the resources and the capability of contributing to the improvement of the communications systems in selected, friendly countries, that capability should be exercised. When USIA is invited by a developing country to help in the training of individuals in the press, radio, and television field, either through the sponsorship of visiting U.S. communications experts who can hold seminars and workshops, or by the International Visitors Program (whereby visits by nationals of foreign countries are invited to visit the United States for 30 days or so for specific purposes), these programs should be given a high priority.

Although AID, as noted earlier, has entered the communications field occasionally—particularly with respect to educational TV—and other international agencies have dabbled in educational TV (as has the U.S. Peace Corps in Colombia, for example), the results have not, apparently, been more than marginally helpful in overcoming social/economic problems. This limited use of television, as an educational tool, while helpful, does not play the same vital role in social/economic/political progress as does the development of a communications infrastructure and the improvement, through training, of the professional qualifications of communicators who can serve all of the varied communications needs of a government and society.

Noted communications theorist Lucian W. Pye, as early as 1963 when he edited a volume entitled *Communication and Political Development*, noted the importance of concentrating on communication networks as essential accelerators of social/economic/political progress. "A strong case could be made," he wrote, "that the two most general and most fundamental problems in political modernization are . . . changing attitudes and reducing the gap between the ruling elites (in developing countries) and the less modernized masses." He added, it would follow that:

> If students of international communications were to shift their emphasis from, say, the problems of communicating the policies and the image of the United States to the emerging countries to the problems of domestic communications within those countries, they could readily make a substantial contribution in the effort to deal with one of the most demanding problems of world politics.[2]

Given the seriousness of the world's economic plight, and the U.S. realization that it is in our self-interest to do what we can to alleviate the problem of the widening gap between the developing and the developed world, especially as our interdependency grows, then all applicable U.S. government resources that can contribute to the formidable task of narrowing that gap should be employed. Although USIA is a relatively small organization—judged by its budget and the size of its staff—its worldwide scope and its experience in intercultural communications technology and practices make it a unique and valuable asset that could be more fully utilized to support U.S. government overseas social and economic objectives. One might not go as far as communications theorist Ithiel de Sola Pool when he said that America's public diplomats "ought to be in the technical assistance field (referring to communications)."[3] But assistance in providing developing countries with information about modern communications technology and practices through demonstrations, printed and audio-visual materials, visiting American communications experts, and educational exchange grants to highly selected foreign nationals in key positions to affect the changes needed to modernize the communications systems of their countries could easily become a greater part of the normal activities of USIA posts in developing countries than they now are. This would add no great pressure on available funds and staff. In short, USIA posts, if encouraged by Washington, could be more responsive to requests for information on the importance of communications in developing societies; on how to obtain communication hardware and software; on new developments in communications technology, psychology and methodology; and on possible sources of financing communications development. However, without a conscious decision to give priority to this theme in the third and fourth world countries where USIA functions, the contibution that U.S. public diplomats make to U.S. objectives in those countries will be far less than what it could be.

As with most things, this idea is not new. But it has to be among the priorities of the USIA Washington leadership if it is to have any impact. At a minimum there should *not* be, as experienced a few years ago at at least one post, a reluctance to allow U.S. communications specialists to conduct USIS-sponsored training seminars and workshops in modern television techniques and technology on grounds that USIA "should not get involved with training," The irony exists that USIA has been, and will be, by the nature of its operations, involved in training of various types. Not only does USIA support of communications training in developing countries assist in the development of those countries, but the genuine show of interest and concern in such local needs cements even further the generally excellent relations between U.S. public diplomats and key local communicators.

In the early days of USIA, at a period in U.S. history when we were going through one of America's periodic upsurges of interest and concern for the welfare of the developing world, one of the priority themes guiding USIA officers was called "national development." With a particularly active U.S. policy designed to assist developing countries, expressed in Latin America, for example, as the "Alliance for Progress," it was natural for USIA to be involved in the public diplomacy aspects of that effort. What we have been discussing here, however, is a much narrower role for USIA, based, as it is, on recent political/economic development theory that asserts that communications development is an important ingredient in modernization. And it is an ingredient that few if any organizations are as experienced, or as well-prepared to help provide as is USIA, with its global connections on the one hand and easy accessibility to modern U.S. technology and methodology on the other.

In discussing our two worlds—the developed and the developing, we have suggested not only why and how the public diplomacy operations of USIA should be performed differently to meet the differing requirements of these major segments, segments whose differences continue to grow at the same time that their interdependency does, but urge that a new priority be given to USIA programs in developing countries. This could be done by including in its programs in developing countries far greater professional advice and guidance in communications theory, practice, and technology, *when requested*, than USIA has, with some reluctance, provided in the past.

In a later chapter we shall discuss a bolder, more innovative idea for contributing to the political, economic, and social growth of developing nations. However, an encouraging sign of growing recognition within USIA of the unique importance of the developing world to U.S. interests was seen when USIA Director Wick announced in June 1982 the formation of "a blue ribbon panel to advise the Agency on public and private means of strengthening Educational Exchange programs." The panel was created to examine ways in which academic exchange can strengthen international understanding between the United States and other nations. Jointly sponsored by USIA, the Board of Foreign Scholarships, and the Conference of Associated Research Councils, the panel was to study "the special needs of developing nations." Communication development should be high on any such list of "special needs."

NOTES

1. *U.S. Development in an Interdependent World*, GIST series, Bureau of Public Affairs, Dept. of State, Wash. D.C., March 1976.

Another "GIST" release, *US Prosperity and the Developing Countries*, June 1981, asserts that the economies of some less-developed countries (LDCs) have grown so large that they are beginning to have a significant impact on global prosperity and business fluctuations (countries like South Korea, Brazil, and Mexico). Citing 1979 figures, LDCs "bought US merchandise worth $63 billion, or about 35% of total US exports, including 40% of all US exports of manufactures . . . LDCs account for two-thirds of US motor vehicle exports (excluding Canada) and about half of all US machinery exports . . . 50% of our wheat exports, 60% of our cotton exports, and 80% of our rice exports. . . . The US imported $95 billion from LDCs in 1979—45% of total US imports. . . . During the last five years (1974-79) LDCs consistently have provided more than 30% of US raw material imports (excluding petroleum) and more than 50% of our food imports. . . . Of the 29 countries which imported US goods worth more than $1.5 billion in 1980, more than half were LDCs, including 6 of the 15 largest US export markets."

2. Pye, Lucian W., Ed., *Communication and Political Development*, Princeton Univ. Press, 1963.

3. Pool, Ithiel de Sola, Professor of International Studies, M.I.T., in an address to the USIA Intercultural Communications Seminar at the American Univ., March 16, 1976.

6

USIA'S INTERNAL DYNAMICS I
PERSONNEL ADMINISTRATION
LABOR-MANAGEMENT RELATIONS
WOMEN AND MINORITIES

A career as a public diplomat in the U.S. Foreign Service can be as exciting, challenging, and enjoyable as almost any career imaginable. Aside from the satisfaction inherent in public service, it brings the adventure of travel, the glamour of representing one's country in a foreign environment, the opportunity of hobnobbing with the most famous and accomplished individuals of the United States and other countries, and exposure to the political, economic, social, military, scientific, educational, and intellectual cross-currents of various cultures, including that of the United States.

Despite these positive attributes, public diplomacy as a profession is not everyone's meat. The bureaucracy of even a relatively small organization like USIA can be utterly impersonal at times, grossly unjust in individual cases, and hamstrung with bothersome government regulations intended to protect the government's interest but which sometimes cause considerable hardship or adversely affect the lives of employees and their families. Regulations that require flying on U.S. carriers, often at considerable inconvenience to the traveller; restrictions on the type and location of housing when assigned abroad; and such regulations as the one only recently changed that prohibited, or at least discouraged, the sale of one's automobile at the fair market value when leaving a post for another assignment because a U.S. Foreign Service officer is not allowed to "make a profit" in this manner, even to offset losses incurred in frequent moves—these and similar regulations and restrictions require of those who choose public diplomacy as a profession have a high degree of dedication, or a well-developed sense of humor, and preferably both.

For many families, life in the foreign service of their country can be an exhilarating, broadening experience. For others it can provide traumatic cultural shocks in the constant moves it entails from one culture to another. Those who stay are those who love that kind of life, and they are many. But there are also some who, sooner rather than later, decide that the advantages of the foreign service life aren't worth putting up with the hassle of the periodic moves and the various restrictions.

The most important element of any organization is the people who make up that organization. For U.S. public diplomacy to be effective it must function with highly qualified, highly skilled professionals who understand other cultures as well as their own, are dedicated to their mission, and are knowledgeable about the methodology and technology of modern communications. Generally speaking, USIA has had no shortage of qualified people, obtained either through what is known as "lateral entry," that is, the hiring of skilled professional communicators or educators from private industry and academia, or through the Public Affairs Training Program, which takes academically qualified individuals and provides them with on-the-job training.[1]

While USIA officials obviously have recognized at various times in various ways—through special awards, supervisory training programs, management-labor relations, its equal opportunity office, etc.—that it is the people who are the most important element of any organization, USIA's personnel system is in great need of an overhaul. In this respect, USIA may not be different from most government agencies, and it has tried, through its "open assignments" system and the earlier establishment of so-called "career counselors" to improve the administration of an admittedly complex mission involving the orderly movement of hundreds of people annually throughout the world. It may well be that in dealing with so many individuals, involving so many different job specialties, in so many different countries, and where timing is important if the more than 100 posts involved are to be adequately staffed at all times, the demands for courage and wisdom are so great that it is not humanly possible to do more than satisfy the most pressing needs of the Service. What cannot be denied, however, is that there is room for improvement. In the opinion of many seasoned USIA officers, as the decade of the 1980's begins there appears to be a far greater need for improvement in the agency's personnel procedures than at any time in recent memory. Proof of this is partly reflected in the large number of senior officers who sought retirement in recent years as much due to disillusionment with the organization and disquietude concerning its aims as for any other reasons. This disillusionment set in as a result of the fuzzily explained purposes of the International Communication Agency vis a vis the introduction of the term "communication tensions"; the apparent absence of strong, professional leadership that could articulate forcefully and clearly its intentions and desires; and a personnel system that functioned in a way that seemed at times to allow for too much indecision and that left many overseas officers with little faith in the much-heralded open assignments system because it appeared to work so rarely. Under Charles Wick's administration—although he caused controversy with some of his tactics, such as the "Let Poland Be Poland" TV spectacular, as well as his heavy emphasis on anticommunism in the agency's program—the morale of agency officers rose considerably as USIA became better known at home and as it received better funding support from the Reagan administration and the Congress than might have been expected during a period of general reductions in government spending. Nevertheless, the personnel system remained a weak, unsatisfactory internal element of USIA, politicized more than members of its career service would prefer, and lacking the degree of input by experienced foreign service personnel that would, in the view of many, have improved its performance.

When USIA was first established in 1953, many of its officers were veterans of the Office of War Information (OWI), which ran the U.S. information effort during World War II. Many were experienced communicators but lacked the management skills required to run USIA at the time. The Public Affairs Training Program, now more than a quarter-of-a-century old, was one of the devices utilized to staff USIA with officers whose experiences differed from those who had been with OWI or had given up private careers in journalism to join the new agency. Now as then, the planning and supervision of diverse informational, cultural, and educational exchange programs requires management skills that do not always come easily to someone, like a foreign correspondent, for example, who is accustomed to working alone with a singleness of purpose and not on the varied, diverse problems apt to be the daily diet of a public diplomat. Because the duties of a public diplomat entail such a variety of activities, the Foreign Service information officers (as they were formerly known) of USIA are called "generalists." They must be able to be information officers (or press attachés) at one time, cultural attachés on other assignments, and eventually, good managers as country public affairs officers in charge of the entire U.S. public diplomacy effort in a specific country.

Recognition within USIA of how important the caliber and dedication of the men and women who carry out USIA's functions are to the achievement of USIA's objectives has been expressed, as noted earlier, in various ways, one of these being special incentive awards of various types. The intention of the open assignments system was good, devised, as it was, to give public diplomats a voice in their own future assignments, as was the establishment of the career counselors, designed to match an officer's personal interests and experience with future assignments. Despite these efforts, however, morale among U.S. public diplomats has suffered since USIA was first established, partly because career counselors in many instances have been unwilling or unable to be as responsive as many USIA officers would wish, and partly for what may be more general reasons.

For an upbeat agency that deals optimistically with U.S. foreign policy, the late 1970s were not among the finest hours of U.S. history as viewed from abroad. In that post-Vietnam, post-Watergate era, the U.S. economy was in serious trouble; Iran was twisting Uncle Sam's tail; few notable foreign policy achievements were visible—relations with China were credited to Nixon and the Panama Canal settlement was highly controversial within the United States; and even American space programs, the symbol of pride in U.S. technological prowess, had bogged down with the consistent postponing of the launching date of the space shuttle, the dramatic Pioneer visits to the planets notwithstanding. In this framework, U.S. foreign policy under the Carter administration, which U.S. public diplomats abroad were charged with explaining, seemed all too often to waver between the White House and the Department of State. If signals were not too clear in the foreign policy field, they were even less clear within what was then USICA, where John Reinhardt was pushing "communication tensions," which no one clearly understood. Perhaps in such a setting no personnel system would have sufficed to uphold morale. However . . .

• when a good officer, with an excellent record, can indicate, long before his tour of duty ends, a willingness to serve at any one of 22 posts throughout the world, all with upcoming vacancies, and then remains unassigned until almost a month before his scheduled departure and is sent to a geographic area completely new to his experience—with no special training or orientation to the new cultural environment—something is wrong with the system.

• when a highly capable, dedicated, senior Latin American expert is pulled off his job and told to either study an exotic Asian language, or leave the agency, something is wrong with the system.

• when an excellent officer who has spent nearly 25 years in Asia, except for Washington assignments, that also dealt mainly with that geographic area, is forced to study a Latin American language and sent to South America, it is not surprising that he decides on early retirement, with the resultant premature loss to the agency of a highly experienced Southwest Asia expert.

These are but a few examples of actual cases of personnel actions that weakened rather than strengthened the foreign service upon which U.S. public diplomacy depends. Understandably, the many competing factors that go into any one assignment—the person's qualifications and experience, the agency's needs, health considerations, family requirements, personal desires, and the timing—cannot all be satisfied. And no unit that must match so many differing personalities with a limited number of positions will ever completely avoid individual frustrations, complaints, and disappointments. But receognition of the importance of personnel to the success or failure of U.S. public diplomacy is essential, and its strength is reflected to a certain degree in staffing patterns as they exist at any one time and by the over-all *esprit de corps*, or lack of same.

Those responsible for personnel matters in USIA might do well to initiate an in-depth review of the career counseling and open assignments systems. If the former is to be retained, it should be more reponsive to individual queries than it has been in the recent past. Nor should a lower-grade officer ever be assigned to advise a higher-grade officer on future assignments, a practice that has occurred in the past despite all attempts to avoid it. If career counselors are counselors in name only, perhaps the system should be abolished and some other assignments process devised.

As for the open assignments system, new guidelines might at a minimum correct some of its deficiencies. It is nonsense to spend so much time and effort and obtain so few visible results. Public diplomats should be given an opportunity to express their personal preferences, but it should be made clear that the needs of the service come first. It is time to return to the old principle that members of the U.S. Foreign Service commit themselves, when they enter this profession, to be ready to serve wherever they are needed.

In talking with one retired public diplomat who left the service early because of disillusionment with the directions USICA was taking in the late 1970s, he remarked:

> The problem as I see it is that we have lost our sense of direction. There has been a loss of leadership as well. The result is that in Washington in particular too many people are putting in their time and worrying about their mortgage payments rather than what the purpose of their job is. Its purposefulness seems to have disappeared.

This is a sad commentary, and goes beyond what USIA's Office of Personnel Services alone might do to bring back to those involved in U.S. public diplomacy the spirit and dedication of earlier years. But the internal personnel system of the agency is a good place to start.

Although, as noted earlier, morale has generally risen in USIA during the Wick administration, failure to continuously focus on good personnel practices can only result in decreased efficiency and lowered morale. Personnel policy becomes even more important, perhaps, at a time when USIA employees at the agency's Washington headquarters suffer from the shock of being uprooted from their favorite haunts on Pennsylvania Ave. N.W., one block from the White House, to take up new quarters crosstown in unfamiliar surroundings, farther from both the White House and the Department of State, with whom USIA works closely. Most employees affected professed opposition to the move though, in theory, consolidation of USIA activities makes a great deal of sense. But as personnel policies and working conditions are the major factors affecting morale, concentration on improved personnel policies at this particular time, both for agency employees at home and public diplomats abroad, also makes sense.

LABOR-MANAGEMENT RELATIONS

There was a time when most professional foreign service officers, including public diplomats, would have been appalled at the idea of a need for a union in the event of a difference of opinion—let alone a confrontation, with management. But times have changed, as has the thinking of many professional diplomats.

While relatively new to the professional Foreign Service, union activity among other federal employees goes back to about 1835, when the struggle for the 10-hour day began. About a hundred years later, in 1932, the American Federation of Labor (AFL) chartered the American Federation of Government Employees (AFGE). Membership in AFGE has grown from 2,500 at its founding 50 years ago to more than 300,000 by 1980, its biggest growth occurring after the issuance of President John F. Kennedy's Executive Order 10988 of January 17, 1962, which established, for the first time, a government-wide policy on labor relations for federal employees.

Changes to E.O. 10988 were made with a new Executive Order, 11491, signed October 29, 1969 by President Richard M. Nixon. Labor-management policy for federal employees was again altered by Executive Order 11616, also under Nixon, and E.O. 11838 under President Gerald Ford. E.O. 11491 authorized negotiated grievance procedures with binding arbitration and the holding of elections among employees for choosing an exclusive bargaining agent. All of the new executive orders kept the long-standing and generally accepted rule that strikes by government employees are illegal.

The U.S. labor movement generally received a boost when Franklin D. Roosevelt was president, so much so that the great strides made by labor unions during the Roosevelt Era were sometimes described as being due to the fact that in that sympathetic, Democratic president the unions had "a bargaining agent in the White House." But it was under a Republican president, Richard Nixon, that, for the first time, rules for employee-management relations in the Foreign Service of the United States were spelled out. This was done in Nixon's Executive Order 11636.

The Foreign Service Act of 1980 (Public Law 96-465 of Oct. 17, 1980 pays considerable attention to labor-management relations, much of its content being based on E.O. 11636. Recognizing that "a career foreign service characterized by excellence and professionalism is essential to the national interest," the Act's preamble goes on to state that the new law is designated "to strengthen and improve the Foreign Service of the United States."

The 1980 Foreign Service Act also makes clear the attitude of the U.S. Congress with respect to government unions, when it states:

> The Congress finds that—
>
> (1) experience in both private and public employment indicates that the statutory protection of the right of workers to organize, bargain collectively, and participate through labor organizations of their own choosing in decisions which affect them—
>
> (A) safeguards the public interest
>
> (B) contributes to the effective conduct of public business, and
>
> (C) facilitates and encourages amicable settlement of disputes workers and their employers involving conditions of employment.

The act further notes that "the public interest demands the highest standards of performance by members of the Service" and, given the unique conditions of Foreign Service employment, "a distinct framework for the development and implementation of modern, constructive, and cooperative relationships between management officials and organizations representing members of the Service" is required. It concludes: "Therefore, labor organizations and collective bargaining in the Service are in the public interest and are consistent with the requirements of an effective and efficient Government."

The exclusive bargaining agent for all USIA employees (except overseas nationals) is the American Federation of Government Employees (AFGE) Local 1812. AFGE Local 1812 represents U.S. *public diplomats* as well as USIA's civil service employees who provide program, logistical, and administrative support to overseas public diplomacy operations.[2]

The exclusive bargaining agent for U.S. *diplomats*, all of whom are employees of the Department of State, is the American Foreign Service Association (AFSA). AFGE and AFSA do not always see eye-to-eye. This was the case with respect to the development of the Foreign Service Act of 1980.

Rightly or wrongly, AFSA is viewed by many as being a "company union." Originally, it was solely a professional organization. AFSA still publishes a monthly professional magazine, the *Foreign Service Journal*, and generally serves as the major professional, in-house organization for U.S. diplomats. Its "union" activities were initiated when E.O. 11636 authorized exclusive bargaining agents selected by the holding of elections among federal employees who were in the Foreign Service. AFSA strongly supported the new Foreign Service Act of 1980.

AFGE Local 1812, on the other hand, while supportive of many of the objectives of the new legislation, nevertheless expressed serious reservations concerning it. First, AFGE questioned the grievance procedures as originally presented in the bill. AFGE was concerned that the new act would deprive members of the Foreign Service of the right to challenge instances of agency misconduct that were grounds for complaint under earlier legislation. Initially an individual complainant was not to have the right to representation of his or her own choice, though the bill, as finally written, guarantees this concept. In addition, AFGE objected to the stipulation in the new law that allows the foreign affairs agencies to appoint the grievance board unilaterally, thus departing from well-established principles governing the resolution of disputes.

AFGE's second major objection, however, was that the act would extend the unproven and controversial concept (at the time) of a Senior Executive Service (created by the Carter administration's Civil Service Reform Act) to a new Senior Foreign Service (SFS). As Abe Harris, president of AFGE Local 1812, expressed in a letter published in the *Washington Post* July 28, 1980:

> Officers reach the senior ranks only after success in constant competition with their peers. They spend a lifetime gaining competence in area and language studies. The bill would place these officers on short-term contracts subject to short renewals.

What AFGE President Harris was concerned about when he mentions "short-term contracts subject to short renewals" was the fact that the new act limited the number of years a member of the Senior Foreign Service could continue in the Foreign Service if not promoted. Management could provide limited extensions in some cases, but the decision was not in the hands of the individual who would have no recourse but to retire if management so decided. Others, of course, saw this as a means of clearing out deadwood at the top and reinforcing a generally accepted Foreign Service concept designed to make room at the top which, over the years, had fallen into disuse.

A third area where AFGE believed the new act was weak was in regard to the question of pay comparability. AFGE, understandably, preferred a formula that would increase to the greatest extent possible the pay scales of U.S. employees in the foreign affairs agencies when compared with those in private industry. The Helms substitute bill, which was defeated, received AFGE's support because it included high statutory pay linkage and 15 percent supplemental compensation for world-wide availability of Foreign Service employees.

From the beginning, it was the belief of AFGE officials that the fundamental aim of the new Foreign Service Act was to enable the Department of State—which was top-heavy with senior Foreign Service officers—legally to remove numerous senior officers from its rolls, since the State Department lacked appropriate positions for many of these officers. AFGE saw this as a problem not shared by other Foreign Service agencies and, therefore, one which should not have required such sweeping, all-encompassing legislation to resolve. Counter to this view, however, was a belief in some quarters that since this was the first rewriting of the law since 1946, it was time for many of the changes strongly advocated by State Department management, most of which had the full and active support of AFSA.

Many diplomats were pleased when, immediately after the act was signed, paychecks of lower and middle-ranking Foreign Service officers were fatter as a result of the new law. Yet the most dramatic effect of the act on the Foreign Service, for better or for worse, was yet to come. The Senior Foreign Service came into being in June, 1981, requiring many new rules and regulations to be issued in conformity with the new law. AFGE held to the view, now academic, that laws benefiting the Foreign Service and its members could have been written that would have provided positive changes without shaking up the whole Foreign Affairs establishment.

Regardless of AFGE's misgivings about the Foreign Service Act of 1980, it is now law. The act continues the prerogatives granted government employee unions earlier, such as exclusive recognition, negotiation of collective bargaining agreements, and acknowledgement that labor practices can be unfair at times, thus providing recourse for employees to file grievances. It established a Foreign Service Labor Relations Board and a Foriegn Service Grievance Board. But differences continue to exist between AFGE 1812 and AFSA, especially with respect to the interpretation of various aspects of the new legislation, which treats diplomats and public diplomats alike. Nevertheless, there were occasions during the lengthy meetings between union representatives and management officials of the foreign affairs agencies, when implementation of the new Foreign Service Act was discussed, that AFGE and AFSA were united on common issues.

In meeting the needs of public diplomats who occasionally find themselves, like other government employees, at odds with a sometimes impersonal, regulation-ridden bureaucracy, at least two complicating factors exist for AFGE Local 1812.

Elsewhere in society there is recourse to the courts as arbiters of justice for the individual. Within USIA, no "ombudsman" or third party stands between management and the employee when, as happens in all human relationships, differences of opinion develop.[3] Therefore, one of the main roles the government union plays is to represent the interests of employees when differences arise that cannot be satisfactorily settled without resort to a third party. But this role is complicated by the fact that U.S. public diplomats who are USIA employees are represented, when a need arises, by AFGE, whereas diplomats who are Department of State employees are represented by AFSA.

A second complicating factor is, as noted earlier, that AFGE represents not only Foreign Service employees—the public diplomats—but also USIA program and administrative support staffs at Washington headquarters who are predominantly Civil Service employees. This situation lends itself to the possibility of a four-way tug-of-war as different interests sometimes seek different priorities. Union leaders must recognize the differing interests of those of its membership who are in the Foreign Service and those who are in the Civil Service; of those who are overseas and of those who are at home; and even of those who are at the Washington headquarters building, and those who are with the Voice of America or with the agency's Television and Film Service at another location. The exclusive representative for all of these somewhat varied groups must provide fair and equal treatment to each, a challenge that is almost as great as that of facing management on behalf of individual employees, or groups of employees.

In any dispute where the union is representing employees, management has far greater resources at its disposal. It has behind it the power of the U.S. government; it can call on an Employee-Management Relations staff as well as USIA's general counsel and his specialized staff to prepare its point of view on specific issues; and has, in effect, all of the USIA's resources of personnel and material. These resources are immense compared with the union's resources.

The union's financial resources come primarily from the dues paid by its members. It has a small paid staff consisting of one attorney and a secretary (in 1983). While it gets some assistance from AFGE's central organization, the AFL-CIO, it is left to dedicated Foreign Service and Civil Service employees of USIA to provide the considerable voluntary labor that a successful union requires. Only in recent years has the secretary on the union's payroll been a full-time employee!

Although AFGE Local 1812 is the exclusive bargaining agent for the roughly four thousand American employees of USIA, only slightly more than one thousand are dues-paying members of the union. Eliminating those defined as managers, some of whom, despite this designation, belong to the union because they believe in its goals, it appears that about three out of four USIA employees get a "free ride" at the expense of their colleagues, enjoying the benefits the union has gained for all USIA employees without sacrificing any time, effort, or treasure.

Some public diplomats and those involved in supporting the efforts of U.S. public diplomacy still believe that a union is out of place in a government organization. Some believe that their profession should not be unionized, though not all of those believe strongly enough in the value of the American Foreign Service Association as a professional organization of diplomats, including public diplomats, to join AFSA while rejecting AFGE. Some, on the other hand, belong to both. And some have not taken the time to understand the importance to themselves and to the U.S. public diplomacy effort that union membership represents.

As mentioned earlier, some "managers" in USIA are dues-paying members of AFGE. Why? While a major purpose of the union's existence is to represent aggrieved employees when it is believed that they have been unjustly treated by the bureaucracy, its other major function is to further the interest of, and seek support for, the Foreign Service community and those associated with it, for example, USIA's Civil Service employees, in those instances where issues outside the Foreign Service impact upon the lives and concerns of diplomats, public diplomats, and their coworkers. It is for this reason that many career Foreign Service officers and Civil Servants who are managers in USIA hold union cards.

Some USIA managers also find it worthwhile to be union members because of USIA's autonomy under the Foreign Service Act of 1980. The new law does not require that the State Department's diplomats and USICA's public diplomats have to be treated exactly alike in all matters pertaining to personnel, but calls for "maximum compatibility" in regulations affecting the personnel administration of each group. Thus public diplomats, whose job responsibilities differ considerably from what one might term "pure diplomats," are not affected by all State Department regulations down to the last "T." Of course, the vast majority of regulations affecting both are either joint regulations or are very similar in content, but the recognition in the Foreign Service Act of 1980 of the autonomy of USICA (now USIA) was sought by the union as being in the individual public diplomat's interest. It implies recognition of the fact that some differences do and should exist between diplomats and public diplomats. While they have much in common, and both are assigned to U.S. embassies abroad, they perform different, distinctive roles.

A unique offshoot of union activities in the U.S. Foreign Service is the Thomas Legal Defense Fund. It was created in 1971 by interested Foreign and Civil Service employees of the Department of State, USIA, and the Agency for International Development (AID). Fund officers work with AFGE and AFSA in an attempt to resolve many issues adversely affecting personnel of the foreign affairs agencies. This is done through consultations and negotiations with management and through lobbying efforts in the Congress. When these channels fail, the Thomas Fund undertakes legal action to correct abuses. Among its many accomplishments during the past dozen years of its existence have been a court order requiring retirement credit for USIA officers who originally were employed by USIA as binational cultural center directors without such credit, a court order in 1973 that declared selection-out procedures at the time as being "constitutionally defective," and court determinations that home-leave expenses of Foreign Service officers should not be taxable because such leave is a legal requirement of Foreign Service employment.

The Thomas Legal Defense Fund is incorporated in the District of Columbia as an independent, nonprofit, tax-exempt institution. All of its officers provide their services voluntarily. In seeking reforms which are intended to improve the foreign service and guarantee the constitutional rights of all of its members, the Thomas Fund depends solely on voluntary contributions to carry out its work.

An important but sometimes unrecognized value of a responsible union operating on behalf of Foreign Service officers of USIA and their colleagues is the effect the union has had on substantive issues affecting USIA as an institution. When there is a budget crunch or when legislation is being drafted in the Congress that affect the agency's operations, union officials are often invited to present their views to congressional committees, or they themselves take the initiative to do so. The testimony of union leaders was taken, for example, during the development and discussion that followed the Stanton and Murphy Commissions' reports on how the U.S. public diplomacy effort should be organized. These contributions have been generally well received, and have been taken into account when drafting new legislation—the Foreign Service Act of 1980 being a case in point.

USIA's administration under Charles Z. Wick tested the mettle of AFGE Local 1812. Management held firm on many issues, one being the question of who should determine bonuses (allowed under the new Foreign Service Act) for outstanding USIA officers who are members of the Senior Foreign Service—their peers, who in the Foreign Service traditionally make recommendations for promotion, or management. By late 1982, this issue had not yet been resolved, and the Wick management tended to adopt a "get tough" attitude in other respects involving the agency's exclusive bargaining agent. By mid-1983, however, the union's position on the bonus issue was finally adopted.

When AFGE Local 1812 takes up an issue with management on behalf of an individual public diplomat who has, perhaps, been caught in a web of impersonal government rules and regulations adversely affecting him or his family, it is a David and Goliath situation. On the side of management as mentioned earlier, are the great power, influence, and resources of the U.S. government. On the side of the individual is a union representative whose resources pale in comparison. But as several U.S. presidents have indicated in their executive orders, and the U.S. Congress has stated most recently in the Foreign Service Act of 1980, "labor organizations and collective bargaining in the (Foreign) Service are in the public interest and are consistent with the requirements of an effective and efficient Government."

WOMEN AND MINORITIES

All government agencies have a variety of goals and interests beyond their primary objectives that must be considered in the planning and execution of their programs. The effort of the U.S. government in recent years to provide greater opportunity for women and minorities is one such goal and it has affected ICA and USIA as it has other U.S. government agencies.

Such historic events as the abolition of slavery in the United States in 1865 and the granting of the vote to women in 1922 marked major advances in the struggle by these two groups to obtain the same equality of opportunity and treatment afforded other Americans. More than a century later, in the case of blacks, and about 60 years later, in the case of women, while much progress has been made, there is evidence that even in a forward-looking, dynamic government organization like USIA attention must continue to be focused on this issue if the ideals of equality that the U.S. government espouses, and that its public diplomacy organization often portrays, are to be realized.

In the late 1970s, the casual observer of the Washington headquarters of what was then ICA (whose presidentially appointed director was a black of considerable experience both as a diplomat and as a public diplomat) might have concluded that ICA had become an institution where blacks and women, and, to a much lesser degree, other minorities, had come into their own. It appeared, to the casual observer, that the pendulum that seems so prevalent in American social phenomena, in swinging from one extreme to another, had made its swing through ICA headquarters in Washington. Yet such a conclusion would not have been completely accurate.

The most visible group of employees to the casual visitor to ICA or USIA headquarters is the agency's secretarial ranks, where change has taken place rather dramatically in the past decade or so. The major influx of black women into ICA headquarters in the 1970s could hardly go unnoticed, especially by the white secretaries who were soon to be outnumbered, and by the majority of public diplomats and Washington-based civil servants in supervisory positions, who also were predominantly Caucasian.

There was some rough going in the beginning. Some of those employed as secretaries appeared to have limited qualifications but were hired because of the urgency felt at the time to statistically raise the number of women and minorities employed, with the result that professional requirements for employment were lowered. Considerable adjustments were required because of either the lack of qualifications in some instances, or the lack of experience, or both, and the fact that the predominantly white supervisors were unaccustomed to working with more than a smattering of black Americans. But if it required considerable adjustment on the part of many supervisors, the adjustment required was probably much greater on the part of many black women who, through their new employment, were entering "whitey's world" for the first time. Eventually, for most, a satisfactory working environment developed, though there was long a need for in-house professional and social training for some secretaries new to government employment. This need, if recognized by the agency's management, was not met. Had it been, the transition, now nearly completed, might have been much easier for all concerned.

While figures regarding USIA's minority employees going back many years are either unavailable or difficult to obtain, the total number of black females employed by USIA at the end of 1973 was 394. Excluding two women who were cultural affairs officers, the remaining black females (392), we can assume, were predominantly clerks, clerk-typists, and secretaries. This was roughly 9 percent of a total of 4,285 American employees in USIA at that time.

Figures made available by ICA for December 31, 1980 (seven years later), show that out of 4,187 total ICA American positions, 570, or 13.6 percent, were filled by black women. This indicates considerable progress in the U.S. government's efforts to provide more representative employment for groups historically discriminated against. It should be noted, however, that this increase occurred in Washington, D.C., where about 70 percent of the population is black. Furthermore, the rather dramatic progress this minority group appears to have made was primarily among the lowest-paid positions, as reflected in the following:

ICA Civil Service Positions (DEC. 1980)

GS-1 through GS-6:	Black females: 285
	White females: 156
	441
GS-7 through GS-11:	Black females: 177
	White females: 215
	392
GS-12 through GS-15:	Black females: 22
	White females: 137
	159

(Spanish-speaking and Orientals accounted for only 18 and 12 employees, respectively, thus totaling 1,022 women civil service employees of ICA in December, 1980.)

Approached from a different angle, it is interesting to note that in December 1973 some 1,352 of USIA's 4,285 American employees were women (31.5 percent). They were in the following categories:

White:	905	(21.1%)
Black:	394	(9.2%)
Spanish surnamed*	19	(0.4%)
Oriental*	33	(0.8%)
American Indian	1	
Total:	1,352	(31.5%)

*Includes aliens working in Washington, D. C.

By December 1980 the total number of ICA American employees (Civil Service and Foreign Service) had been reduced slightly to 4,187. Of these, 1,612, or 38.5 percent, were women.

Looking again at the agency's December 1980 figures for Civil Service women employees (GS-1 through GS-18), we note the following percentages:

White:	508	(28.6 %)
Black:	484	(27.3 %)
Spanish Speaking:	18	(1.0 %)
Oriental:	12	(0.7 %)
American Indian:	—	—
Total:	1,022	(57.5 %)

(Of the 1,776 Civil Service employees of ICA in December, 1980, there were clearly more female employees than male employees, i.e., 57.5 percent females, 42.5 percent males.)

The number of American women employed as public diplomats in the Foreign Service of ICA in December, 1980, were as follows:

Foreign Services Information Officers

	Total	Women	
Senior positions:	151	5	(3.3 %)
Mid-career positions:	556	78	(14.0 %)
Entry:	122	46	(37.7 %)

It can be seen from the above figures that, while progress is being made in providing the same opportunities for women as for men, women as a group still have a long, long way to go. Looking at the *total* number of ICA employees (Civil Service and Foreign Service) in December, 1980, the picture that emerged was very close to the percentage seen among entry-level employees who were Foreign Service Information officers, i.e., 37.7 percent of entry-level positions in the Foreign Service of ICA were held by women while women held 38.5 percent of *all* ICA positions (the Foreign Service and Civil Service combined), as noted below:

	Total	Women	
Senior level:	223	11	(4.9 %)
Mid-career:	2,001	447	(22.3 %)
Entry-level:	1,357	691	(50.9 %)
Support staff:	606	463	(76.4 %)
Totals:	4,187	1,612	(38.5 %)

In recent years, women and minorities have not only been especially sought for employment by the federal government, but they are being promoted at a faster rate than their white male colleagues. Yet, as Mike Causey in his popular *Washington Post* column, "The Federal Diary," has noted, "they have a long way to go to match white males in the pay, grade and clout department."[4] The figures for ICA cited above certainly bear this out.

Causey quotes an Office of Personnel Management study for the period July 1, 1978 to June, 1979, which states that women received 46 percent of all promotions during that period, although they held only 37 percent of the U.S. government's 2.1 million non-postal jobs. (Interestingly, this compares with 38.5 percent of all ICA jobs.) The same study cited by Mr. Causey stated that 52 of every 100 persons hired by the government during the one-year period under review were women. The study also noted:

—One in every four women in government received a promotion during the one-year period compared to promotions for one in every six men.

—Twenty-one percent, or about 83,000 of the promotions during the period, went to minorities—a percentage point jump from the previous year.

—But despite their higher rate of promotion, eight of every ten women upgraded in government are in Grade 8 ($16,826 to $21,875) or below, most still concentrated in clerical jobs. Sixty percent of all promotions were from one clerical-type job to another; only 7 percent of the promotions for women were in professional-type jobs.

The effort of Uncle Sam to encourage more equitable treatment of women and minorities in U.S. society as a whole, and the federal government in particular, manifests itself in USIA in various ways, not least of which is in the activities of USIA's Office of Equal

Employment Opportunity (OEO). OEO was established in 1972 following the enactment of the 1972 Civil Service Law, which required the federal government to concentrate on hiring larger numbers of women and minorities, and to assure equal opportunity for members of these groups who were already employed. The first director of ICA's OEO was George Haley, the brother of Alex Haley, author of *Roots*. George Haley, a lawyer from Kansas who had unsuccessfully sought to become a congressional candidate, was a political appointee. He was given the title of assistant director of USIA for equal employment opportunity, an indication of the importance assigned to this subject, since other assistant directors of USIA headed the geographic area programs of the agency and provided the major services for the overseas public diplomacy efforts at that time.

In 1978, the position of director of the Office of Equal Employment Opportunity was downgraded from an assistant director of the entire agency to an office director, but so also were all but four of the 16 positions that were assistant directors at the time that George Haley was. So the change was not necessarily due to a downgrading of the efforts to provide preferred or special treatment for women and minorities, but was the result of a generally welcomed rationalization of the organizational structure of ICA that its director, John Reinhardt, initiated.

The changes that have occurred since special efforts were begun to recruit and advance women and minorities in ICA and USIA were not accomplished without some cost to job efficiency and to the morale of some who contended that these efforts resulted in considerable "reverse discrimination." Yet, as we have seen, the employment statistics with regard to women employees of ICA are very similar to those of the U.S. government generally (in 1979 women held 38.5 percent of ICA jobs and 37 percent of total U.S. government non-postal jobs).

USIA continues to maintain special recruitment programs for women and minorities. The Comprehensive Minority Recruitment and Training Program (COMRAT) "is designed to recruit well-qualified men and women with minority backgrounds (Afro-American, Hispanic-American, Asian-American, and Native American)" and was established "to increase applications for professional careers in the agency's Foreign Service." Applicants must fulfill a minimum age requirement of 21 and a minimum educational requirement of a bachelor's degree. Women and minorities are also sought for mid-level positions in the Foreign Service requiring academic, professional, or managerial backgrounds. Their qualifications are examined in written and oral tests, and successful candidates are appointed.

In addition to special recruitment efforts, USIA pursues other affirmative action and upward mobility policies for its employees. The results of these policies, even though not yet overly visible in the higher grades, are evident in the promotion lists of recent years. To assist in assuring equal treatment within USIA of women and minorities, there are 12 equal employment opportunity counselors who hold various jobs throughout the Washington headquarters of USIA. These volunteers offer help to any employee who believes that he or she has been discriminated against in a job-related activity, in which case counselors sometimes discuss the situation with supervisors, or, as a last resort, assist the employee in filing a grievance if it appears to be warranted. Grievance boards weigh the merits of each individual case and decide whether corrective action is warranted. The decisions of grievance boards are binding.

There are few people, in the United States at least, who would not admit that the history of the treatment of women and minorities in the world generally has been one of injustice and discrimination, which continues to this day and is far worse in some societies than in others. In the United States, the struggle for equality continues. In 1978 the United States Supreme Court, for example, said that public colleges in the United States could legally consider race in deciding whom they would admit, in order to provide greater opportunities for minorities. In 1979, it said employers and unions could take race into account in making training and promotion decisions. In 1980, it ruled that the government could use race as a criterion in handing out federal contracts. But today, with the adoption of "quotas" in some instances, there are those who contend that the pendulum has swung too far. For example, the Reagan administration's regulatory relief task force, when first established, let it be known that it would focus specifically on regulations issued by the Labor Department's Office of Federal Contract Compliance programs—the agency that has required federal contractors and subcontractors to establish hiring plans that include specific goals and timetables for employment of women and minority group members.[5]

Particularly strong reaction was voiced in some quarters when, just before President Jimmy Carter left office, the Justice Department signed a consent decree that in effect required that any examination used to select persons for the Civil Service would result in the hiring of minorities in the same proportion as those who took the test. According to Shattuck Professor of Government at Harvard University, James Q. Wilson, the panel on social justice of Carter's Commission for a National Agenda for the Eighties said that the object (of this decree) is not equality of opportunity, but an increase in the number of blacks, Hispanics, women, and minorities in a particular labor force. In criticizing any system of quotas to alleviate past and present injustices, Wilson argues that "We do not wish to be served by a 'representative' collection of brain surgeons, or naval aviators, or physicists, but by the very best such persons we can obtain, provided that no one has been unfairly excluded from consideration."[6] The same, presumably, would apply to public diplomats. Thus, while the statistics presented earlier clearly indicate that a tremendous task lies ahead in bringing more women and minorities into the higher echelons of USIA and its Foreign Service, extremist approaches, such as a quota system, are highly problematical.

In the early 1970s, USIA participated in a program for minorities that provided a fully paid, four-year college program after which the participant entered on duty as a junior officer trainee in USIA's Foreign Service. One capable young man of Hispanic origin not only obtained his college education at the taxpayers' expense under this program, but also obtained a graduate degree paid for by USIA while he was in a training status in Washington. Just before it was time for him to go overseas to begin fulfilling his obligation as a Foreign Service officer for USIA, he resigned from the agency. Thus a five-year investment, while great for him, did little for USIA. This kind of experience eventually resulted in the abolishment of this particular program, since it failed to require some years of service in return for funding.

In the attempt to correct the inequalities of the past, a few individuals reached were allowed to attain positions of responsibility in which they were expected to represent U.S. government abroad as public diplomats but lacked the knowledge, skills, dedication, or judgment to perform the required duties in a satisfactory manner. Poor judgment by a Foreign Service officer can lead to ridicule and disdain, hardly the goals of U.S. public diplomacy. If poor judgment is countenanced or excused because of race or sex, the values and standards of the Foreign Service, the U.S. government, and Americans generally can be called into question. The effort to move further ahead in creating conditions of equal opportunity for women and minorities must continue, but extreme measures can be costly and even counterproductive.

Former HEW Secretary Joseph Califano, in his book *Governing America: An Insider's Report from the White House and Cabinet*, depicts the effort made at the highest level of the U.S. government during the Carter administration to offset the historical imbalance in the number of women and minorities employed by the United States. Discussing the cabinet meeting of July 17, 1979, in which the president asked his cabinet both to resign in order to give him a free hand, and to review the work of their top assistants, Califano wrote:

> He wanted us to review the work of our subordinates, and 'get rid of all of those who are incompetent, except minorities and women.' No woman or minority member could be fired; their situations were to be discussed with the White House, the president said.[7]

Hopefully the time will come, though we are not yet there, when women and minorities will no longer require such special treatment.

Those in USIA charged with increasing the opportunities for women and minorities have good reason to feel that they have made considerable progress, as the figures cited earlier bear out. They contend that one of the difficulties faced in recent years in not achieving even greater success in recruiting women and minorities is that highly qualified individuals who might be candidates for work in the field of public diplomacy have been attracted to higher salaries elsewhere. There are, of course, other reasons as well, but the matter of salary was a contributing one, in their view, particularly in the late 1970s. However, USIA seems to have done as well or better than the U.S. government as a whole in efforts to right past injustices caused by discrimination and in moving forward in the continuing struggle for more just and equitable treatment of women and minorities in U.S. society.

Finally, if public diplomats generally can be considered in a relatively new profession, this is even more true of those women and minorities beginning careers, or planning to begin careers, in USIA's foreign service. For while progress admittedly continues to be made, the conclusions reached by the authors of a report based on a *Washington Post*/ABC NEWS opinion survey in 1981 provides little cause for complacency. The survey attempted to explore U.S. race relations in that year.

"On the whole," the *Washington Post* staff writers concluded, "the results suggest progress and improved relations." But, they added, "nevertheless, Americans, white and black, continue to use race as a principal factor in defining fellow citizens." This being so, it must be said, once again, that while progress has been made, in USIA and elsewhere, there is still a long way to go.

NOTES

1. The trainees, who in recent years generally have at least a master's degree and often a doctorate, while technically termed "Public Affairs Trainees" until 1981, were originally called "Junior Officer Trainees," or "JOT's." Efforts to abolish this redundant term over the years had little effect—though some are former college professors, they are still often referred to within USIA as "JOT's."

Their training period generally lasts 4-6 months in Washington, often including language training, and 8-12 months overseas before placement in a regular position. Now called "career candidates," participants in this program are hired permanently after three years or dropped from the USIA roles, depending on their performance.

2. The National Federation of Federal Employees, a small, independent union not affiliated with the AFL-CIO, represents the VOA's Master Control technicians.

3. In 1981, Director Charles Wick created the position of "ombudsman" for ICA. By 1982, however, the incumbent resigned alleging that his advice was being ignored by management

4. *Washington Post*, Feb. 18, 1981.

5. Reid, T. R., "Affirmative Action Is Under a New Gun," *Washington Post*, March 27, 1981.

6. Wilson, James Q., "Equal Merit, Equal Opportunity," *Washington Post*, March 4, 1981.

7. Califano, Joseph A., Jr., "Getting Fired by Jimmy Carter," excerpts from his book "Governing America: An Insider's Report from the White House and Cabinet," *Washington Post*, May 24, 1981, p. C-5.

7

USIA'S INTERNAL DYNAMICS II
USIA ON THE MOVE

The administration of the U.S. government's public diplomacy agency is a complicated business, given the variety and complexity of its operations in more than 120 countries. Aside from the challenges inherent in a personnel system that must move men and women into and out of approximately one thousand positions in those countries as frequently as every two years in many cases, as discussed briefly in Chapter 6, the administrators of USIA must concern themselves with the movement of household effects of the agency's public diplomats and overseas specialists and their families; must process shipping and travel documents; must maintain payrolls; must help arrange security protection for personnel and property; must order and control equipment, supplies, and furnishings for their offices in Washington and abroad, as well as for some government-owned or leased houses overseas; must assure that all contracts are written in accordance with government standards and regulations; must approve and advise on new construction projects and major alterations of current facilities in various parts of the world under differing conditions; must make sure that its communication and mailing systems operate as efficiently as possible between its Washington headquarters and its overseas posts and among the various elements of the agency; must maintain adequate training and recruitment of personnel; and must develop systems technology and methodology consistent with rapid technical changes in automatic data processing, word processing, communications, and related fields. This is a tall order.

All of USIA's administrative matters are the responsibility of the associate director for management, one of the four associate directors established when the U.S. International Communication Agency was created in April, 1978. Programs that had not been under an overall administrator in the past, such as the Office of Equal Employment Opportunity, the Office of Inspections, and the Office of Personnel Services, were, at that time, placed under the overall supervision of the associate director for management. In theory, this made sense. In practice, the same close contact between the director of the agency and the director of personnel services, as well as the inspector general, seems to have continued.

The complexities of administering an organization of roughly 8,000 employees scattered throughout the world notwithstanding, one area in need of strengthening is the internal administration of USIA. With the move in 1983 to a new building, where many of the agency's Washington headquarters' activities will be consolidated, an unprecedented opportunity has been provided to make improvements in the physical appearance of USIA offices in the nation's capital and in administrative support activities.

With public diplomacy here to stay, USIA has long needed a home of its own, but locating a building that might house all U.S. public diplomacy activities under one roof, with the possible exception of the Voice of America operations, and which would enable continued easy access to the Department of State and other key government agencies, seemed like an impossible dream. As late as 1982, ICA was operating out of nearly a dozen buildings spread across the Washington, D.C. landscape.

The oldest of these buildings was located at 1776 Pennsylvania Ave. N.W., at the corner of 18th Street. This section of the famous avenue that runs between 17th and 18th Street, a block from the White House, is not long. It is bordered by about ten large office buildings on each side. In addition to its offices in "1776," the director's office, the geographic area offices, the agency's library, and offices for many other of its activities were located next door at "1750," a more modern edifice—though with elevators that were just as fickle as those in "1776." It was a thoughtful person who recommended, many years ago, that the street number of USIA's main office building be changed to "1776." This is a number no American can forget, even if few Americans knew what ICA stood for when it occupied that building, and far fewer knew what

ICA did. An occasional passer-by entered "1776" when he saw the sign "International Communication Agency" outside the building and asked if he could send a telegram. Some asked if ICA was an office of the U.N. After all, the World Bank is located just on the other side of 18th Street, and the headquarters of the International Monetary Fund is in the same neighborhood.

USIA has spent millions of dollars overseas throughout the agency's history constructing and renovating buildings that put America's best foot forward—buildings in which to show audiences abroad the wonders of the United States and in which, through its libraries and by other means, U.S. culture and policies are presented in attractive surroundings. Though the United States is the wealthiest country in the world, the officers of the headquarters of America's public diplomacy agency have been a collection of hodgepodge spaces in a collection of hodgepodge buildings, due probably as much to the lack of attention this subject received in the past as to the lack of financing, among other causes. Considering the creaky, old elevators and many other signs of age of "1776"; some of the windowless, dungeon-like rooms of the relatively new Patrick Henry Building that houses the motion picture and television offices of the agency; or the crowded caverns that house the VOA offices in the old Health, Education, and Welfare building across the mall from where most of USIA's other offices were formerly located, there has long been a need for a master plan for USIA housing. Admittedly, political considerations have also, perhaps, discouraged the construction or occupation of a building that could house all USIA activities.

By mid-1982, this long-standing need for centralization of USIA (ICA) activities in Washington received the attention of Charles Wick. In testimony June 2, 1982, before the House Foreign Affairs Committee's Subcommittee on International Operations, held to consider plans for the consolidation of ICA (later USIA) in a complex in Southwest Washington, Wick told members of Congress that "an approach to USICA consolidation" has been developed that is "both workable and cost effective." He outlined aspects of the proposed consolidation, which would include the relocation of certain agency elements in a new building across from the Voice of America studios in the HHS (Health and Human Services) North Building. The General Services Administration had already begun the process of obtaining the necessary concurrence of the Public

Works Committee to lease the building for ICA at the time of Wick's appearance before the Subcommittee on International Operations. Wick stressed that the proposed consolidation could be expected to result in better policy and managerial effectiveness, enhanced professional interaction, and increased administrative efficiencies.

The Motion Picture and Television Services, which Wick placed under the supervision of the director of the VOA, would remain in the Patrick Henry Building, but most other USIA operations were to be consolidated in the new complex. Also excepted would be the agency's Foreign Press Center, which will stay in the National Press Building, easily accessible to the foreign press corps, and a photographic facility that would be too costly to move. As is the case with all changes, there were those who were not pleased with the idea of moving from northwest to southwest Washington. Some USIA staffers expressed the view that moving farther away from the foreign policy formulaters at the Department of State and from the White House could cause serious problems for USIA programming. However, others believe that the advantages of consolidation will outweigh the disadvantages of the new location.

Movement into the new USIA building at 400 "C" Street, S.W. began in December 1982, and was to be completed in about six months. Aside from the increased efficiency that should result from having most of USIA's varied activities together under one roof, the new building should also provide a few amenities such as an employee's cafeteria and space where America's public diplomats can entertain visiting foreign dignitaries appropriately. Such amenities are available to Department of State employees, all Washington-based international organizations, congressional employees, and many private firms and institutions, but USIA has always remained an orphan in this regard.

With a major step taken toward the consolidation of agency activities (though this has only been partially achieved, and in a building and location that many consider as being less than ideal, thus subject to continuing controversy), agency administrators should concentrate next on some of the stubborn administrative problems they have long faced.

It is the responsibility of the Congress to watch over the spending of the public treasure and to pass laws that protect the public interest. But there are times when, in seeking to protect the interest of the U.S. government, the congressional cure is worse than the disease. Three particularly questionable regulations prescribed by the Congress that affect both diplomats and public diplomats and that tend to create more problems than they resolve are: (1) the attempt to control overseas housing assignments not by cost but through square feet restrictions based on equating housing in Washinton, D.C. with housing in the rest of the world, despite the marked physical and cultural differences between cities and countries throughout the world; (2) the "Fly America" Act, which often forces foreign service employees and their families to travel to and from overseas posts at highly inconvenient times or via inconvenient places; and (3) the restriction levied on foreign service personnel that discourage the sale of personal automobiles "for a profit" when leaving a post on transfer, even though such sales might be at the prevailing market price.[1] While USIA administrators are not responsible for these questionable, restrictive regulations, they have never voiced any great concern with or disapproval of such picayunish rules, which directly, needlessly, and adversely affect the morale of foreign service officers and their families. Restrictions on housing could much more easily be controlled by price limitations; the Fly America Act, originally designed to help the U.S. balance of payments, ends up probably costing the U.S. government more in the long run; and the no profit regulation not only made dupes of diplomats who, as a result, often sold their personal cars at below-market prices when leaving one country to go to another, but meant that the U.S. government lost revenues it would otherwise collect as income tax. U.S. government employees, regardless of where they live and work, pay income taxes—unlike U.S. citizens who work for private industry, who do not pay such taxes if they reside overseas for 18 months or more.

Within USIA, there are a number of administrative rules and regulations that could be modernized and streamlined; those governing the management and administration of travel vouchers present one outstanding example.

Public diplomats, by the nature of their work, must travel extensively. This being the case, one might expect that USIA, with its long experience of moving people around the globe, would be able to do so quickly and efficiently and would have an efficient system to maintain records and to pay the financial obligations incurred by its official travellers. Alas, such is not the case, at least not in recent years.

Planning to get there is one thing, and for years this was handled by qualified staffers at USIA headquarters who had become highly efficient in their tasks, learning through experience the unique conditions of travel in remote corners of the world. In a change designed to let private business handle the travel arrangements of agency personnel, in the belief, perhaps, that such an arrangement would result in savings to the government, in 1982 a private travel agency was invited to take over this important administrative task. Unfortunately, the new firm had far less experience than USIA's travel specialists, who had routed public diplomats around the globe for a quarter of a century. The result was less than satisfactory, and it was not long before the new firm was replaced by another. While the effort to have private industry replace government where-ever and whenever possible is a basic tenet of a Republican admini-tration, this may be a case where the government's unique experience cannot easily be replaced.

Another administrative problem concerning the travel of USIA personnel that needs attention is the tedious task of processing travel vouchers. Whenever government employees travel on govern-ment business, they submit expense vouchers when their trip is completed. This travel voucher is inspected for accuracy and legitimacy, and the traveller eventually receives reimbursement for funds spent on behalf of the government or in conducting the government's business. At ICA headquarters in Washington in the early 1980s it was taking about six months between the time an official traveller submitted a travel voucher upon the conclusion of a trip and the time reimbursement for expenses incurred was received. In effect, the travelling public diplomat or ICA employee was being asked to carry the expenses accrued on behalf of the U.S. government for a six-month period. While this is sometimes avoided by obtaining funds beforehand, known as a "travel advance," this is not always possible or convenient and, in any event, adds more paper to an already overburdened bureaucratic system.

Within ICA Washington there was an added reason in the early 1980s for the inefficient handling of travel expenses. Protecting the substantial sums of government funds spent on official travel is a complicated process if waste and occasional fraud are to be held in check. But in the late 1970s, within ICA there was a general downgrading of clerical and secretarial positions. With the down-grading of positions was a growing inefficiency in the processing of travel vouchers. Aside from the factors already mentioned, it became increasingly difficult to recruit employees for the extremely low grades of the positions in the ICA office charged with processing the agency's travel vouchers. As experienced employees sought other jobs that offered advancement opportunities, opportunities unavailable in that particular office, backlogs grew, as did the frustrations, both of those responsible for reviewing and authorizing payments, and those awaiting the return of the funds they had spent on the government's behalf. Downgrading and deadending, i.e., leaving no room for an individual to hope for a higher salary no matter how well a job is performed, contribute to inefficiency in any office. The travel unit of ICA found itself in such a situation. The solution for the particular problem of delayed travel voucher payments lies not only in simplifying the procedures, but also in grading the positions of those who must process vouchers more in line with their responsibilities.

This is but one of a number of administrative items that cry for corrective measures to make the internal administration of USIA more responsive to the needs of its personnel and thus more efficient. Of course, the smooth functioning of services to keep an organization of more then eight thousand employees involved in diverse activities is only slightly less of a challenge than the personnel administration of USIA under the circumstances described in Chapter 6. But the need for agency administrators to focus on a number of stubborn problems, such as those cited in this chapter, has long been felt by agency insiders. Hopefully, the move into the new headquarters building of USIA in 1983 will provide the inspiration needed to tackle such internal administrative problems. Increased administrative efficiency should redound substantially to the benefit of the agency's external mission.

NOTE

1. In 1983 this restriction was finally lifted after more than a decade of criticism by the foreign service employees affected.

8

THE PUBLIC DIPLOMAT'S BASIC TOOLS
INFORMATION ACTIVITIES

The basic tools of the public diplomat are almost as varied as the cultures in which public diplomats operate. Although some specialization is required to make optimum use of the varied communications media now available in the modern world, the most successful U.S. public diplomats are those who consider themselves to be "generalists," i.e., as knowledgeable about press, radio, and television techniques as they are in administering programs of the performing arts, exhibits, or educational exchanges. While one person may be particularly strong in press or radio due to a background as a former journalist, for example, and another may administer educational exchange programs with great knowledge and gusto because of a background as a former college professor, the fact is that, despite the 1980s being an era of specialization, public diplomats must be "generalists." They must have the capability and versatility to move from the information side of programming to the cultural side, and vice versa, depending on the requirements of any particular job.

The relatively few public diplomats (in terms of global responsibilities) who foster U.S. interests abroad must and do rely greatly on their national employees in each country. Not only do these national employees understand their own cultures far better then most outsiders ever could, particularly given the limitations of the two-to-four-year tour standard for most USIA officers, but many are highly skilled professional communicators who are attracted to employment with USIA because the work is interesting, fairly well-paying, attractive, and, as a rule, benefits their own countries since the "product" they are handling is generally accurate, useful information or cultural and education activities of positive value.

The information activities that are the standard tools of the public diplomat's "trade" are press, publications, radio, motion pictures, television, and videotape recordings. The cultural activities that public diplomats administer include libraries, various other book programs, lecture, and seminar programs, English teaching, support to bi-national cultural centers, support to American Studies programs, educational exchange programs, and cultural presentations involving both the performing and nonperforming arts.

One activity that can fall administratively into either the "informational" or "cultural" category is that of exhibits. Some USIS posts find it more convenient to place exhibits under the responsibility of the information officer, though many others consider it to be among the cultural officer's responsibilities. This is a matter of convenience.

Some have argued that by delineating "cultural" from "informational" activities, problems are created that could be avoided if these terms were avoided. This has been attempted at some posts by assigning "program officers" whose duties encompass both functions. Thus, for example, a program officer at such a post who has the responsibility for mounting an exhibit on, let us say, advances in solar energy, might also have the responsibility for press releases and other publicity concerning the exhibit. In the more conventional organizational arrangement, the press unit of a USIS information section would simply be asked to carry out the publicity aspects of the exhibit as part of its normal information activities.

Throughout the history of USIA, the question of what is a "cultural" activity as opposed to an "informational" activity has often been debated. It has been pointed out that information activities frequently are "cultural" in nature, such as the distribution of a press feature on modern U.S. dance, for example. At the same time, many activities described as being cultural, such as a lecture, are just as accurately described as informational when they deal, for example, with U.S. foreign policy.

The argument as to whether an activity is informational or cultural is sterile. There is little question but that cultural and informational activities are a mixed bag. Such activities are usually a combination of both, but there is little to be gained in arguing which is which. The content of any of the activities practiced by public diplomats can be either or both. However, there is a value in categorizing informational and cultural activities from the point of view of administering these activities within an organizational framework. Thus, those activities categorized as cultural affairs officer, who is also generally known as the cultural attaché. Those activities categorized as informational are normally the responsibility of a post's information section, headed by the information officer (I.O.), who is also often generally known as the press attaché.[1]

PRESS

A radio-teletype network emanating from USIA headquarters in Washington, D.C., sends regional transmissions five times weekly to five geographic areas of the world. Known to its users as the "wireless file," (WF) it contains policy statements, the texts of major speeches by U.S. political leaders and other notables, special features, commentaries, and interpretive articles. More than 150 USIA posts abroad receive the wireless file, since it goes to many branch posts as well as those offices attached to U.S. embassies in all of the world's capitals where the United States enjoys normal diplomatic relations.

The wireless file has long been described as one of the most useful tools of public diplomats. By providing up-to-the minute information on foreign policy decisions, important U.S. government domestic activities, and other vital information such as verbatim texts of public statements by top U.S. officials, this radio-teletype network is indispensable for providing the kind of information most useful to anyone wishing to know where the United States stands on issues of global, regional, or local concern. Not only is the wireless file useful in providing host governments and local media representatives, among others, with the latest, authentic information about U.S. policies and actions, but it also provides a highly practical means for keeping U.S. ambassadors and their staffs informed in greater detail on various issues of interest to them than might otherwise be available through regular diplomatic channels. Most U.S. ambassadors would agree that this daily file is "must reading" for them.[2]

It is this channel of communication that provides the majority of the material used in the USIS press releases issued by individual posts throughout the world. Items are chosen that are, or could be expected to be, of interest to the host country. These are distributed to the local media and selected individuals, as, for example, local government officials. In many countries these releases are often reprinted in the local press or find their way into local radio and television newscasts. Sometimes they provide local editors with excellent background information for their editorials.

In a survey of practicing public diplomats made by USIA some years ago, the wireless file received the highest grade of any single item in the agency's list of public diplomacy instruments. It was the one vehicle of communication most valued by overseas posts above all others. As noted earlier, it has consistently been considered as the most important tool available to U.S. public diplomats for bringing needed information quickly and efficiently to important audiences abroad.

Due primarily to financial restrictions, USIA has not been able to keep pace with the changing communications technology; faster and more efficient reception of the wireless file could be achieved if outdated equipment were replaced. Constant progress is being made, however, in updating equipment, in making greater use of satellites, and in utilizing word processors to print multiple copies of this popular and highly useful "file."

An exciting, new computer-age development is the transmission of USIA's wireless file to selected overseas posts by utilizing computers, satellites, and available telephone lines. In 1982, experiments utilizing the new system met with complete success. As a result, USIA plans to expand the system to an ever-increasing number of posts, though the rate of expansion is dependent upon budgetary factors, the availability of direct dial circuits and ability to maintain them, and the continued free flow (in countries where there are no restrictions) of the transmission of data over direct-dial circuits.

The WF is currently transmitted to overseas posts via several mechanisms: radio frequency, shared U.S. Department of State lines, and land lines. The maximum rate of transmission for land lines is approximately 75 baud.[3] Consequently, the normal transmission of the WF may span a three-to-four-hour period or longer which, in turn, subjects the transmission to numerous errors and failures. Once received at the post, the WF must be either manually cut and pasted or retyped to produce a clean copy for reproduction and distribution to end users.

The new system uses available telephone lines that allow USIA to transmit information between the overseas post and Washington at either 300, 1200, or 2400 baud. This significant increase in the transmission rate significantly decreases the time needed to receive the file. The entire WF can now be received utilizing this system in a ten-to-thirty-minute time frame depending upon the size of the file and the transmission speed used.

The higher rate of transmission is accomplished by using not only more advanced equipment, but by employing a different communication discipline. In other words, it is not only the technology that makes the difference, but the methodology as well. This discipline, called binary synchronous transmission, allows the equipment to verify the content of all data and request retransmission of any characters that were not received correctly due to problems on the telephone line. Thus, the overseas USIS post receives the WF free of any erroneous characters caused by communications problems. If the connection is so poor that data cannot be received properly, the equipment automatically disconnects the line and informs the operator. A new connection can then be established by redialing.

In addition to the tremendous savings in time and labor that this new communications system provides, as more and more USIS posts come into the system a substantial monetary savings will be realized. For example, the cost of transmission of the WF to some overseas posts using a combination of satellite feeds and land lines is as much as $100,000 annually. With a 12-minute telephone call costing in the neighborhood of $30 or so, the annual cost of the WF transmission to some countries can be reduced to about $6,000 to $8,000.

PUBLICATIONS

There are 14 magazines in 16 languages published and distributed by USIA, plus a few others at major posts. Most of the articles in these publications are selected from major U.S. magazines and periodicals. With almost all of the mammoth production of America's communications-saturated society to choose from, many of these are outstanding articles by outstanding specialists in various fields. The content is heavy, as one might imagine, on U.S. culture, politics, economics, and international affairs.

There are two major publications edited by USIA's Washington headquarters. *America Illustrated*, a monthly magazine in Russian, is distributed in the USSR while an equal number of the Soviet Union's magazine for American readers, entitled *USSR*, is distributed in the United States under an agreement between the two countries. The other major USIA publication is *Dialogue*, a scholarly quarterly that has received high praise for its content from its many readers throughout the world. It is published in English, French, Spanish, Polish, Romanian, Russian, and Greek. Without doubt it is the agency's most prestigious magazine for global distribution, devoted as it is to intellectually challenging articles that often present various points of view.

In 1979, while John Reinhardt was director of ICA, it was decided to change the format of *Dialogue* from a smaller, two-color, unpretentious magazine to a larger, multi-color one that could take advantage of spectacular color photos and more dramatic artwork. Some of the funds for this changeover became available by abolishing a bi-monthly publication of the agency, *Horizons USA*. This latter publication had been published for a number of years in English, Spanish, and 13 other languages. But it was not particularly popular among many public diplomats abroad charged with its distribution to foreign audiences. Its critics were of the opinion that it lacked the scholarship of *Dialogue* and the splash of *America Illustrated*. As an "in-between child," few lamented its demise when it disappeared. But the changed format of *Dialogue* was met with some misgivings.

There were those who felt that *Dialogue*'s dramatic change in format placed too much emphasis on design and layout, and that while its photography and artwork are highly impressive, providing, as they do, an example of the ultimate in modern printing capabilities, this tends to detract from the content of the articles presented therein. The content of the less pretentious earlier issues of *Dialogue* had, so to speak, stood on its own for so many years, yet had clearly reached countless readers throughout the globe who had grown accustomed to *Dialogue*'s conservative format. Proof of their general satisfaction and the fact that *Dialogue*'s articles were being digested was evident in the numerous letters received by its editors, commentary in newspapers quoting articles which appeared in *Dialogue* in various countries of the world, requests for reprints, and in other ways. "Why disturb a good thing?" critics of change asked, with some pointing to the continued global popularity of the ubiquitous *Reader's Digest* as a reason for not changing *Dialogue*'s format.

It is very American to want to change, however, even when it is a good thing that one has going. Many were convinced at the time that USIA (then ICA) should have stayed with the old format because it emphasized the content. One of the problems with the agency's publication *Horizons* and, perhaps, the reason it never truly got off the ground in a number of countries, is that earlier editions were so striking in their format that "format" seemed to have a much higher priority than content.

One element, however, that encouraged the change was the practical advantage of producing all or most of the agency's magazines in similar sizes in order to increase printing efficiency by cutting down on paper waste. U.S. ingenuity was at work here. Another reason for the change was the desire to present U.S. visual arts in their true color and dimensions. To do this required a new format as well as greater emphasis on artistic themes. In the final analysis, perhaps *Dialogue* gained rather than lost readership following its major change in format. In any event, it remains a highly readable commodity and one of the best products produced by USIA. One of its greatest selling points is its generally objective approach to a great variety of topics of interest to scholars and intellectuals the world over. Without doubt it is one of USIA's least "propagandistic" vehicles. It is this that provides its strength and high receptivity.

USIA publishes two magazines that are designed for special audiences. *Economic Impact* is a quarterly that is published in English and Spanish. Its impressive, authoritative articles on economic subjects have been well received for many years by those interested in economics and related fields. Sometimes articles from *Economic Impact* are reprinted in local newspapers and magazines at the request of editors, columnists, or economists who believe that a particular article should receive wider circulation.

The other speciality magazine of USIA is *Problems of Communism*. This is a scholarly, bimonthly publication that presents timely as well as theoretical articles relating, as the title indicates, to communism and, of course, communist societies. It is the only regular publication of USIA, except for *English Teaching Forum*, which is for teachers of English as a foreign language, that the Congress allows to be sold and distributed within the United States, presumably because of its subject and its scholarly approach. As a result, it is available to scholars and students in most of the university libraries in the United States.

Since the subject of communism, important as it is in today's world, does not turn everyone on, some public diplomats suggested years ago that the title of *Problems of Communism* should be changed and the content of this publication broadened. Envisioned was a publication that might have been entitled "International Politics" or "International Problems" and which might have created greater interest to larger audiences, particularly if, while dealing with "problems of communism," it also dealt with other political philosophies. It might do with politics what *Economic Impact* does with economics. While this idea has been discussed within the agency at various times, it has never been adopted. A perceptive Asian once commented on "Problems of Communism" as a title by noting, "What makes the U.S. think that only communism has problems? Perhaps a more fitting title would be 'Problems *with* Communism'."

Four major magazines that USIA publishes for specific geographical regions are *Topic*, published eight times a year in English and French and distributed in sub-Sahara Africa; *Al Majal*, a monthly published in Arabic for Near Eastern and North African countries; *Trends*, published in Japan; and *Span*, which is published in India and distributed in that country.

Most of the agency's magazines are printed at two regional service centers for this purpose, and located in Manila and Mexico City. A third center located in Beirut for geographic and other advantages, had to be closed due to the Lebanese political situation.

FILM, TELEVISION, AND VIDEOTAPES

The three audio-visual vehicles of films, television, and videotapes are related, and thus managed by one office in USIA under the direction of the director, Television and Film Service. Just as the technology moved from film to television to videotape, and as these media gained in importance, organizational changes occurred in USIA.

As early as 1952, when the Voice of America studies were still located in New York City, USIA's original television service became part of VOA. When the VOA staff moved to new studios in Washington, D.C., the television staff moved with them. At the time, except for the United States, only the United Kingdom and West Germany had regular television broadcasts, so the agency's television role was a minor one. In 1958, a separate Television Service (ITV) was established and, by 1963, its staff had grown from 40 to 115 persons. It was concerned mainly with contracting and packaging programs. Much later, the agency began to produce its own shows, and ITV expanded as television expanded, both at home and abroad. In late 1965, the Television Service was merged with the Motion Picture Service.

In 1982, the year that Charles Wick achieved the goal of abolishing the International Communication Agency as the name of America's public diplomacy organization, returning to the old names of USIA at home and USIS overseas, he also returned the agency's Television and Motion Picture Service to the jurisdiction of the VOA, where it had been at its inception 30 years earlier. Like some of the other actions taken since Wick became director of USIA, this was applauded by some, criticized by others. The critics felt that television was too important as a leading communications vehicle in the modern world to come under the wing of the Agency's radio section. After all, the U.S. Advisory Commission on Public Diplomacy describes television in its 1982 Report to the Congress and to the U.S. president as being "perhaps the most complex and powerful means of communicating with foreign audiences when it is used wisely and well."[4] If this is so, critics argue, there is good reason to maintain its organizational independence from the VOA. In fact, the 1982 decision to place the Motion Picture and Television Service under the VOA was reversed less than a year later, on July 24, 1983, when the Television and Film Service was again established as a separate element within USIA.

In its 1982 report, the Commission also expressed publicly the same concern about the agency's failure to adequately use the full potential of television, a shortcoming at times expressed privately by some public diplomats.

"In the Commission's view," the report states, "the Agency has not yet realized the exciting potential of this medium." While commending its initiative in creative television programming by citing such uses of satellite television in 1981 as President Reagan's State of the Union message and foreign press interviews with senior government officials, the commission's report urges that additional steps to achieve the full potential of television technology be taken. In addition to calling for a major study "to ensure that the Agency realizes the full potential of television programming and remains completely abreast of technological advances," the commission's only other "recommendation" regarding television is to welcome increased cooperation between the agency and the private sector while "it opposes (private sector) funding of major programs, particularly those articulating U.S. foreign policy." Its concern here is that the funding methods used for the Agency's "Let Poland Be Poland" global telecast (about 90 percent of the estimated $500,000 cost was covered by the business community, foundations, and private individuals) not become a precedent. "The possibility that such products (as "Let Poland Be Poland") could be improperly influenced motivates our concern," the report states.[5]

The development of videotaped programs within USIA began, as did television, not within the Motion Picture Service as one might have expected, but elsewhere—in this case in the Cultural Service. Initially it was almost a one-man operation, but it quickly became so successful in providing programs in this new medium, at a time when the medium itself was taking off, that it soon became imperative for more funds and personnel to be assigned to this activity in order to greatly enlarge the agency's videotaped programs. Reluctantly, the unit in the Cultural Service that had pioneered VTRs (videotaped recordings) transferred its equipment and materials to the motion picture service. The era of videotaped programming within USIA began in earnest.

As new technologies develop, old techniques disappear. In the mid-1950s when USIA was new and relatively inexperienced, the "mobile unit" of the Motion Picture Service was a stock item at many USIS posts. It was standard practice in the developing countries, which were and still are the majority, to load the USIS mobile unit with a projector, films, and a gas-powered portable generator and take off for the hinterland to show U.S. films, primarily documentaries, to people in remote towns and villages, many of which did not boast a single motion picture theater of their own. Thus, when the USIS operator showed up at the town square for an open-air film showing, a good percentage of the community turned out to see the wonders of the silver screen. It really didn't make much difference to most of the audience what was being shown, for in most of these villages there was little or no competition in the way of entertainment. A combination of the growth of television, and the realization in later years that this was not an effective method of bringing U.S. views to national leaders, finally brought about the demise of the mobile units.

The use of videotape as a tool of public diplomacy has also undergone changes as experience with this medium has increased. When the potential of videotaping first came to the attention of USIA's leadership, it was looked upon somewhat as a panacea—the answer to a public diplomat's dream! It provided such an easy way, it seemed, to bring U.S. policy statements and other information to the attention of leaders and movers in societies around the globe. All one had to do was to bring an assistant secretary of state, for example, into the studio at the Patrick Henry Building, where the Motion Picture Service is located, run the cameras while a few questions are being answered, and there you have it—U.S. policy right from the horse's mouth! But then some problems developed. None were as unique as that which occurred on the day one of the agency's policy officers escorted an assistant secretary of state to the new Patrick Henry Building for a taping session. After being unable to readily locate the building in downtown Washington, the unhappy assistant secretary demanded that he be returned immediately to his own office across town, a demand that was immediately complied with. Later the chagrined policy officer realized that he had taken the assistant secretary to Sixth Street in southwest Washington instead of Sixth Street in northwest Washington!

Most problems that developed with this new communications medium when it was first introduced were much more common. The agency's leadership quickly became enamoured with the videotape technique. This, plus the fact that it was so easy to interview many of the numerous leaders and specialists who inhabit or transit Washington, resulted in a flood of videotaped programs to the field—many more than could possibly be effectively used—unless all other types of programs were reduced or halted. And because, initially, almost all of the videotaped programs were interviews conducted in the Washington studios of the Motion Picture Service, they were generally "one on one"—consisting of an interviewer and the person being interviewed. These shows became known, somewhat perjoratively, as "talking heads."

With so many programs being produced, and on a great variety of themes, there were bound to be some that were outstanding and some that were simply mediocre. It was possible, of course for each overseas post to be highly selective about what it chose or did not choose to program. Yet problems developed in arranging as many videotaped showings to key audiences as Washington officials had originally anticipated.

There are few individuals who, assuming they are not camera shy to begin with, do not relish the idea of being filmed, or, if you wish, videotaped. Most people in this category, particularly top government officials, love it. The same cannot always be said for those who are invited to view the results. One really has to be interested in the subject to focus attention on a talking person for any length of time, particularly when the opportunity is not provided to talk back. Yet USIA officials, when they first moved forward in earnest with this new communications medium, and despite general recognition of the importance of dialog, expected their public diplomats to achieve great results with videotaped programs—immediately.

The first problem was to get busy, important leaders to sit still for 25 or 30 minutes to watch a videotape. In those early days of VTRs, videotape machines were rare, so the machines were generally available only on USIS premises or at the homes of public diplomats, though they could also be moved to other locations if necessary. In addition to having to go to where the machine was located, the subject in question had to be one of priority interest to attract and hold the interest of viewers. Once the audience and the machine were brought together, the next problem was to expect the audience to remain silent during the program. Not only do leaders in all fields tend to be good talkers, but as soon as two people are in a room looking at a small screen, only the most interesting or entertaining of programs will prevent the normal gregariousness of human beings from expressing itself in conversation, to the detriment of the message coming from the tube. Another problem that soon became evident was that not only is time required to plan, invite, and hold a videotape showing for a highly selective audience, but it is often appropriate, possibly even necessary, to make the occasion a social event as well. It was soon discovered that although "talking heads" were easy to produce, they were not so easily utilized.

As time went on and the glamour of this new medium wore off, these problems sorted themselves out. Videotaping became more selective, both on the production side and on the distribution side. The quality of the productions improved, the number of "talking heads" diminished, the number of videotaped films and television programs increased, and the demands for placement became more practical, leaving the final word, as it always should be, to the discretion of the public diplomats on the spot. Furthermore, more videotape machines became available. Today it would be inconceivable to public diplomacy practitioners to think of carrying out their activities without the use of videotapes. For highly selective audiences they are an invaluable tool.

USIA started out with videotapes using half-inch reel-to-reel tapes The technology then advanced and the decision was made to switch to 3/4 inch cassettes, which were much easier to handle and became a standard at many television stations, particularly in developing countries, though the two-inch tapes were the mainstay of large stations. Their use by TV stations was a major reason for the adoption of this format by USIA. Of the three television systems in common use in the world today—the U.S. system, NSTS, which is also used by Japan: the German system, PAL; and the French system, SECAM—the first two are the ones most widely used in those countries where USIA has the greatest possibility of placing its programs on local television stations. With home videotape machines becoming more and more popular throughout many countries of the world, USIA might well study the feasibility of doing more in the line of producing and distributing its programs in half-inch cassettes for these home system. This would enable key contacts in many countries to borrow these programs for viewing in their homes.

USIA still operates its audiovisual programming in the Patrick Henry Building in northwest Washington, where its studios are located and it produces and ships out hundreds of films and videotaped programs yearly. Almost 200 videotaped shows alone are produced in these studios annually, and many more copies of news-oriented U.S. network programs are acquired, videotaped copies of which are distributed to USIS posts abroad.

With regard to motion pictures, about 100 films in all categories are produced yearly by USIA and more than 300 films are acquired from private U.S. sources. The copyrights for some of these are obtained, after which they become part of the permanent collections of USIA's overseas posts. Others are borrowed for periods of 30 to 90 days, but due to copyright rules can be shown only as specified under the loan agreements. Thus copyright restrictions, and the high cost of obtaining rights, preclude the agency from making available to foreign television stations many of the commercial and noncommercial films produced in the United States.

The most famous film ever made by USIA was *Years of Lightening, Day of Drums*. Produced by George S. Stevens, Jr., who was, at the time, director of the agency's Motion Picture Service, it depicted the life, times, and death of President John F. Kennedy. By a special law of Congress the agency was granted permission to allow the showing of this film within the United States. As a rule, however, agency-produced materials such as films and publications (*Problems of Communism* is an exception) cannot be distributed within the United States. For many years agency officials have sought a liberalization of this restriction on the distribution of their products in order that U.S. taxpayers, who finance the agency out of the taxes they pay to the federal government, might more easily examine what this branch of the U.S. government produces and distributes. Only on rare occasions have they been successful in this effort, which is one reason why so few Americans know what their public diplomats do, and how they do it.

The history of motion pictures is so identified with U.S. culture that it is rather surprising that U.S. public diplomacy has not made greater use of this medium. Many other nations, proud of the achievements of their film industry and fully aware of the impact of film as a means of demonstrating a country's culture, often sponsor their own film festivals in foreign countries. These festivals usually generate a great deal of interest in, and empathy for, the sponsoring nation. While it is true that U.S. films dominate most of the world's commercial markets, including television, and Hollywood producers frequently participate in commercially sponsored international film festivals, only infrequently do totally American film festivals take place overseas. If ways could be found to make outstanding Hollywood productions more easily available for such film festivals, which could be sponsored by USIS or the U.S. embassy in selected countries, it would provide another highly welcomed means of communicating with foreign audiences.

One of the running debates within the agency among those particularly interested in film has to do with the role of agency-produced films. In recent years the argument has been advanced that, given the high cost of film production today, and the wealth of films now being produced privately and commercially in the United States, USIA productions should be held to a minimum. The problem with this argument is that, while a tremendous number of films are in fact produced in the United States, the vast majority are geared to specific purposes and specific audiences, neither of which may fit the particular needs and audiences that most interest public diplomats.

An example of this can be seen in the history of a film USIA produced on illegal drug trafficking. For the past decade, this subject had been of growing interest to the U.S. government, as international drug trafficking has grown to alarming proportions. The cost to U.S. society as a result of this illicit trade, in terms of wasted lives, deaths, injuries, and increased crime rates, is incalculable, although the figure of $17 billion annually was cited for many years. In the early 1970s, as interest in this subject continued to grow, a number of U.S. filmmakers began producing films which, they hoped, would meet the new demand for more knowledge about this problem. Unfortunately, as one narcotics expert remarked, "Some of these films are worse than the drugs themselves." While that may have been an overstatement, the fact is that counteracting the drug explosion is a complicated enterprise involving education, prevention, rehabilitation, and many other elements, any one of which, let alone several, would be exceedingly difficult to portray on film—even assuming that accurate information was available to the film producer. Equally important is the fact that none of the films already produced or those scheduled to be produced at that time was apt to carry the message that U.S. public diplomats believed most important if U.S. cooperative antinarcotics programs were to succeed in selected countries—the message that narcotics was not a problem solely for the United States.

In the early 1970s, for example, it was a common belief in most Latin American countries—even in those which were major sources of illicit drug trafficking—that the narcotics problem was a "U.S. problem," not one with which they needed to be too concerned. Unfortunately, as time and experience proved, they were wrong. The youth of other countries, particularly in those countries engaged in drug trafficking, also became afflicted with the drug disease. In addition, the huge sums generated by the narcotics trade eventually produced negative economic factors, such as increased inflation, in many societies. Yet there was not a single film available to USIA at the time that could carry the message the United States wanted to convey—that the adverse effects of illicit drug trafficking could become as damaging to other countries as they were to the United States.

After much planning and urging by those interested in this problem, USIA finally produced its own film on illicit drug trafficking. Entitled *The Trip*, it was the creation of one of the few film producers employed by USIA, Ashley L. Hawken. Soon after its completion it became one of the most sought-after films by the growing number of individuals and groups throughout Latin America who recognized the drug problem for what it was and what it could become.

As a case study of the effects of drug trafficking on individuals, families, and society generally, *The Trip* provided a realistic portrayal of what was happening in one Latin American government, it provided a clear lesson that was well received in an idiom with which Latin American audiences could easily identify. Though now somewhat outdated, *The Trip* continues to be used because so little else of equivalent effectiveness is available even today. It thus remains an outstanding example of why America's public diplomacy agency should not rely entirely on what can be acquired from outside sources. There will always be occasions when an "in-house" production, designed with specific audiences in mind, though costly, is the best means for delivering a specific message. Not until 1983, a dozen or so years after *The Trip* was produced, and despite the continuous growing concern and negative effects of illicit drug trafficking, did USIA plan to produce another film on this theme.

It is television, however, that has become the major audio-visual tool of public diplomats today in most countries. Today satellite programs are increasingly common, though they are still costly enough to preclude their being used as extensively as radio. Most programs that warrant the kind of expenditure by USIA that satellite telecasting requires are major policy statements or major events of political significance. Not infrequently, however, what may seem of utmost importance in Washington is seen as being far less important in other areas of the globe. As a result there is a tendency on the part of Washington bureaucrats to occasionally lose perspective. This occurred, for example, as far back as President Eisenhower's day, when *all* of his press conferences were filmed and sent to USIS posts abroad, where they saw less and less use until the idea of filming every one of his press conferences was finally abandoned. It is somewhat surprising that it took so long to realize that a press conference, even at that time, rapidly grew stale. In the early 1980s, there continued to be occasional attempts by USIA to send by satellite press conferences or speeches by top U.S. government officials which, while possibly earthshaking in Washington, were less so elsewhere, warranting at best a minute or less of prime newstime in most countries overseas—thus expensive satellite telecast.

One of USIA's earliest attempts at satellite telecasting was during Henry Kissinger's first visit to Latin America as secretary of state. He made a major foreign policy address on U.S.-Latin American relations while visiting Caracas, Venezuela, his first stop. With the cooperation of the Venezuelan government, the telecast emanated from a Caracas television studio and was sent by satellite to more than a dozen countries in Latin America in three languages—English, Spanish, and Portuguese. At the time there was possibly more interest in the technique than in the content of the program, and though there were some technical difficulties, which resulted in the soundtracks getting mixed, the telecast was a notable "first" in public diplomacy. It was the beginning of a technique that perhaps saw its culmination, as far as public diplomacy is concerned, about a decade later when, on January 31, 1982, the International Communication Agency sponsored a program called "Let Poland Be Poland."

"Let Poland Be Poland" was beamed by satellite to more than 30 countries around the world where it was seen, in whole or in part, by an audience estimated at more than 170 million people. Additional millions saw all or part of it later by videotape on other television stations and on closed circuit receivers.

"Let Poland Be Poland" was a highly controversial project that caused considerable comment and discussion, including a number of editorials about its technique, its taste, and its effectiveness. Most would agree, however, with the *Toronto Star* when that newspaper noted that "it also happened to be a well-done example of propaganda at the highest level." "Well done" and "highest level" are, of course, subject to one's own interpretation.

Whether this global television effort influenced the Russian and Polish governments to soften their harsh policies toward the Polish people, or the Western Europeans and others to more actively support U.S. policies toward those two governments is problematical. Some would argue that it appears to have served little purpose other than to demonstrate what can be done with modern communications technology. Others argue that it kept the problem of the Polish people alive in a world where attention spans are extremely limited. And still others argue it resulted later in Polish government restrictions on USIS Warsaw operations that might not have occurred if USIA (ICA) had "Let Poland Be Poland," or at least had been more subtle in its approach to this issue, in television and other media.

The program was estimated by USIA officials to have cost about $500,000, much of which they said, was not charged to the U.S. government, but this figure certainly does not include the time and effort put forth by U.S. public diplomats throughout the world and the vast number of communications to and from Washington generated by the planning, last-minute changes, and execution of such an earth-girdling undertaking.

"Let Poland Be Poland" was produced in the Reeves studios in New York, where technicians who received and recorded scores of statements by world leaders and cultural figures worked round-the-clock. According to USIA, they taped scenes of rallies and demonstrations in favor of Polish freedom. They recorded performances by noted artists and readings of well-known personalities. This material was assembled into a continuous, 90-minute-long production that was broadcast to the world via satellite in seven languages (English, French, Spanish, Portuguese, German, Italian, and Arabic). Technical planning and supervision was by USIA (ICA) personnel, while Pasetta Productions of New York actually produced the program. USIA reported that more than 345 people, both from government and from the private sector, were involved in making the program. In New York, producing the program required all seven floors of the Reeves facilities as well as a large studio in downtown Manhattan.

In the main satellite broadcast at 1900 GMT January 31, 1982, different European language soundtracks were broadcast simultaneously and in synchronization with the video image. The program was subsequently repeated via satellite at 2400 GMT in Arabic.

All translations were prepared by a staff of some 40 professional translators, hired by ICA's televison and film service, for the task of working under tremendous time pressure in Reeves' studios.

As the program was sent out by satellite, it also went from New York by landline to ICA headquarters in Washington, to PBS Washington, to Canada, to UPI TV News in New York, to Home Box Office in New York, to German Television in New York, and to NBC New York. All five INTELSAT satellites were used at one time or another in transmitting the program. The Voice of America also broadcast "Let Poland Be Poland."

A special technical problem that had to be overcome was that of converting program material from U.S. to European technical standards. Not only was this necessary for the live satellite transmission, but also for many of the tapes air-shipped to countries that had requested videotape instead of satellite coverage. The necessary conversion for satellite transmissions was performed at receiving earth stations overseas. The tapes were converted in the offices of companies in New York and Florida and then sent to Washington for overseas shipment.

Whenever "Let Poland Be Poland" is discussed in the future, there will probably be arguments as to whether it was worth the high cost, the time, and the effort. A few days before the scheduled telecast the program's length was extended from 60 to 90 minutes, in itself a questionable move when satellite time and program time had already been allotted in so many countries and was difficult to change on such short notice. There is also the greater question of whether information policies can ever be placed before political policies, as some contend was the case in this instance.

The program brought fame of sorts to ICA, as well as tremendous publicity to Poland's plight. But did it bring any second thoughts to Soviet and Polish leaders? Did it make the Western Europeans any more willing to associate themselves with U.S. policies toward Poland at a time when the Europeans had adopted a much more cautious stance than the United States? And what of its effects on the Polish people themselves—positive initially, no doubt, but what then? Full answers to these questions may never be known. What is certain is that a giant step in the use of worldwide television for public diplomacy was taken with this unique program. This step, like others before it, is but one of many more which will follow as the communications technology already available to us shrinks our globe, and makes events more instantaneous for more people than ever before.

After discussing one of the latest experiments in satellite telecasting, it may appear nostalgic to mention a slower-paced, earlier television technique of public diplomacy—that of the television series. Although this is no longer as widely used by the U.S. public diplomats as in the past, there are still opportunities where a television series can be a good means of reaching wide audiences in the developing world.

The value of producing various series of television programs, such as the *Ahora* (*Now*) Series which was produced by USIA for many years more than a decade ago, was often debated within USIA. (*Ahora* was produced in Spanish for Latin American audiences.) The value of such a series is that, by offering a television station 13 completed programs and in getting an agreement from the station to present each program weekly in a specific time slot, placement is assured and the series becomes a ready vehicle for what is known in the trade as "freight." Too much "freight," and the program cannot be "sold" to television station managers. This happened once, in the case of the *Ahora* series, at a time when the Panama Canal issue was a major problem in U.S.-Latin American relations. By devoting an entire program in that series to the Panama Canal, the "freight" proved to be too much for at least one Latin American country, which decided to cancel the entire series.

While the *Ahora* series served U.S. public diplomats very well for many years by bringing to thousands of Latin American television viewers interesting presentations of U.S. culture, and occasional programs regarding issues of concern to Latin America and the United States, there was always a running debate within USIA between those who sought more "freight," and those who believed that the entertainment value had to be at a high level for the program to be accepted by station managers. As a rule the policy and geographic area representatives sought more messages in these programs while the producers, wishing to exercise their creative and artistic talents to the fullest, argued strongly about the necessity of making the shows entertaining as well as informative if they were to be placed on leading stations and in good time slots. Of course, if these programs delivered no "freight," there would be no reason for public diplomats to sponsor them. In fact, they usually contained a fair mixture of entertaining features and presentations of serious subjects of interest to both the U.S. and Latin America, though the debates regarding the right "mix" never ceased.

As Latin American television generally became more sophisticated, the *Ahora* series was moved more and more away from prime-time placement. Because of this trend, many who believed that this type of programming served the agency well in the past, by the late 1970s argued that it was time to go on to other things. Others, however, argue that there are still many places in the third world where a series like *Ahora,* in the local language, would be welcomed and useful.

There are many excellent educational television programs and documentaries that have been produced commercially or by private groups in the United States that would be highly useful if rights could be obtained for their placement by USIA in countries where commercial placement is impossible or improbable. Generally, however, the copyright costs are prohibitive, though there have been exceptions. One outstanding exception was the Alistair Cooke series, *A Personal History of the United States.* Shown widely in the United States and in many other countries, this series depicts (in the usual 13 episodes) the dynamism as well as the problems encountered in the growth of the United States from 13 weak colonies to today's superpower status. When the rights were obtained by USIA for Peruvian television in the late 1970s, for example, this series was so popular that it was shown twice nation-wide at a time when that country was struggling to return to a democratic form of government. Without USIA's assistance, this excellent program may never have become available to Peruvian television audiences.

Finally, one of the more unique ways in which USIA helps to present U.S. views to foreign television audiences is to provide what is known as "facilitative assistance" to foreign TV teams who come to the United States to produce their own programs about the United States. These teams are often welcomed in Washington by USIA's motion picture and television service and assisted by arranging interviews for them, by providing studio space, and in other ways. The visiting TV crews interpret what they see as they see fit, but because they are able to talk to key, knowledgeable individuals and gain access to places they want to film, their final product is apt to be more accurate and objective than it otherwise might be. In this way, as with USIA's foreign correspondent centers in Washington and New York, where correspondents are welcomed and assisted, and where special press conferences with top U.S. officials are often held, public diplomacy is practiced at home.

RADIO

Numerous USIS posts in the developing world produce their own radio programs in local languages using their local employees or professional radio talent under contract arrangements. Often these local programs contain Voice of America taped shows in whole or in part. By tailoring these locally produced programs to local interests and by maintaining a high quality of production, many radio stations find them to be attractive additions to their regular programming schedules. Some of these programs enjoy great popularity, in part due to the considerable amount of resources which are available for their production. These resources include the wealth of VOA materials and the creative talents and technical skills of USIA's local radio unit, which is attune to local needs and interests.

One controversy which has raged within the public diplomacy community for many years with respect to the use of radio as one of the "tools" of public diplomacy in developing countries is the role of popular music. In earlier days programs devoted primarily to U.S. popular music were distributed far and wide. As budgets faced reductions and more and more sophisticated programming was developed, the pattern changed. At one point popular music programs almost became taboo as more and more public diplomats asked, "What's in it for us?" Others conceded that "a little sweetening" is needed to place other programs on local stations which carry considerable "freight." There were still others who believed that the job of America's public diplomats was as much to spread U.S. popular music as a reflection of our society, as it was to present any other facet of U.S. culture, and there are also those who contend that U.S. popular music is already so popular in most countries that there is little reason to spend time and effort in this field when there are so many other needs and interests. This latter view has become the prevailing one today.

One radio technique that has been particularly successful in bringing global news and features about the United States to ever-widening audiences is the "correspondent's report." Using VOA transmitters at times when regular VOA broadcasts to a particular region are off the air, a live report by a Washington correspondent is beamed from Washington to Latin America or other areas. These reports, which generally tend to be from two to four minutes long, are then picked up on short-wave receivers either by the individual radio stations which use this service, or by the local USIS radio units. In either case the transmission is taped for rebroadcast later, often within regular news shows. The beauty of this system is that it provides many stations with their own "Washington correspondent," which they could not otherwise afford. In a sense this performs a service similar to that of a syndicated columnist in a newspaper whose column appears simultaneously in many dailies at the same time.

In one Latin American country, the USIS information officer who was in charge of the post's radio programming determined, through a survey and by other means, that the audience he was interested in reaching seldom listened to local radio stations except for music and the morning newscasts. He decided to eliminate all USIS radio placement under his jurisdiction except for that which could be placed on morning news shows, which was not a great deal. Although he was probably correct in his assumptions, and the time and effort of his staff was more effectively utilized in other media efforts, it was not long after he had left on an assignment to another country that the post's radio programming began to return, under the supervision of a new information officer, to where it had been before—making and distributing programs to local radio stations that used them at odd hours of the day or night. The results of the survey mentioned earlier were ignored or forgotten. The local staff was geared to produce and distribute radio programs, so as soon as the opportunity presented itself to do so, they were going to do their thing. That opportunity came when the information officer who had so drastically reduced radio programming was replaced by another who either did not know, or did not share, the conclusions of the survey. Since there are few hard and fast rules in conducting public diplomacy, this was a case where two pioneers in public diplomacy had two differing views on how best to make use of radio.

Radio in most developing societies continues to be the greatest source of information for the greatest number of people. The sensitivity of authoritarian governments in particular to the power of radio is sometimes seen in the greater restrictions such governments place on radio programming than on the press or television, and the fear some governments demonstrate by jamming outside broadcasts.

Fewer people regularly read newspapers than listen to radio in developing countries, though almost all literate people are regular newspaper readers, while television, as impressive as it is, is nowhere in the developing world as accessible as radio. Thus radio remains an important tool for public diplomats in most developing countries, at least those where local governments are receptive to the types of programs USIS posts offer. In the information-laden developed world, public diplomats seldom include radio among the tools of their trade. The competition, with few exceptions, is far too keen.

One cannot mention radio in connection with public diplomacy without, of course, discussing the Voice of America. However, the VOA is a subject in itself, being better known than USIA and, in a way, more independent. Given the importance of the VOA, its ramifications, its size and its at times controversial history, this giant broadcaster merits a separate chapter—which follows.

NOTES

1. At large posts there may be two officers or more in the Information Section, one who fills the position of information officer (I.O.) and has responsibility for all information activities while another may be the press attaché who reports to the I.O. but may be only responsible for press and related matters. The press attaché works closely with the ambassador on public statements, interviews requested by the press, etc., whenever the ambassador is involved. There can also be one or more assistant information officers who may specialize in radio and television placement or publications.

2. In recent years the wireless file has increasingly been used for other things in addition to providing the press file. Lists of books and articles which are recommended and available, personnel assignments, the "open assignments" listings, and other administrative matters now appear on regular and special files. As the speed of transmission increases, additional uses can be expected to develop.

3. A *baud* or *baudot* is a variable unit of data transmission speed, usually equal to one bit per second.

4. *Report of The United States Advisory Commission on Public Diplomacy, 1982*, Government Printing Office, Wash. D.C. 1982, p. 29.

5. *Ibid*. pp. 29-30.

9

THE VOICE OF AMERICA

During a visit to South Asia of a high VOA official, a regular VOA listener who was becoming increasingly concerned about VOA broadcasts to that part of the world in early 1983 told the Washington visitor: "There are only two things wrong with the Voice of America—its content and the low quality of its signal." He might have added a third if he were more familiar with VOA operations—the problem of personnel. In recent years the inability to attract and hold highly qualified professional and technical personnel has contributed, perhaps, to the other problems at the "Voice," though budget considerations, political influences, policy questions, changes in the White House, and VOA's high visibility have also been important in focussing greater criticism of the VOA than USIA and ICA have received.

On February 24, 1982, the Voice of America celebrated its fortieth anniversary. Older and better known than its parent agency, The VOA sends out more than 950 hours of globe-girdling programs every week in more than 40 languages. Total broadcast time in early 1983 averaged 957 1/2 hours per week. These programs reach an estimated audience of more than 100 million listeners with news, news analyses, official policy statements of the U.S. government, editorials, and features on almost every aspect of American society, including music, science, education and technology. In addition to being the best-known activity of USIA, it is the most expensive and the one that has the highest number of employees. The VOA employs about 2,300 persons, of which 1,560 are located in the United States. But even if one were to add the costs of Radio Liberty and Radio Free Europe, two stations not connected with VOA but involved in public diplomacy efforts, the United States is far behind the Soviet Union in international radio broadcasting activities.

The VOA was first organized as a government-sponsored short-wave radio service in 1942, less than three months after the Japanese attack on Pearl Harbor. This was five years after the British launched the BBC external service, which, to this day, critics both within and without VOA look upon as a model for the "Voice."

When VOA's programming began, it began with the pledge that "daily at this time, we shall speak to you about America and the war. The news may be good or bad. We shall tell you the truth." The desire to tell the truth has remained throughout the four decades of VOA's existence, though even this has not been without controversy, as some critics believe the VOA has at times leaned too far over in an effort to maintain objectivity. For example, Kenneth Adelman, writing in the Spring 1981 issue of *Foreign Affairs,* suggested that the VOA "could allocate slightly less time to Western economic woes, crimes and racial unrest—not because these put America in an unfavorable light but simply because the Soviet press already gives them sufficient if not inordinate play."[1] Yet he admits that VOA "has gained and deserved a high reputation for presenting the news fairly, regardless of whether it puts U.S. policy in a favorable light," and adds, "it has been credible." USIA Director Wick, aware of the importance of credibility, has said, "The greatest asset that the Voice of America has, and the BBC, is credibility . . . it is of paramount importance that credibility be maintained." Credibility as a goal is without controversy. The type and tenor of the programs broadcast, however, are subject to many varied opinions.

When the VOA was launched 40 years ago, it soon began building an audience throughout the world, particularly in areas under the control of the Axis powers. Today its largest audiences are in areas controlled by communist governments. Wherever totalitarian regimes treat their own citizens like little children from whom the harsh truth must be hidden, there is were the VOA and other international broadcasters will continue to find their largest audiences. Of VOA's estimated 100 million listeners in the early 1980s, about 70 million are in communist countries.

Region	Estimated audience
Sub-Sahara Africa	6,730,000
Latin America	4,830,000
East Asia/Pacific	1,985,000
China	18,000,000
Near East/South Asia	19,691,000
Western Europe	2,239,000
Eastern Europe	17,945,000
USSR	32,274,000
Total	103,784,000[2]

The use of electronic devices to drown out broadcasts from other countries, known as jamming, is a major item of expense for the Soviet Union and some of its allies. As an outgrowth of World War II, during which jamming was used by Nazi Germany, Stalin in 1948 ordered it done to VOA and BBC broadcasts in Eastern Europe. A year later, the U.S. government established Radio Free Europe, which was much more difficult to jam and which specialized in news for and about Eastern Europe. Then in 1953, Radio Liberation, renamed Radio Liberty ten years later, began broadcasting to the Soviet Union.[3] These stations, which are still functioning today, might never have been established had it not been for the jamming tactics of the Soviets.[4]

During the period of detente, the Soviet Union stopped jamming the VOA for about seven years. But with the Soviet invasion of Afghanistan, and the consequent cooling of relations between the two superpowers, Soviet jamming resumed. The Polish crisis of December 1981, when martial law was declared in that country, brought about increased jamming. Despite this increase, an expanded Polish-language service enabled the VOA to continue to be heard by many Poles.

Jamming, besides being expensive, is not always effective. Cuba has jammed U.S. broadcasts for years, but its jamming is far less effective the farther one gets from Havana. Taking a leaf out of the pages of post-World War II European history, the Reagan administration announced that it would like to establish a "Radio Free Cuba" to be known as Radio Marti. Like Radio Free Europe and Radio Liberty, Radio Marti, as originally planned, would be managed by the U.S. government, but would be independent of the VOA and would focus on Cuban news and features of interest to Cuban audiences.[5]

When the Cuban crisis first flared in the 1960s, the VOA broadcast a special program to Cuba using medium-wave transmitters in the Florida Keys. Later, when it appeared for a while that Cuba and the United States were moving toward "normalization" in their relations, special programming to Cuba seemed inappropriate and was replaced by the VOA's regular broadcasts to all of Latin America. Now the pendulum has swung back again. The new station was expected to be much harder hitting in its commentary and newscasts than the VOA. There are those who still believe that this type of programming is inappropriate for a U.S. government-sponsored station. Others believe that, with Cuba's record of support for terrorist groups fighting so-called "wars of national liberation" in Central America and elsewhere, and the sending of Cuban troops to African countries, it is time for the United States to take off its gloves, at least in the information field. What finally occurred with Radio Marti, however, was that on September 13, 1983, the Senate approved establishment of Radio Marti *under VOA*. The Senate compromise legislation, following earlier approval by the House, ended a two-year struggle by the Reagan administration to get Radio Marti established. Opposition to Radio Marti centered mostly on fears that the Cuban government would retaliate for the broadcasts by jamming broadcasts of U.S. commercial stations. When, on October 4, 1983, President Reagan signed the legislation creating Radio Marti within the Voice of America, he noted that the new broadcast facility will help "to break Fidel Castro's monopoly on news and information within Cuba." The president added that he would have preferred that the facility be placed under the Board for International Broadcasting but that he was "satisfied" that the new service would be operated "while maintaining the historic high standards of the Voice of America for accuracy and reliability." Radio Marti would operate on the frequency used by the VOA at its facilities in Marathon, Florida, 125 kilometers north of Cuba.

The VOA's problems for the past few decades, and much of the criticism that has been directed at the VOA in recent years, concerns how it is organized, the content and tenor of its programs, its mission, how it is administered, its personnel policies, its signal strength, and its effectiveness.

When USIA was established in 1953, the VOA came under its wing. At that time VOA studios were located in the radio capital of the United States, New York City. Moving the VOA to Washington, D.C. a few years later was undoubtedly even more traumatic for VOA staffers than the trauma suffered by the State Department's "CU" personnel when, in 1978, they had to move six or so blocks to become part of the International Communication Agency. In 1953, Washington had a reputation for being a desert, culturally, where the "Blue Laws" made the city even more dead on Sundays than it was on weekdays, and where the sidewalks were rolled up daily almost as soon as the government bureaucrats turned off the office lights. Some VOA staffers refused to make such a radical change from New York City and resigned. Most moved to the nation's capital, however, and as Washington changed and grew, so did the VOA.

For the past quarter of a century, the issue as to whether the VOA should be independent; a part of the Department of State; or a part of USIA and, later, ICA, has been debated. The highly publicized March 1975 report by the Panel on International Information, Education, and Cultural Relations, known as the Stanton Commission, recommended that the VOA be made a separate agency outside of both the Department of State and the information-cultural agency, though "closely linked" to both. This recommendation was not accepted, serious doubts about it being raised by the General Accounting Office in its report of May 5, 1977, and elsewhere.[6] The debate is still going on, however, and each view has its advocates. In the meantime the VOA remains the radio section of the agency responsible for America's public diplomacy. Though this organizational arrangement has not endured without frictions and serious internal administrative and personnel problems, throughout the VOA's history, the VOA has, on balance, performed in an outstanding manner, as judged by the size of its audience, the maintenance of a high degree of credibility, and its relatively smooth functioning despite a number of different USIA, ICA, and VOA directors.

The argument that VOA should be completely independent leaves many public diplomats cold. It is one thing to be independent in newscasts, which make up a large percentage of broadcast time, and with which few would disagree. It is quite another to be independent from the U.S. government, which pays the bills for VOA operations from funds that come, of course, from U.S. taxpayers. Unless the VOA exists, like its parent agency, to foster U.S. policies abroad, there ceases to be any strong justification for the American taxpayer to support this activity. On the other hand, if the VOA were placed under the Department of State, as some have suggested, it would almost surely be subject to much greater bias in its programming as it sought to emphasize U.S. foreign policy objectives to the exclusion or, at least, the detriment of other objectives. This would endanger its most valued asset—its credibility. Furthermore, at a time when educational and cultural exchange programs have so recently been transferred from the State Department to ICA, it would be rather inconsistent to go in the opposite direction with regard to radio broadcasting.

Not all of the difficulties between VOA managers, located as they were until recently crosstown from USIA headquarters, and USIA's top administrators can be attributed to the physical separation of the two, but certainly the physical separation has tended to keep the two groups, especially when USIA was ICA, from a closer and smoother association. The Television and Motion Picture Service of the agency is also physically separated from USIA's headquarters building, yet the same frictions that have marked VOA relationships with top agency officials, in the early 1970s in particular, have not emerged in the case of the former. That only VOA has its own charter, a unique fame, its larger size, and a constituency that includes important members of Congress help account for VOA's special situation vis a vis USIA's top management. VOA staffers also have a tendency to believe themselves as being very special because their product does not have to be filtered through either the Washington bureaucracy at home, or U.S. public diplomats at posts abroad. This is not to say that policy statements and program content are not discussed and cleared with USIA's policy office, but it must be greatly satisfying psychologically to know that one can communicate directly with Soviet, Polish, African, Asian, or Chinese citizens, which is what VOA does. All other products of U.S. diplomacy are much more closely controlled at home, and generally screened for suitability at overseas posts.

Aside from making policy decisions, USIA's managers must assure themselves that the VOA is in tune with the efforts being made by other media elements of the agency. But if USIA pursues its objectives via the VOA in too forceful a manner, objective newscasts and other programming of vital importance in maintaining VOA's audience interest and credibility can be adversely affected.

When USIA leaders told congressional leaders in the summer of 1981 that they intended "to hone the agency into a 'cutting edge' in making America's foreign policy work," such a combative U.S. information policy designed to challenge the Soviet Union, Cuba, and other Marxist countries, if carried to the extreme, could easily damage VOA's reputation and image. Already some regular VOA listeners are concerned that the emphasis on Poland, Afghanistan, and Soviet "disinformation" activities has been so great that they are switching more frequently and in greater numbers to the BBC and other international broadcasters who seem to be more entertaining, and maybe even more informative, and certainly not as hung up on anticommunism. While the VOA has a long way to go to be as boring and repetitive as Radio Moscow, too much of anything, particularly negative commentary, turns listeners away.

The concern in some quarters that the VOA might endanger its credibility by concentrating too much on anticommunist themes was clear when the 1982 Report of the United States Advisory Commission on Public Diplomacy published its recommendations for the Voice of America.[7] "The Commission recommends that USICA (USIA) take greater care to avoid actions and policies that can be easily misinterpreted and cast doubt on VOA's commitment to accuracy and objectivity," the report noted.[8] Arguing that VOA's credibility is "its most precious asset" but that that credibility "is a fragile thing," the Commission stated that VOA news must not only be accurate and objective, "it must also be perceived as such." The strongest language indicating the concern of commission members regarding this issue was the following:

> Some observers have expressed concern that the integrity of VOA's news programs has been undercut by more strident programming policies and a series of recent senior management changes which have received national media attention. Others have suggested that VOA's coverage of world events is unbalanced and even at times inimical to the best interests of the United States. Still others believe that the Voice should be more hard hitting and aggressively propagandistic as a foreign policy instrument.[9]

A strong advocate for a more rather than less confrontational approach is Kenneth Adelman who, writing in *Foreign Affairs*, calls for more programming on the declining economic fortunes of Vietnam under communist rule and on Cuba, including Cubans stationed in Africa.[10] The problem with focussing so much on anticommunism in VOA broadcasts is not only that the question of credibility is raised, but equally important is that many listeners are turned away. The one-track programming of Radio Moscow, for example, keeps potential listeners to that giant broadcaster away in droves. The BBC, on the other hand, continues to be the most popular international broadcaster in the business, not only because it is generally recognized as being objective (the Falklands crisis not withstanding) but, equally important, it remains entertaining and informative.

The VOA has, in recent years, become so highly politicized in its programming that, despite its high listenership, it is losing listeners to other stations. For example, the BBC consistently gains and keeps listeners by drawing on the rich British literary heritage, which the United States could and should do with respect to our literary achievements, but seldom does. Having gotten away from radio dramatizations, perhaps in the belief that to do so reflects the modern style of U.S. domestic radio, by 1983 the VOA was using more and more editorials on U.S. policy than ever before, leaving little time for cultural, scientific, educational, and lighter subjects in which many worldwide listeners are much more interested and which, in the long run, may be much more effective. Many of the BBC's entertaining programs, which are aired fairly regularly, are usually followed by news, commentary, or other "freight." Incidentally, the BBC also almost always summarizes the main points of the news following each newscast, a technique that VOA frequently ignores, leaving late tuners frustrated.

The VOA always has a need for new ideas, which usually comes with new blood, but some of its language services are so in-bred and in need of new faces that new ideas are rare indeed. The VOA originally signed contracts with nationals from various countries to work for the Voice in Washington as translators, broadcasters, etc., on two to four year contracts. Today many contract employees from abroad were expected to return to their homelands upon completion of their contracts, or after one extension, to be replaced by others fresh from overseas, thus keeping up with language and social developments in their homelands (though in the case of communist countries this is hardly possible). Unfortunately, as bad as some say the working conditions at the Voice are sometimes alleged to be for these foreign nations, life in Washington is such that once employed there with the VOA few ever want to leave. Many manage to find ways, sometimes with the help of their union, to stay on indefinitely. Enforcing the original intent of contracting overseas VOA employees is necessary for language and other reasons. Stimulating a greater number of exchanges as VOA now does with some countries would also be beneficial to VOA programming.

Commenting on the influence of VOA's personnel problems on program effectiveness, the GAO report to the director of the U.S. International Communication Agency in July 1982 noted that many of these problems have existed a long time and added: "The current management has had success in implementing some corrective actions—establishment of an independent personnel office and the acquisition of additional physical space." It went on to say that "other problems, including vacancies in key management and staff positions, continue to limit the effectiveness of VOA and its ability to maximize efficiency and economy in programing and operating technical facilities."[11]

The lack of continuity in the office of the director and other key positions of VOA is cited in the report for the period March 1980 through July 1982, when VOA had a series of directors as shown here:

March 5, 1980	January 20, 1981	Director
Jan. 20, 1981	August 6, 1981	Acting Director
August 6, 1981	March 22, 1982	Director
March 22, 1982	July 1, 1982	Director (Designate)
July 1, 1982	Present	Director

Also, during this period there was no director of programs for ten months and the position of director of engineering and technical operations was vacant from November 1979 to June 1982. In January 1982, VOA had some 200 positions or 10 percent of its non-administrative positions vacant.[12] This kind of personnel turnover at the top and in many key positions is hardly conducive to good administration.

VOA's Washington studios transmit their programs to various locations in continental United States via telephone landlines and microwave and by satellite to the West Coast. Programs are broadcast directly from the U.S. transmitters as well as to the VOA's relay stations abroad. VOA transmitters in the United States are located at Bethany, Ohio: Delano, California; Marathon, Florida; Greenville,

North Carolina; and Honolulu. The foreign transmitters are located in Liberia, Morocco, Germany, mainland Greece, the Greek island of Rhodes, Great Britain, the Philippines, Thailand, Sri Lanki, Okinawa, Botswana, and Antigua. Some 15 satellite circuits are used to feed VOA overseas relay stations. While the technology has been developed that allows direct satellite transmissions to individual receivers, the political implications of such transmissions have so far inhibited such broadcasts by stations like the VOA. Some day this as well as direct international television broadcasts from satellites may become common, but as of the early 1980s, the VOA used satellites only to relay its programs from one ground station to another.

The technical quality of VOA broadcasts leave much to be desired in many parts of the world. Because of the geographic location of the United States, separated as it is from much of the rest of the world by two major oceans, agreements must be made and maintained with foreign governments willing to allow VOA transmitters on their soil. Furthermore, the high cost of transmitters results in the VOA installing fewer new transmitters and modernizing its equipment less frequently than it would like. In comparison, the Soviet Union's geographic location, and its ability to spend whatever amount of money it wishes on international broadcasting without regard to congressional appropriations, places the Soviets in an enviable position when it comes to global radio broadcasts. The mammoth radio operations of Radio Moscow reach most of the far corners of the earth loudly and clearly most of the time, and the Russians never have to be concerned about jamming since Western nations find jamming repulsive. Of course, sound is not enough. Radio Moscow's geographic and financial advantages over the VOA, the BBC and other international broadcasters are offset by the dullness of most Radio Moscow programming, music programming being an exception.

The GAO's July 1982 report on VOA criticized the Voice for having "given little consideration to long-range planning for technical requirements" and found that VOA had "embarked on a number of piecemeal modernization projects which could cost more than $325 million." It urged that the Voice update its construction practices to include new concepts, such as colocating receiver and transmitter plants, and using rapid deployment stations and standard-designed buildings at relay stations.[13]

Arguing that VOA has yet to achieve full benefits from new technology that is now available, the report notes that since satellites were first used by VOA in 1977, they have proven their utility by providing increased reliability and a better quality of service than the more traditional methods. Today, VOA leases 18 active satellite circuits and two additional satellite circuits were scheduled to be completed in 1983. Costs for these circuits in Fiscal Year 1982 were estimated at $4.3 million.[14] While citing controversy within VOA about the use of these satellites, centering around their reliability because of technical outage, vulnerability to potential interference from foreign governments, and cost compared to the use of shortwave transmitters to relay programs, the report presents solid evidence of the reliability of satellite transmissions.

A 1980 report by the VOA Office of Administration on the use of satellites stated that the circuits to the Philippines for a 1-year period had a reliability factor of 97.2 percent. In October 1981, a VOA evaluation of all its satellite circuits disclosed that reliability for a 6-month period was in excess of 99.7 percent.[15]

Because of the reliability of satellites indicated above, the GAO recommends elimination of backup shortwave transmissions which could save $1 million in annual operating costs, funds which could be used for other purposes.

Despite problems of low morale; differing viewpoints at times between the VOA's foreign nationals, civil servants, and Foreign Service officers; concerns that the VOA broadcasts "in the shadow of the State Department;"[16] concerns that uptown USIA bosses haven't always seen eye-to-eye with the VOA hierarchy downtown; and the failure of the VOA to keep up with modern electronic technology as it operates under financial restrictions imposed by the U.S. Congress and the administration, the VOA is still one of the most popular, reliable, and credible radio stations in the world today. It is frequently quoted in the third world press as a reliable source, and all indications are that although the Soviets spend more on jamming (an estimated $250 million annually according to the CIA) than is spent on VOA broadcasting, the VOA is still a primary source of news and information in the Soviet Union, Eastern Europe, and many other areas.

The Near East, North Africa English-language Service alone receives an average of 2,000 letters weekly from listeners. In Latin America, in the late 1970s, more letters were received from Cuba than from any other single country in that part of the world. Letters are constantly received at VOA headquarters in Washington from listeners throughout the world, a clear indication that there are a lot of people out there tuned in to what the VOA has to say.

Mail from VOA's worldwide audience, totalling approximately 185,000 pieces in 1981, was not centrally analyzed or used to identify program interests of listeners when GAO's 1982 report was published. In October 1982, the Office of the Director of Audience Relations was established. Though its purpose was described as being "to develop and direct a comprehensive program of overseas advertising and promotional activities," it might presumably include centralization of audience reaction and program suggestions reflected in VOA's mail, as recommended by the GAO. With this addition, and the inclusion of USIA's Television and Film Service under the associate director of USIA for broadcasting (VOA director), the agency's broadcasting organization was comprised by 1983 of six offices: director of programs, director of engineering, director of administration, director of personnel, and the two new additions, director of television and film,[17] and director of audience relations.

In past years the Office of Research of USIA conducted surveys of VOA listenership. In Latin America these surveys usually demonstrated that audiences were small in that part of the world during normal times, ranging from 1 percent to 3 percent or thereabouts of urban audiences. This was sometimes used to argue that VOA broadcasts to Latin America were unimportant. Such arguments ignored the placement of VOA taped programs on local radio stations, correspondent reports, VOA segments used in programs produced by USIS posts, and the importance of VOA, with a consequent dramatic jump in listenership, whenever a crisis of international significance or an event such as the launching of a major space vehicle occurs.

What the United States does is important to the rest of the world. People in other countries want to know what and how the United States is doing politically, economically, and militarily. The VOA has been, and will continue to be, a primary, immediate source for that kind of information.

NOTES

1. Adelman, Kenneth L., "Speaking of America: Public Diplomacy in Our Time," *Foreign Affairs*, Spring 1981, Vol. 59, No. 4, p. 921.

2. U.S. General Accounting Office. Report to The Director, U.S. International Communication Agency, *The Voice of America Should Address Existing Problems to Ensure High Performance*, July 19, 1982, CAO/ID-82-37, p. 17.

3. In addition to Radio Free Europe and Radio Liberty, one other radio station which came into being in the aftermath of World War II is RIAS (Radio in the American Sector). RIAS has operated since 1946 for listeners primarily in East Germany, where it apparently has a large audience. Although its director is a U.S. public diplomat, the rest of its staff are West Germans and it is the West German government that finances it today. Located in West Berlin, its programs consist of news, music, and entertainment.

4. Jamming involves placing loud radio signals on the same frequency as the broadcast that is being blocked. Sometimes the jamming signal consists of distorted Soviet domestic radio programs and sometimes it is just a buzzing noise. Either way, it has only one purpose—to prevent normal radio signals from being understood. The Soviet Union spends far more to interfere with a VOA or other Western broadcast than the originating government spends to transmit its program in the first place. Jamming is inconsistent with the agreements signed by the Soviet Union in the Helsinki Final Act to encourage the free exchange of information.

5. Radio Marti was among the casualties in the lame-duck session of Congress in December 1982 when the Senate declined to join the House in approving start-up costs for the new station. In early 1983 the Reagan administration indicated, however, that it would continue to seek congressional approval for the establishment of Radio Marti. One concern voiced by U.S. radio broadcasters was that the new station would cause Cuba to retaliate to the detriment of U.S. stations. One U.S. station, WHO in Iowa, was especially concerned because Radio Marti would be on a frequency identical to that used by WHO.

6. U.S. General Accounting Office report, op.cit.

7. Section 8, Reorganization Plan No. 2 of 1977, and Public Law 96-60 require the United States Commission on Public Diplomacy to submit reports to the Congress and to the president of the United States on the U.S. International Communication Agency (now USIA). The 1982 report was the second report of the Commission. At the time Commission members consisted of Leonard L. Silverstein, Chairman, an attorney and president of the National Symphony Orechestra Association; Tom C. Korologos, vice president and director of Legislative Affairs of Timmons and Co., Inc.; Olin Robison, professor of Political Science and president, Middlebury College; Lewis Manilow, attorney and former president of the Chicago Museum of Contemporary Art; Jean McKee, director, Government Relations of General Mills Restaurant Group; Neil Sherburne, chairman, Association of Governing Boards of Universities and Colleges and retired secretary-treasurer, Minnesota AFL-CIO; and Mae Sue Talley, retired business executive, publisher and civic leader.

8. Report of The United States Advisory Commission on Public Diplomacy, 1982, Wash., D.C., p. 16.

9. *Ibid.* p. 17.

10. Adelman, op.cit., p. 932. He also advocates targeting broadcasts at Cubans stationed in Africa, with special emphasis devoted to the casualty rates

and their discontent at being there as well as the declining fortunes of Cubans at home. He suggests interviews with "some among the one million of Cuba's citizens who became refugees" and citing such things as World Bank statistics which show Cuba's per capita gross national product declining 0.2 percent per year since 1960 despite enormous outside assistance. "In sum," he says, "there is grist enough for a public diplomacy campaign toward Cuba, should policymakers adopt a more confrontational approach." In early 1983 Adelman was President Reagan's nominee to be director of the U.S. Arms Control and Disarmament Agency, a job which includes being principal advisor to the president and the secretary of state on arms control matters. After considerable controversy concerning his nomination, he received the Senate's approval.

11. U.S. General Accounting Office report, op. cit., p. i.

12. *Ibid.*, p. 9.

13. *Ibid.*, p. ii.

14. *Ibid.*, pp. 23-25.

15. *Ibid.*, p. 26.

16. Fenyvesi, Charles, "I Hear America Mumbling, Why the Voice of America Won't Win Any Emmys This Year." *The Washington Post Magazine*, July 19, 1981, pp. 22.

17. As noted earlier, on July 24, 1983, the Television and Film Service was again established as a separate element of USIA thus no longer under the jurisdiction of the VOA director.

10

THE PUBLIC DIPLOMAT'S BASIC TOOLS
EDUCATION AND CULTURAL PROGRAMS

In the opinion of the U.S. Advisory Commission on Public Diplomacy, USIA's educational and cultural *exchange* programs are as indispensable to the effective conduct of public diplomacy as media efforts.[1] Most public diplomats would agree but would add—so are such cultural activities as USIS libraries, various other book programs, lecture and seminar programs, cultural presentations, English teaching, support to binational cultural centers, and support to American Studies programs at overseas universities and institutions. However, in the U.S. General Accounting Office report to the director of USIA of Feb. 11, 1982, the GAO concluded that USIA's cultural program support, "with few exceptions, is apparently failing to satisfy the overseas missions' planning requirements." The report notes that "some cultural events are largely superfluous and duplicative of those already available in-country."[2] In other words, as important as cultural programs are, there is, apparently, a need for considerable improvement in USIA's planning and execution of cultural programs, at least so far as the GAO is concerned.

The public diplomat's tools to be discussed in this chapter all fall under the rubric of cultural, and most are viewed as "long range" in concept when compared with such "fast media" information activities as press releases and radio and television programs. The designations "cultural" and "informational," as noted earlier, are primarily organizational designations which enable a logical distribution of workloads among those responsible for creating, developing, and managing the great variety of activities that public diplomacy entails.

Whether a particular program is more cultural than informational makes little difference to most public diplomats. It tends to make a difference, however, to many academicians and others who participate in educational and cultural exchanges sponsored by USIA, since most insist, and rightly so, that their independent views not be compromised by the acceptance of U.S. government grants. Some see culture as good and information as propaganda. The fact is that many of USIA's cultural activities are informational—i.e., libraries with books on U.S. policies among many other subjects, and USIA-sponsored lecturers, some of whom attempt to explain U.S. policies, etc.,—while many information programs are cultural, i.e., USIA magazines that report on U.S. literature, art, music, dance, and so forth.

LIBRARIES

More than 125 libraries and reading rooms are maintained by USIA in nearly 90 countries. Some of these are major institutions that play an important role in the communities they serve, such as the Benjamin Franklin Library in Mexico City, the Thomas Jefferson Library in Brasilia, and the Abraham Lincoln Library in Buenos Aires. These are major resource centers for educators, writers, intellectuals, researchers, and students, and have gained their well-deserved reputations after years of providing easily accessible, accurate, and objective information about the United States, its people, history, and policies. If information sought in these libraries is not available locally, efforts are often make by the library staff to obtain materials from the United States.

In many of the countries where USIS libraries are located, few if any free public libraries are available; thus the USIS libraries are novelties. While some, like those mentioned above, occupy their own buildings and are devoted almost exclusively to library operations, many other smaller libraries are located in multi-purpose cultural centers and in binational centers. Some can best be classified as reading rooms, given their small number of volumes and the small size of their staffs. Regardless of size, however, most of these libraries are popular among the people who have access to them, and exemplify the quest for knowledge, the freedom of ideas, and the egalitarian concepts found in U.S. society. Most of these libraries welcome the general public. A new concept, however, is that of the small reference library, such as the one in Lima, Peru. Because of its limited size and staff, membership is restricted to writers, editors, professors, graduate students, researchers, and others who have a genuine need for timely research materials on the United States, or from the United States. Those with only a general interest in the United States have access to the library of the Peruvian-American Cultural Center in Lima, a former USIS library. The idea of a USIS reference library like the one in Lima is to provide information which may not be available from any other source in the host country.

Many of the tools used by public diplomats are focussed on the leaders and movers of a foreign community, i.e., the *fuerzas vivas*, but most of the libraries of USIA are available to anyone interested in their contents. As might be expected, they are particularly popular with students.

Whether it is the power of the printed word that some disenchanted, criminal elements fear, or simply the high visibility of these facilities, which seem to offer easy targets to vent frustrations, the fact is that occasionally USIS libraries are physically attacked and damaged or destroyed. Since the host government has the responsibility for protecting the property of foreign governments accredited to them, not only do the culprits who cause such destruction deprive local citizens of useful information and knowledge, but they place an additional burden on the local governments, as it is the local government that has to pay the repair bill. Often the proceeds received are used in the construction of more modern installations to replace the old ones. Because of this, among other reasons, the type of terrorist activity that seeks to blow up books is usually counterproductive.

There was a time in the history of U.S. public diplomacy when Senator Joseph McCarthy was riding high and, for a while, the U.S. government was as guilty as others who burn books. In the early 1950s, under prodding by Senator McCarthy, numerous titles were removed from USIA libraries on specious grounds. Fortunately, the McCarthy Era has long since passed. This does not mean that any and all books are now to be found in USIS libraries. These libraries are, after all, highly specialized. They are intended to provide information about the United States, its people, its policies, and its culture. While this covers a broad spectrum, it does not compare with the almost universal interests of a typical library in a typical U.S. community. Yet USIS libraries tend to serve far more generalized interests of foreign citizens than any other single activity conducted by America's public diplomats overseas.

Some libraries formerly managed exclusively by USIA or ICA have been transferred to the jurisdiction of binational centers or other institutions. Where this has occurred it has usually been for budgetary reasons. The result has often been a downgrading of the quality of service of the library affected, brought about by reductions in the funds available for new books, staff reductions, and other factors, including less support from USIA's Washington headquarters.

In the General Accounting Office's February 1982 report, two reasons are given for the dramatic reduction in the number of USIA libraries and reading rooms from some 426 between the years 1946 and 1978, to 129 in fiscal year 1981, a reduction of about 68 percent. In an era of continuously shrinking budgets (in terms of constant dollars), a first source of cuts was the budget for libraries. While this was occurring, the number of American professional librarians employed by USIA dropped from a high of 53 in the mid-1950s to 18 in 1979. These two factors, the GAO contends, were responsible for the disappearance of many USIS libraries and reading rooms. USIA did not make a deliberate decision to phase out USIS libraries overseas, "but the apparent neglect of their needs has created such deterioration of their condition that their maintenance may no longer be justified," the report states.[3]

The role of USIA libraries, like almost every other activity of USIA, has been debated for years. What aspects of the United States the libraries should present, what books and periodicals they should distribute, and what audience they should serve are among the questions repeatedly raised when discussing USIS libraries. In certain areas, like Eastern Europe, many public diplomats consider them essential; in developing countries many consider them extremely important; in developed countries many consider them to be superfluous. Others, preferring collections and services geared to narrowly targeted audiences, denigrate them for their "shotgun" approach of trying to reach mass audiences with unfocussed book collections. In any event, USIA libraries in their totality, according to agency statistics for 1982, contain about 1.6 million volumes and

22,000 periodical subscriptions which are used by nearly 9 million library visitors annually. In the prior fiscal year USIA spent about $9.5 million for salaries and related costs of American and foreign national employees associated with libraries, and about $6.5 million for the purchase of books and periodicals, rent, and other support for its libraries.[4]

In June of 1982, in response to the GAO's recommendation that the USIA director examine the usefulness of the overseas libraries and eliminate those no longer considered useful, Director Charles Wick and Associate Director for Educational and Cultural Affairs Ronald L. Trowbridge took a hard look at the agency's libraries and book programs generally. They concluded that USIS libraries have "a unique contribution to make to our short-term information and policy objectives as well as to our long-range objectives."[5] In providing their officers in the field with a revised Library Policy Statement for USIA, the first such statement in many years, they noted that the U.S. government and USIA has, for many years, "vigorously promoted the international flow of books and information, and our libraries play a crucial role in this effort—a role recognized recently in a resolution by the American Library Association."[6]

While noting that differing conditions and special circumstances will be reflected in each country where USIA maintains libraries, the agency's new library policy states that its library programs should, wherever possible:

—Provide the latest and most accurate information about the U.S. government and its policies.

—Provide in-depth information about American values, history, culture, and character.

—Promote the use of program-oriented materials by those audiences and institutions identified as important to ICA (USIA) objectives.

—Facilitate the use of the library by a self-selecting audience. No patron with serious interest in the United States should be denied access to the library.[7]

—Provide adequate funding, training and policy orientation to enable library staff members to effectively maintain and promote the collection and provide high quality reference and outreach services.

—Ensure that the physical facility is attractive, functional, and appropriate to its national environment.[8]

FIGURE 1
Western European USICA Libraries Attendance Figures (1954-1981)

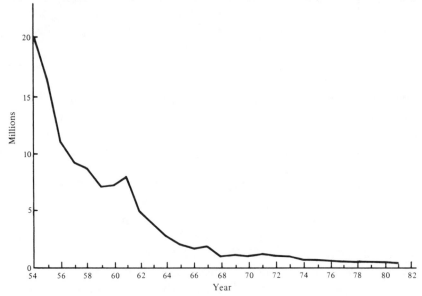

Source: USIA

While USIS libraries continue to play a particularly important and effective role in developing countries, attendance at USIS libraries in Western Europe has fallen continuously and dramatically since USIA was established in 1953. There are many reasons for this, nor should this trend be expected in information-laden societies like those of Western Europe. The statistics clearly indicate that while libraries remain a major element of USIS programming in developing countries, they are no longer a vital part of USIA programs in the West European nations where so many other sources of information exist.

OTHER BOOK PROGRAMS

In addition to libraries, public diplomats make use of books in several other ways. Books on subjects that are known to be of interest to host government leaders or local writers, journalists, intellectuals, educators, etc., are obtained, generally from Washington, and presented to the interested person or institution. This activity is known as the agency's "Presentation Program."

The U.S. Congress in its wisdom some years ago decided that this type of activity is a "give-away program." Unfortunately, this connotation ignores completely the reason books are given away, on a highly selective basis, by America's public diplomats. The same mistake is made when U.S. economic assistance programs are referred to in the same manner, despite the fact that they benefit the U.S. almost as much as they benefit the recipient countries by generating employment within the United States, etc. In fact, most of the activities of public diplomats could be described as "give-away programs"—press, radio, television, libraries, lecture programs, etc. They all give away information in different forms—it is their *raison d'être*. Why pick on books? Yet as a result of this narrow congressional view, for years USIA had to spell out special justifications for any book, or group of books, presented to important contacts overseas if the cost was $25 or more. This limit has now been raised to $100. Requiring overseas posts to justify the reasons for presenting books is not necessarily a bad idea, but it was initiated for the wrong reasons. Worthwhile presentations were discouraged when one had to justify to Washington, in writing, almost every book intended to serve mutual interests by presentation to key individuals or institutions.

Another program involving books is the Donated Book Program of U.S. publishers. This activity has been somewhat misused in some instances when posts end up with many more books on some rather esoteric subjects than they could possibly use effectively, though generally this program has served USIA well. The program works by receiving from U.S. book publishers donations of their surplus stocks, which are distributed by USIA overseas. Until recently the publishers could consider their donations as gifts, thus providing them with tax breaks, while the public diplomacy agency obtained, at no cost, certain books that advance U.S. objectives. The problem is that there is still some cost involved to the agency for handling and shipping charges, thus great care must be exercised to be sure that the books obtained by this means are truly of interest to USIA objectives. In the past, some books that were of little interest, or were outdated were sometimes accepted. Obtaining such books, or more books than can usefully be donated to key individuals and institutions, only serves the interests of the U.S. publishing industry, not that of the U.S. government. And since almost all of the donated books are in English, this must be considered when judging the utility of any one book for overseas audiences.

Still another book program, though one which has been sharply curtailed since the mid-1960s is USIA's Book Translation Program. The purpose of this activity is to encourage the translation, distribution, and sale of books that have been published commercially in the United States and that cover themes of interest to U.S. public diplomacy objectives but which might not ordinarily be translated and published abroad. Obviously best sellers are seldom included in this program since they usually are easily marketed commercially in most major languages and are seldom what those in the (public diplomacy) trade would call "program books." Prime candidates for USIA's Book Translation Program are titles of a serious nature that discuss some aspect of U.S. history, culture, or foreign policy. Books on economics and politics are among those most frequently translated, as are books on American literature.

The Book Translation Program operates by bringing to the attention of overseas publishers certain titles in which, for one reason or another, USIA has an interest. A foreign publisher is approached and an offer is made to guarantee the purchase of a certain number of copies, for example, five hundred or so, if the publisher agrees to translate and publish the book in question for the commercial market. The copies purchased by USIA are used in USIS libraries and for presentation to selected individuals and institutions. USIA has no control over the contents of the books chosen for this program. They have already been published and, though deletions might be made in the translated editions, American abhorrence of anything that smacks of censorship would make such changes unacceptable. However, given the difficulty of translating U.S. jargon into other languages, arranging thorough checks of the translations of books published under this program is one of the more important tasks of a USIA book officer.

USIA has had book translation programs in Spanish, French, Portuguese, and Arabic for many years. By the early 1980s, the agency spent about $700,000 annually for the publication and distribution of U.S. books in translated editions, far less than in earlier years.

The Spanish program began more than 20 years ago and has generally been restricted to Latin America where, when it first began, it was intended not only to serve the purpose of providing another vehicle for U.S. ideas through the publication of U.S. books, but also to assist the nascent book publishing industry of the Americas,

TABLE 1
USICA Book Publishing Program

	Translation Program	P. L. 480 Textbooks	Published* In U.S.	Total
FY 1950	10,000			10,000
FY 1951	1,730,000			1,730,000
FY 1952	3,310,000			3,310,000
FY 1953	5,820,000			5,820,000
FY 1954	4,360,000			4,360,000
FY 1955	5,131,496			5,131,496
FY 1956	5,987,666		633,624	6,621,290
** LPB FY 1956-1960	4,346,800			4,346,800
FY 1957	7,359,238		1,904,962	9,264,200
FY 1958	6,814,890		873,046	7,687,936
FY 1959	3,873,550		830,875	4,704,425
FY 1960	4,746,350		659,867	5,406,217
FY 1961	3,129,950	142,350	672,149	3,944,449
FY 1962	3,545,422	476,150	1,082,624	5,104,196
FY 1963	5,287,900	775,805	1,456,971	7,520,676
FY 1964	8,317,151	1,078,396	1,776,196	10,801,743
FY 1965	10,244,342	1,215,116	1,325,197	12,694,655
FY 1966	8,855,243	789,100	1,599,016	11,243,359
FY 1967	6,913,109	792,000	1,597,223	9,302,332
FY 1968	4,999,557	696,052	835,310	6,530,919
FY 1969	3,202,001	952,623	653,077	4,807,701
FY 1970	2,593,922	1,761,806	517,723	4,873,451
FY 1971	2,089,650	364,030	517,706	2,971,386
FY 1972	2,029,840	1,436,519	655,170	4,121,529
FY 1973	1,528,544	272,244	415,903	2,216,691
FY 1974	1,256,390	229,202	620,374	2,105,966
FY 1975	1,130,181	402,311	296,181	1,828,673
FY 1976-5-Quarter FY	1,344,546	441,195		1,785,741
FY 1977	881,229	106,500		987,729
FY 1978	768,204	23,275		791,479
FY 1979	565,087	16,750		581,837
FY 1980	502,040	23,000		525,040
	123,674,248	11,994,414	18,923,194	154,591,856

*Consists of student and ladder editions published for export sale.
**Low Priced Book Program in Translation done through New York firms.
P.L. 480 Textbooks, primarily in English and in India, were financed by foreign currency generated from the sale of agricultural products.

Source: USIA

125

particularly Mexico where a book officer was stationed to manage the program. A book officer was also assigned to Buenos Aires, the other major publishing center of Spanish-speaking Latin America, and a third book officer was stationed in Rio de Janeiro for the translation and publication of books in Portuguese. When political conditions became so bad in Argentina in the mid-1970s that terrorist activities evolved into attacks on Americans, including the kidnapping and murder of a U.S. consular agent in Cordoba, Argentina, the book officer was transferred to Santiago-de-Chile as were other positions considered "nonessential." At the height of the Spanish Book Translation Program, a fourth book officer for Latin America was stationed in Bogota, Columbia, though by 1982 there were only two, one in Buenos Aires (which had quieted down by then) and one in Mexico City. With the continuous budget reductions for the agency's book translation programs on the one hand, and the growth of the book publishing industry in Latin America on the other, the value of having full-time book translation officers stationed in Latin

FIGURE 2
Agency Sponsored Book Translations into European Languages
(Numbers of Titles: 1954-1981)

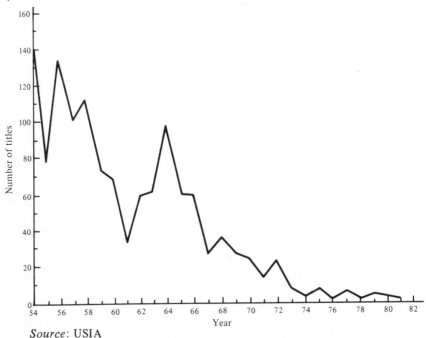

Source: USIA

America is questionable. Perhaps one person, operating out of Washington or Miami, could handle the entire limited program, using resources available to public diplomats and their staffs already stationed in Latin America.

Attempts have been made, seldom with much success, to stimulate greater commercial sales of "program books" in Latin America, but the barriers to book sales throughout the area are formidable. Until fairly recently, books published in Mexico seldom reached the southern cone of South America, at least in any substantial quantities, and book publishers in Argentina found their markets in the north to be fairly restricted. Aside from marketing arrangements, which was a major problem, the vagaries of Argentine Spanish compared with the vagaries of Mexican Spanish discouraged interchange. The marketing and language problems have been greatly overcome by some publishers who publish their books simultaneously in Buenos Aires, Mexico City, and Barcelona, Spain.

The first and foremost publishing center in the Spanish-speaking world has historically been Barcelona, Spain. This would have been a natural place to foster the publication of "program books" in Spanish. But, for a variety of reasons, none of which ever seemed valid to the author, the agency never moved in that direction despite Barcelona's many assets as a publishing center: a language acceptable throughout Latin America, the existence of a highly-experienced publishing industry, direct trade routes to all Latin American countries, relatively low production costs, and other advantages. The one exception to USIA's reluctance to engage in a book translation program in Spain was a small textbook translation program in the early 1960s which enabled 41 titles to be translated and published in about a two-year period, utilizing PL480 funds that were at that time available for such purposes.

In July of 1981, USIA took a long serious look at all of its book programs. The committee established to do so concluded that the agency's book activities had diminished steadily since the mid-1960s and that the distribution of serious American books overseas (both in English and in translation) was losing ground to books from other major nations. The committee argued that the time had come for USIA to stem the decline of its book activities, to improve the use of books in its programs, and to upgrade the distribution of American books in general through more effective cooperation with the U.S. book publishing industry in an effort to improve the general distribution of American books abroad.

FIGURE 3
Spanish, French and Arabic BTC Costs—Per Book
Book Translation Program Cost Per Program Book, FY 1979, Spanish,
French and Arabic Only*

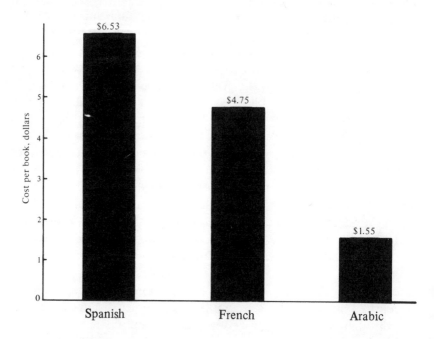

*These regional programs account for approximately 55% of total USICA translated books, the rest being post-controlled individual translation programs. Figures are based on data supplied by ECAIX. They exclude domestic salary costs.

Source: USIA

The history of USIA's book programs is spotty. From 1956 to 1960, a Low-Priced Book Program was designed for the publication of 4,346,800 books, of which about 40 percent were sold and as much as 20 percent may not have been printed, the remainder being presented or used in USIS libraries. These books were published in Japanese, Chinese, seven or eight languages in India, Thai, Urdu (for Pakistan), Arabic, Greek, and Turkish. Subsidized at 100 percent to reduce retail prices, publishers were left with very little incentive to sell what they produced, while many other problems ensued, resulting in the cancellation of this program four years after its inauguration.

The same low-priced book concept produced a program of full-length American books in English, known as "Student Editions." The Student Editions were terminated in 1967, when agency officers who managed the geographic area that included India decided to withdraw funds from this program in favor of a new "package approach" to programming. Without the Indian market, the high cost to USIA of smaller editions suitable for the rest of the third world, where English is the major common language, made it impractical to continue this program.

Another book program of the late 1950s was that of the "Ladder Editions." These were paperback editions of American books abridged and adapted in controlled vocabularies of 1,000 to 5,000 words for the use of readers of English as a second language. This program began in 1957 as a means to introduce students or persons who had studied English as a second language to U.S. culture. The idea for Ladder Editions originated with USIS Tokyo, when it was discovered that Japanese students without U.S. books in English on their level of competency were reading about the lives of Lenin, Marx, and Stalin. Given the wider market for these books, the Ladder Editions flourished and distribution was extended to Latin America. In 1975, however, despite the program's success, it was terminated due to budget cuts. In Korea and in Japan where, as noted above, the Ladder Series concept originated, the Ladder books continue to be published and sold but without USIA support.

Other major agency book translation programs existed in India in various languages of the subcontinent, in France for French-speaking Africa, and in Chinese, Japanese, and Arabic. But USIA's Book Translation Program was reduced from a peak of more than 12,690,000 books published in fiscal year 1965 to about 525,000 in fiscal year 1980. As the 1981 report of the Agency's Book Committee notes, "Under USIA auspices books have been published in 57 languages and English since 1950; in 1980 there were 14 foreign languages plus English and only seven languages exceed 15,000 copies (Arabic, Chinese, French, Spanish, English reprints, Korean, and Portuguese)."[9]

Not everyone shares the view of the book committee, which recommends expanding translations. The individual cost of books has increased tremendously from the 1950s and 1960s. There are those who believe funds now spent on book translations might better be spent in other programs. This would not prohibit occasional titles from being translated, but it is obvious that USIA's leadership in recent years has not been enthusiastic about the book translation program; otherwise it would have received much more attention than has been evident.

In the mid-1960s, USIA arranged the publication of a small, unattributed book concerning the crisis in the Dominican Republic in which the United States became militarily involved. It was to be the first, and possibly the last time, that America's public diplomats were to attempt such a technique. It rubbed the U.S. Congress the wrong way, since it was not identified as a product of the U.S. government. Also it ignored the unwritten rule that has guided U.S. public diplomats since the formation of USIA: that their products must be "attributed or attributable." Since then, the agency has stayed away from publishing books on its own, while all pamphlets and magazines USIA publishes are attributed.

There will always be programs that serve a highly useful purpose under certain circumstances, but which, when circumstances change, should also be changed or abolished. A good example of this was the *Informational Media Guarantee Program* (IMG). The IMG Program began in the late 1940s and was designed to overcome the postwar shortage of U.S. dollars abroad with which to purchase U.S. educational, informational, and cultural materials. Because of the nature of its objectives, it became a USIA program when USIA was established in 1953.

Under IMG, publishers sold books and other materials abroad for blocked currency and then applied to USIA for conversion of the nonconvertible foreign currency proceeds to dollars. The foreign currency was then deposited in a U.S. Treasury account where these funds became available for use to finance U.S. government activities in the countries of origin. Although the program was successful in promoting the overseas distribution of U.S. books through commercial channels (from 1949 to 1967 about $83 million worth of materials were sold), fluctuations in exchange rates produced substantial losses on subsequent sales of currencies for dollars. These losses were charged to USIA which, at the end of the program in 1967, required the agency to borrow from the Treasury or assume indebtedness of $31,620,170. Appropriated funds were sought to reimburse the Treasury, a practice which some members of the Congress found objectionable as it was outside a regular appropriation, thus the program was terminated. In early 1983, in one country alone, Pakistan, about 1 million dollars in rupees remained in the old IMG account, funds which could be used for much needed books,

FIGURE 4
Cost Per Book
Total BTP budget* divided by total number of books produced
worldwide by all book translation programs, all countries.

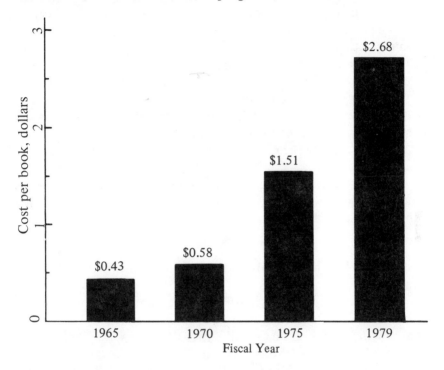

*Excluding salary costs.

Source: USIA

perhaps textbooks, for that developing country, or for other educational or cultural purposes of mutual interest, if a way could be
found to do so. Since the IMG program ended more than 15 years
ago, these funds have lain dormant in a Karachi bank.

Despite the fact that we live in a world where the audio-visual
arts seem to be dominant, and despite reservations about the
Agency's book translation programs, books are still a vitally importance in public diplomacy. However, in today's computer age, how
much of USIA's limited funds should go into book translation
programs remains problematical.

LECTURE AND SEMINAR PROGRAMS

USIA often provides speakers and participants for seminars, which are held either in foreign countries, or in the United States for foreign visitors. Political and economic development are popular themes, but anything from such broad subjects as "communications" to "U.S. perceptions of Islamic institutions" have been subjects of lectures and seminars that USIA either sponsored or to which it provided at least one speaker. At seminars sponsored by USIA in the United States, specialists from various countries or a geographic grouping of countries are invited to attend. Often, when seminars are being held abroad by other organizations, a USIA grant is what enables one or more Americans to attend. Individual USIS offices also take advantage of the presence of visiting Fulbright scholars and professors by contracting them to lecture in the host country on subjects of mutual interest.

ENGLISH TEACHING AND THE BINATIONAL CENTERS

English is today the language most common to the modern world. It is certainly in the interest of the United States to encourage the growth of English among all nations, while at the same time the people of the United States should be expanding their knowledge of foreign languages. Unfortunately, as the Perkins Report revealed in 1979,[10] there were fewer university and secondary school courses in foreign languages being taught in the United States at that time, and fewer students learning foreign languages, than at any time in recent U.S. history, yet the demands for foreign language scholars are increasing.

There is little or nothing that public diplomats can contribute to solving this internal problem for the United States, but public diplomats are involved in supporting the teaching of English in many countries throughout the world. This is done through USIA's English Teaching Division, which supplies overseas posts with background materials for the teaching of English, as well as English teaching specialists who assist foreign educational and cultural institutions, and governmental educational organizations, in developing and improving their English teaching capabilities. A special magazine on new techniques and other items of interest to teachers of English is published quarterly by USIA. Entitled *English Teaching Forum*, it is in great demand overseas. Most USIS posts do not become directly involved in teaching English, though there have been times when exceptions have been made in order to provide, for example, private lessons to a minister of foreign affairs or other high government officials. In short, the role of U.S. public diplomats in the field of English teaching is not to teach, but to encourage and support the teaching of English by others.

The United Kingdom as well as the United States share an interest in fostering the teaching of English in other nations, thus USIA works closely with the British Council, whenever possible, in supporting indigenous efforts aimed at broadening this activity. There was a time when some people argued that British and American English are so different that they are incompatible. However, most would agree that, except for a few hundred words that are different, the British and Americans essentially speak the same language, even if some words are pronounced differently. Host countries interested in improving the language capabilities of their citizens can only benefit from the increased resources resulting from cooperative efforts of the British Council and USIA in the teaching of English.

English teaching has become big business in many parts of the world. This has come about not only because of the need to understand the latest developments in medicine, science, technology and many other fields, where a knowledge of English is essential, but also because of the desire of many to travel to the United States and other English-speaking countries.

In many areas of the world, and particularly in Latin America, the popularity of the English language has enabled binational cultural institutions to be created and to flourish in scores of cities. More than a hundred binational cultural centers, the vast majority in Latin America but many in other countries as well, conduct classes in the English language for thousands of students daily. Most are young secondary school and university students and there are generally more women than men who seek knowledge of this sort. In some centers, special classes are held for journalists, medical doctors, and other specialists interested in learning, for very practical reasons, the specialized terminology, in English, of their profession.

Most of these binational cultural centers receive some support from USIA, such as guidance and advice about the most modern methods for the teaching of English, the assignment of USIA English-teaching specialists, or, occasionally, through provision of U.S. equipment and materials; the main source of income for these non-profit, cultural/educational institutions, however, comes from the tuition payments of the students who want to learn English.

In earlier years, the directors of many of these institutions were U.S. public diplomats assigned to administer their academic and cultural programs as well as their business affairs. In recent years, as USIA and ICA suffered budget cuts, the public diplomats were pulled out of most of these centers and replaced by locally hired nationals. In some cases local political and labor problems arose that also made it desirable that public diplomats vacate the director-ships in order to let national directors run what are essentially national institutions, despite their binational character. This has worked out well in most cases, though not in all, but it was prob-ably a necessary development as funds for America's public diplo-macy efforts constantly diminished in real terms during the past decade.

The director of most binational cultural centers, whether an American or a foreign national, reports to a board of directors, half of whom are generally citizens of the host country and half of whom are Americans resident in that country. One of the board members is often the cultural affairs officer, who provides USIA support and keeps the USIS post informed of the center's needs and problems. Frequently the president of the board is a national and the vice-president is an American, though sometimes these positions change every year or two. In any event most boards try to be binational in character and tend to attract professional and business leaders from both the local and American communities, individuals who welcome the opportunity to serve the educational and cultural interests of their respective countries. While English teaching is a primary goal of these binational centers, and though tuition payments, their major source of capital, the teaching of English is not their only goal. Most centers have auditoriums, thea-ters, or multipurpose rooms where both national and American performing artists are presented and where lectures, seminars, motion pictures, and videotaped programs are held; exhibit areas where the works of national and American artists are shown; and libraries or reading rooms for the use of members and students. Thus, in addi-tion to learning the English language, these institutions provide additional opportunities to learn about the United States through the various activities mentioned above. They also provide opportunities for Americans visiting or resident in those countries to learn more about the local culture.

Top officials of America's public diplomacy organization have grown hot and cold with respect to binational centers over the years. Those most familiar with them generally agree that they are highly worthwhile and effective vehicles, not only for the teaching of English to many thousands of foreigners by modern means, but also because they create long-range, positive interest in the United States. They do this at very little cost to the U.S. government, since most centers are managed sufficiently well, and the demand for English-language training is so high that most centers are self-supporting.

Sometimes these centers, like USIS libraries, have been targets of criminal elements who physically attack them for political reasons. Though due as much, perhaps, to their vulnerability and high visibility, this is also due to their being recognized as highly effective vehicles of U.S. culture and ideas.

There have been times when the political relations between a host country and the U.S. government, for one reason or another, have soured to the point where the local communications environment becomes unreceptive, if not downright hostile, to the efforts of U.S. public diplomats. Often in such situations the binational centers, which are neither directly financed nor controlled by the United States, continue to carry on with the teaching of English and other cultural activities, though usually on a reduced scale. When the political climate between the two countries warms, as so often happens after a coldspell, the binational centers are there to move forward in a new era of closer, more positive relations. In short, for a relatively small investment on the part of the United States, binational centers generally provide a large return in terms of their service to the long-range interests of both countries.

Unlike the USIA library study of 1981 mentioned earlier, by early 1983 no such study had been reported on the binational cultural centers that receive various degrees of support and assistance from USIA. The February 1982 GAO study of USIA programs notes that "with no clearly stated policy regarding the purpose of the Centers, their relationships to USICA (USIA) have often been uncertain and difficult for the (USIS) post to understand." The GAO report bemoans USIA's lack of coherent and uniform programming policy and administrative controls" with regard to the centers. Furthermore, "lack of a clear objective" for the relationship between USIA and the centers, the report states, has produced an attitude toward them on the part of USIA officials of "benign neglect."[11]

The U.S. government's involvement with binational cultural centers began in 1941 and has shown a continuing trend toward less USIA support and control. In Fiscal Year 1981 the Agency spent about $800,000 in support of the centers. When John Reinhardt was director of ICA, various public affairs officers expressed interest in obtaining a clearer understanding from Washington as to what the relationship between their posts and the centers should be. One paper that was drafted in an attempt to clarify that relationship never left the office of the deputy director of ICA. Thus the GAO, in its February 1982 report, felt justified in arguing that uncertainties and difficulties for USIS posts in understanding their relationship to the centers existed "because USICA has never clearly stated a governing policy regarding the purpose of the Centers."[12] The GAO report recommends that the USIA director "develop a policy outlining the responsibilities of the overseas missions toward the Centers." When this is done, it should be a great help to USIA field officers, though the controversy among those who believe the binational centers should have a more prominent role in USIA activities, and those who think otherwise, is likely to continue.

EDUCATIONAL EXCHANGE PROGRAMS

There are two major types of educational exchange programs administered by USIA. The International Visitors (IV) Program enables leaders, potential and emerging leaders, and specialists to visit the United States for three to four weeks on programs designed to accommodate their interests and specialties. At the same time, they are exposed to American progress in their chosen fields and American culture generally. By 1982, former IV grantees who have risen to national leadership included Anwar Sadat of Egypt, Helmut Schmidt of Germany, Valéry Giscard d'Estaing of France, Margaret Thatcher of England, Indira Gandhi of India, and some 30 other heads of government. Within the French Cabinet and National Assembly in 1982, there were 54 members who had visited the United States on IV grants. Developing countries also have participated extensively and fruitfully in this program. In Zimbabwe, for example, former IV grantees included (in 1982) President Canaan Banana, five cabinet members, three members of parliament, two ambassadors, and more than 50 government officials.[13] Although funding for this program was doubled when ICA inherited it from the Department of State in 1978, by the early 1980s increased air fares and other inflationary costs resulted in reductions in the annual number of grantees.

The second major educational exchange program of USIA is that of academic exchanges, usually referred to as the Fulbright Program, in honor of former Senator J. William Fulbright. Legislation that he sponsored at the end of World War II made possible the use of funds generated from the sale of surplus war material and equipment to pay for Europeans to study and conduct research in the United States, and for Americans to study in Europe. Later the Fulbright Program utilized funds obtained from Public Law 480 sales of surplus agricultural products. Like the IV Program, the Fulbright Program was administered domestically by the Department of State until 1978, when it came under the complete jurisdiction of the newly formed International Communication Agency.

The transfer of the Fulbright Program to ICA caused considerable consternation. There were those who believed that placing this program, which was noted for its adherence solely to educational and intellectuals dictates, under the direction of ICA, would politicize it. Many critics of this change, which included Senator Fulbright himself, a great many academics, and a number of congressmen, either were not familiar with, or simply ignored the fact that throughout the history of USIA, ICA's predecessor for a quarter of a century, the Fulbright Program, had been administered by USIA officers overseas. Furthermore, while a binational commission is in charge of these programs in each country, the membership of each commission always includes at least one U.S. public diplomat, usually the cultural attaché, and often a second public diplomat who frequently is the treasurer of the commission. Since the major decisions of a country program are made by this binational body, the change that appeared to be so worrisome to so many was not really that much of a change. Experience to date has indicated that the commissions continue now, as they did prior to the creation of ICA, to adhere strictly to the idea that the Fulbright Program must serve the academic and intellectual interests of both countries, rather than being a political vehicle of either.

The 1982 report of the U.S. Advisory Commission on Public Diplomacy treats this theme by noting that its reports to the Congress must include, as a statutory obligation, "assessments of the degree to which the scholarly integrity and nonpolitical character of the educational and cultural exchange programs vested in the Director" of USIA have been maintained.[14] In carrying out this responsibility, correspondence was conducted with the chairmen of some 42 binational Fulbright commissions abroad as well as with cultural affairs officers in approximately 75 countries where there are no binational commissions. That was in 1979. In 1980, the advisory commission sent questionnaires to about 6,000 members of the Fulbright Alumni Association. Commission members also met with members of the Board of Foreign Scholarships, with career public diplomats, and with representatives of U.S. organizations outside the federal government engaged in the administration of ICA's exchange programs. "The results of these inquiries," they note, "indicate that to date the scholarly integrity and nonpolitical character of the peer review process and other procedures by which academic exchange program grants are awarded is being maintained."[15]

The transfer of the Fulbright and IV programs out of the Department of State to ICA was a particularly trying experience for the employees of the State Department who were transferred. They were uprooted from their offices at the State Department and squeezed into offices in the oldest USIA building in Washington, about a half-mile away, at 1776 Pennsylvania Ave. N.W. Little planning, apparently, had been done to accommodate them. Not only were some of the State Department "CI" employees, as they were known, appalled at the idea of joining what some viewed as more of a "propaganda" organization than an educational one, but they had earlier believed, with good reason, that the Stanton Commission recommendation would prevail whereby USIA employees would become Department of State employees rather than vice versa. While many CU officials reluctantly, in most cases, moved into ICA, others transferred to various units of the State Department, some in order to avoid association with the propaganda arm of the U.S. government. An indication of how unprepared the new ICA was to receive this influx of new employees was the fact that, initially, some were assigned to the geographic area offices to function as liaison with the educational exchange unit of the agency. This experiment did not work and was soon terminated.

Under the International Visitor Program, invitations are extended annually by U.S. chiefs of mission to some 1500 to 2,000 foreign leaders and specialists in government, the mass media, labor, science, education and other fields to visit the United States to exchange views with their counterparts. About 500 of these foreign leaders annually participate in multiregional or regional projects—seminars, meetings, and conferences on such topics as energy, economics, environment, communications, etc. These regional and multiregional projects enable the participants to exchange views not only with Americans but with their counterparts from other countries as well. By bringing together specialists from a number of countries at one time, in one place, the attendance of the highest-qualified U.S. experts in chosen fields is facilitated. The learning experience at such gatherings is, of course, a two-way street. Individually tailored programs are also arranged for IV grantees who are not involved in multiregional projects. While this is sometimes more fruitful and, at times, more satisfying for some individuals, it can be more costly. However, in a study entitled "The International Visitor Program: A Review," which was completed in April 1981, and written by a committee chaired by Richard Arndt of the associate directorate for educational and cultural affairs of ICA, it is noted that "groups are *not* cost effective unless the numbers of participants are high," meaning a group between nine and 14. This study makes a number of worthwhile recommendations concerning the administration of the IV program.

The number of annual IV grantees dropped from a high of 2,171 in 1978 to 1,579 in 1981. While costs rose dramatically in the past decade, the IV Program stagnated at slightly more than $9 million in 1974 constant dollars.[16] Because of this, and because many ambassadors and other observers expressed to advisory commission members their belief that the IV Program "provides American taxpayers with the best return on their dollar in the foreign policy field," their 1982 report calls educational exchange and the international visitors programs "the most effective tools of public diplomacy." They recommend that these programs be "materially strengthened."[17]

In 1981, when the budget of ICA was undergoing review by the administration and the Congress with an eye to cutting it drastically, a scheme was devised to battle the proposed budget cuts by suggesting that *if* severe cuts were implemented, ICA would be forced to drastically reduce one of its most popular and effective programs—the Educational Exchange Program. This ploy, in the view of some observers, was another "Washington Monument Game," as William Greider calls this type of tactic in "The Education of David Stockman." "The Washington Monument Game," Greider says, is "a metaphor for phony budget cuts, in which the National Park Service, ordered to save money, announces that it is closing the Washington Monument."[18] This, in a sense, is what ICA Director Charles Wick did when he told the Congress that his only alternative for meeting congressional budget cuts for his agency was to cut the educational exchange programs. This brought forth a storm of editorials and commentary in praise of this highly valued activity, since educational exchange programs have a much larger constituency than most USIA activities. Not only are these programs highly respected on their own merits, but there are many thousands of former Fulbright students, scholars, and researchers in the United States who have benefitted from these exchange programs, and many others who hope to benefit. The furor raised was just what Charles Wick sought. As a result, the cuts were far less drastic than might have occurred had the agency's response to the Congress been different. At the same time, it is true that had the 12 percent budget cut, which was what was being demanded, been made by across-the-board reductions for fiscal year 1982, coming after years of continuous budget cuts, many of the agency's information "tools" would have been seriously weakened.

USIA is small as U.S. government bureaucracies go, and given the product it delivers overseas—ideas and information—it generally lacks a constituency of any size at home. This is one reason why U.S. citizens seldom objected to the constant cutting of USIA and ICA budgets during the past decade. However, since educational exchange programs involve many Americans who meet and greet and act as hosts to the thousands of visitors who come to the United States under the exchange programs, they constitute a constituency for the managers of these programs.

Some Department of State officials view the transfer of CU activities to ICA as unfortunate mainly because it also transferred CU's constituency to ICA. While the educational exchange programs were administered at home by the Department of State, the more than 700,000 U.S. volunteers throughout the nation who assist in entertaining foreign visitors maintained a close association with the State Department.[19] Many are leading citizens in their communities or associated with important local institutions. Interested generally in foreign affairs, they provided sounding boards for U.S. foreign policy. These contacts also provided a means for U.S. diplomats to readily and easily feel the pulse of America, since these citizens who volunteer their services come from all walks of life and all geographic areas within the United States. With the administration of the IV Program within the United States moved from State to ICA, these volunteers now became associated with ICA (and, later, USIA) rather than with the State Department. In assisting international visitors by providing home hospitality, arranging speaking engagements, arranging interviews with local leaders, tours of business, educational, and professional institutions, etc., most of them were members of the National Council for Community Services to International Visitors, known as COSERVE. COSERVE worked closely with Washington officials in planning the programs of official visitors. Today this organization is known as the National Council for International Visitors (NCIV). NCIV has its headquarters at Meridian House,1630 Crescent Place, N.W. in Washington, D.C. The thousands of volunteers throughout the United States in the network that NCIV maintains to assist foreign visitors have now joined USIA's constituency.

The first major exchange program to be sponsored by the U.S. government was the Fulbright Program, which was established in 1946. More than 130,000 American and foreign teachers, students, and researchers had participated in this program as "Fulbrighters" by 1980. Since 1980, about 3,500 persons annually have utilized Fulbright grants. The presidentially-appointed, 12-member Board of Foreign Scholarships supervises the program in the United States. Overseas there are commissions in more than 40 countries, composed, as noted earlier, of Americans and foreign nationals who supervise the programs in each country.

In recent years USIA officials have been rightfully concerned about the reduction in the number of grants for academic exchanges. This has been brought about not only by the lack of an adequate budget to keep up with constantly rising costs, but also because some 30 new countries, including the People's Republic of China, along with several in Eastern Europe and Africa, have been added to this program since its inception.

The Fulbright Program peaked in 1966 at $76 million (in constant 1972 dollars) and 9,000 persons. In 1980, the Japanese government, recognizing the mutuality of interest in these exchanges, agreed to match the American contribution of $1 million. In 1980, the West German government paid 77 percent of the $4.3 million required to support German-American Fulbright exchanges. In 1972 constant dollars, the American contribution, which had been $29.4 million in 1959, dropped to $19.7 million in 1980, while foreign contributions increased. In fiscal year 1981, the $77.3 million Fulbright Program received 65 percent of its funds from the U.S. government, 20 percent from foreign sources, and 15 percent from the American private sector. In number of grantees, American Fulbrighters plummeted from a high of 904 in 1966-67 to 364 in 1980-81. The number of French grantees, for example, fell from 309 to 63 per year in the past decade.[20]

During the decade of the 1960s, AID, the Ford Foundation, and the Fulbright Program, all with fairly large exchange programs, had a profound effect on the education and educational systems of countries that are of growing importance to the United States in the 1980s. Indonesia is an example of a country where many leaders participated in these programs. But with the programs of AID and the Ford Foundation greatly diminished, as well as the Fulbright Program, in the future Indonesian leaders will probably not receive as much U.S. educational exposure as in the past.

This decline in academic exchanges also adversely affects the ability of the United States to maintain a pool of Americans competent to help achieve American goals in increasingly important third world relationships. In 1979, USIA officials have pointed out, for example, that only seven doctoral candidates went to Africa from the United States under Fulbright auspices, and of these few, none to a country as important as Nigeria. In addition, many scholars at U.S. university area studies centers, persons who are primary candidates for Fulbright grants, are not refreshing their knowledge or acquiring basic language skills. An earlier survey indicated that only three in five can read, speak or write any language in their areas of competence. Another indication of what is being lost by not providing greater numbers of exchanges can be seen by the same study with regard to research papers by U.S. scholars which were surveyed. Only one research paper in three on the USSR or China, countries of great importance to the United States, had original source citations indicating that the researcher had competent knowledge of Russian or Chinese languages.

Perhaps more than any other tools in the public diplomat's "kit," academic exchanges serve the interests of both the United States and the host country. The Board of Foreign Scholarships in Washington, the joint commissions overseas, and the individual public diplomats charged with administering these programs all persistently and passionately pursue the ideal that Senator Fulbright advocated—that they be completely academic in nature and non-political. In so being, and yet serving the interests of all, it may well be that the holders of the purse strings in Congress and the administration will, by recognizing their high value, maintain the strength of these academic exchanges and eventually reverse the downward trend by increasing the amount of funds available for them.

AMERICAN PARTICIPANT PROGRAM

Annually USIA sends approximately 500 Americans abroad to explain U.S. policies and society to overseas audiences.[21] Those who participate in this program, which is known as the American Participant Program, are U.S. professors, as well as specialists in various fields from government and private industry. They generally visit two or more countries in one or two geographical regions, where the local USIS posts arrange lectures, seminars and meetings to exchange views with their foreign counterparts. While political scientists and economists predominate, an American Participant can be an expert on almost any subject of mutual interest such as solar energy, communications, education, business administration, modernization, narcotics, etc.

CULTURAL PRESENTATIONS— PERFORMING AND NONPERFORMING ARTISTS

Presenting American performing artists abroad under Department of State auspices had been a common practice for many years, until ICA was born, after which the responsibility for such performances became an ICA (and, later, USIA) function exclusively. As with educational exchanges, the cultural exchanges had formerly been managed overseas by public diplomats of USIA but administered within the United States by Department of State employees.

Cultural presentations have long been recognized as an "international language" that transcends politics and brings people together in a positive, enjoyable way. However, they are costly, their impact is often short-ranged, and often they communicate in one direction only. However, whenever major U.S. artists perform, they are generally well-received and long remembered.

The high cost of top-quality performers, along with ever-increasing travel costs, particularly for large groups, greatly limits the number and quality of performing artists who can be sponsored by USIA. In recent decades large groups of performers fully sponsored by the U.S. government were sent mainly to Communist countries, where other avenues of communication such as the local press, radio, and television are closed. Even this avenue came to an end, however, with the Russian invasion of Afghanistan and the cooling of relations between the East and West, followed by the cancellation of cultural exchanges.

In other parts of the world, particularly in the developing countries, small performing groups or single artists are frequently sponsored by USIA in order to expose foreign audiences to American music, dance and theater, and through these performances, to the thoughts and ideas of American culture. Many times American performing artists travelling abroad on their own commercial tours can be obtained at far less cost than if the U.S. government had to pay their full travel expenses. Sometimes USIA subsidizes groups of U.S. performing artists on tour in a particular geographic region who might not otherwise visit a nearby developing country for fear of not being able to cover their expenses. In such instances, in addition to helping defray expenses, USIS posts also provide publicity through their media contacts; help in obtaining many of the support services needed by visiting artists, such as local co-sponsorship by indiginous cultural entities; and help in locating suitable places in which to perform.

Communist countries almost always insist on "cultural agreements" in order to maintain the controls they believe are necessary in their societies, and to obtain a quid pro quo. While cultural presentations receive a high priority among the limited activities of U.S. public diplomats in their approaches to audiences in Communist countries, since, as noted earlier, most other avenues of communication are closed, Communist nations also place great emphasis on cultural presentations in their approaches to democratic countries. This is not only because of the intrinsic value of cultural activities, but also because the mass media in democratic countries are likewise "closed" as far as Communist propaganda is concerned. The competition in a free society is generally far too keen for more than a smattering of Communist propaganda to be placed in the mass media of most democratic societies. This is particularly true in the United States.

Most *developed countries* have no shortage of performances by U.S. artists as many can and do finance themselves through commercial tours which thrive in those countries. It is the *developing countries*, along with the Communist countries, where problems exist in presenting American performing artists. In these countries there are either financial or political restrictions that, without the help of USIA, would generally prohibit U.S. performing artists from being presented. This is another example of the need to recognize that public diplomacy approaches to the developing, the Communist, and the developed worlds, differ.

Occasionally, through a great deal of effort and the combined resources of various interested groups, sufficient funds can be garnered to enable a large symphony orchestra or a major American dance group to perform in a developing area of the world. Generally, however, U.S. public diplomats must continue to rely on smaller, less costly groups in their efforts to demonstrate the vitality, versatility, and variety of U.S. performing artists.

If the break in cultural exchanges between the Soviet Union and the United States continues for any length of time, it would be well for USIA to use this time to send some major performing groups to those areas of the third world that have seldom if ever seen a live performance of one of America's hundreds of symphony orchestras or one of its major dance companies. When U.S. and Soviet relations return to some degree of "normalcy" once again, as hopefully they will, few would argue that, given a limited budget for performing American artists, they should, as in the past, concentrate on tours to the Soviet Union and to other closed societies.

With respect to nonperforming artists, presentations of their works fall under the rubric of "exhibits," discussed briefly below.

EXHIBITS

Exhibits, whether they are the presentation of the works of one American painter or an elaborate, specially-designed exhibition on a theme of international interest such as energy or economics, constitute another of the public diplomat's tools. As in the case of performances by major American artists, major exhibits have been important vehicles of communication with Soviet and Eastern European audiences, although they have also been used effectively, though generally on a smaller scale, in other parts of the world. As in the case of performing artists, the more elaborate they are the more costly they are, and their impact may disappear when the exhibit ends. Furthermore, exhibits by their nature demand considerable time and effort in both the planning and operating stages. Taking all this into consideration, many public diplomats are less than enthusiastic about employing this technique in their program plans. If it is the right place, at the right time, with the right exhibit and the right audience, that's fine. But too many times, except for small exhibits that are easy to mount and easy to handle, their cost-effectiveness is questionable.

In recent years, according to USIA sources, the agency produced an average of ten major exhibits annually, including solo exhibitions and participation in international trade fairs and special international promotions. About 75 smaller exhibits are also circulated by the agency annually throughout the world.

AMERICAN STUDIES PROGRAMS

There is a natural interest on the part of U.S. public diplomats in supporting the study by other peoples of American history and institutions. While not a major program of U.S. public diplomacy compared with many other activities, there has been a steady effort by USIA to foster and support American Studies programs abroad. A small unit at the Washington headquarters of USIA follows developments in this field, obtains materials for interested posts, and provides guidance when asked. This unit also provides liaison between American and foreign universities, academic institutions, and scholars interested in American Studies.

OTHER ACTIVITIES

There are two educational activities which merit some comment in this analysis of the standard programs of U.S. public diplomats. The first of these is that engaged in at the East-West Center, located at the University of Hawaii.

The U.S. Congress, through Public Law 86-472, established the East-West Center as an educational institution in order to promote better relations and understanding between the United States and the nations of Asia and the Pacific through cooperative study, training, and research. Known formally as the Center for Cultural and Technical Interchange between East and West, it was created in 1960. USIA serves a liaison function for the center and foreign universities, academic associations, and scholars. Both Americans and foreign nationals from Asian and Pacific countries participate in the Center's activities.

Funding for the center comes from a separate account in USIA's budget. In Fiscal Year 1983 USIA requested $18.2 million for the center's federal appropriation, which makes up about 80 percent of its budget.

In the 1982 Report of the U.S. Advisory Commission on Public Diplomacy, the commission questions what it calls the "disproportionately large" federal contribution in comparison with the 20 percent received from the private sector and other governments. In Fiscal Year 1981, for example, approximately $4 million was received from a variety of individual, corporate, and U.S. government grants, while Asian governments contributed about $500,000.[22] The commission concludes that in view of the center's budget and potential, it is time for a comprehensive evaluation of its effectiveness. Not only would this be helpful in determining if the U.S. government is getting its money's worth, but it would be helpful in determining whether similar centers, dealing with Latin American-United States, or African-U.S. issues, would be worthwhile. From one point of view, a number of university and other institutions, both public and private, which specialize in specific geographic area studies, may be the best vehicles for study, training, and research beneficial to both Americans and foreigners. Those who believe that the less government can be involved in anything the better would favor private enterprise in this endeavor if it can be shown that U.S. government support, while helpful, is not vital.

AMERICAN SCHOOLS ABROAD

American schools abroad are another institutionalized educational activity which, while having no formal connection with USIA, is a subject which merits attention in any discussion of public diplomacy. Ironically, the American schools in foreign countries provide a case, perhaps, for more U.S. government involvement rather than less.

When U.S. educational and cultural exchange programs were administered by the Department of State, roughly $2 million annually were alloted to more than 50 American schools in countries where the United States maintained diplomatic relations. These schools serve a dual object. They are intended to increase mutual understanding by demonstrating American educational ideals, practices, and instructional materials to foreign students, at the same time that they provide elementary and secondary-level educational facilities for dependents of U.S. government employees stationed abroad. Because they provide an American type of education which prepares students for U.S. colleges and universities, they are especially attractive to nongovernment Americans living and working overseas, as well as foreign nationals who either want their children to learn English, since the courses are taught in English, and/or want to prepare their sons and daughters for enrollment in U.S. universities.

In many developing societies, these schools are among the best in the host country. For this and the reasons mentioned above, the host country students who attend these schools often come from the families who are the movers and shakers of their societies. Many can be expected to eventually inherit their parents' positions of power and influence.

The British, French, and German governments have long recognized the value of supporting their own schools abroad and have for years dedicated considerable resources to such schools. Unlike the American government, they seem to give greater importance, and thus greater financial assistance, to their schools in foreign countries than the United States does.

In the majority of American schools abroad, American students are outnumbered by local nations and third country nationals—Canadians, Scandanavians, and Japanese being especially well-represented in many countries. But because American students are there, and USIA must guard against "propagandizing" its own citizens, a question arises as to what connection USIA should have, if any, with these schools. Some might say "none," yet many of the materials—educational, cultural, and informational, that USIA distributes, such as films, books, pamphlets, videotapes, etc.—provide factual information about the United States that can be invaluable as teaching aids to the faculties of these schools, not to mention their value to American students who, living in another culture, usually do not have ready access to American movies, television, libraries, etc.

Given the importance and influence of many of these schools for generations of influential foreigners, consideration should be given to strengthening them by providing greater access to the educational, cultural, and informational materials of USIA. Informal arrangements with many of these schools have been made with overseas USIS posts in the past, and this has been helpful to some. It is time, however, to consider moving the administration of the limited support funds that are now administered in the Department of State to USIA. This would more closely associate USIA with these schools. After all, as educational institutions overseas they are essentially in the same category as the educational and cultural exchange programs, which also involve both Americans and foreigners, as do these schools, and which were transferred from the State Department to ICA when ICA was created in 1978. The time has come for Washington officials to study this possibility as being in the best interests of the students, their parents, the school administrators, as well as that of the U.S. government.

AN EXPANDED YOUTH EXCHANGE PROGRAM

In 1982, because of a growing concern among some American political leaders that the "successor generation" among America's staunchest allies, in Western Europe in particular, was becoming less and less knowledgeable about the United States and its historic commitment to a world of free and independent nations, President

Reagan initiated an expanded youth exchange program for the Western European countries, Canada, and Japan. He named USIA Director Charles Wick as his personal representative to carry out this project. To provide guidance and raise funds for the next exchange program, the President's Council for International Youth Exchange was established. Some 22 leaders from private industry were named to the Council by President Reagan.

During its first three years of operation, the USIA director announced in November 1982, the new program would seek to double the number of exchanges among 15-to-19-year old youths representing Canada, France, Italy, West Germany, Japan, Great Britain, and the United States. With a three-year, $10 million fund provided by the government, an equal amount would be sought from the private sector. To accommodate the 5,000 exchange students expected annually, who would come to the United States for several weeks to a year, some 15,000 American families would be invited to host them. What makes the new exchange program unique are its emphasis on youth and its emphasis on nations of the developed world, all of whom are among the staunchest allies of the United States.

PERSONAL CONTACT

This "tool of the trade" has been left for last, since it belongs in a category by itself and is not an activity per se in the way the "tools" described earlier are. Personal contact is important for at least two reasons. It is a means to convey substantive messages, and it enables doors to open that might otherwise be shut.

The personal touch in carrying out the variety of programs we have been discussing is without question an extremely important factor. While the Chinese are credited with calling the first step the most important one of a thousand-mile journey, it was Edward R. Murrow who, as director of USIA during the Kennedy presidency, reflected that it is "the last three feet" that count in delivering a message. This was his way of saying that, in the end, it is personal contact that counts. Without it, little can be done to place a radio or television program on a local station, to arrange for the local sponsorship of a cultural presentation, to influence an editor to at least consider one's point of view, or to do any of the many things a public diplomat is expected to do to get his country's policies publicized and, hopefully, understood.

There are times when bureaucrats in Washington tend to preach to the converted, and in no field of public diplomacy does this seem to me more true than when it comes to the role of personal contact. Field officers are not only reminded again and again of how important it is for effective programming to establish and maintain personal contacts, but systems are devised by the Washington bureaucracy to assure that this important facet of public diplomacy is not left to chance.

The system that USIA uses to assure that its public diplomats stay in close personal touch, to the greatest extent possible, with the leaders and opinion molders of the host society, is known as the "Distribution and Record System" (DRS). This system has been refined during the past two decades to the point where, theoretically, the movers in any society can be identified. These are the individuals who must be reached by the efforts of public diplomats if those efforts (combined, of course, with those of traditional diplomats) are to have positive results. They are the people who can either act upon the ideas and policies brought to their attention, or are in positions whereby, actually or potentially, they can influence others to act.

The DRS begins with what is called the "Influence Structure Analysis." As the term indicates, it is an analysis of the structure or make-up of the society in a given country. The society is first examined with regard to the issues, problems, and concerns which country X has in relation to the United States. Then a closer examination is made by the categories or types of individuals who hold positions of power or influence in national affairs. These categories, in the system used by USIA in the early 1980s, are as follows:

Media
Academic
Government/Political
Security/Defense
Cultural
Business/Professional
Labor
Community Leaders/Social Involvement
Students

Within these categories institutions are listed, then positions within these institutions, and, finally, the individuals who occupy those positions are listed. These individuals are described as "participants." It is hoped that they will "participate" in some way in the programs designed by public diplomats. Ideally, this participation will be through personal contact, which is generally considered as being the most effective means of influencing individuals. This is, of course, not always possible since the higher an individual is in the hierarchy of a given society, the more inaccessible he or she is likely to be, particularly in medium to large-size countries. Yet almost all participants can be expected to read newspapers, see television programs or listen to the radio at various times. They can, therefore, be reached through the mass media if by no other means. Between personal contact and the mass media are the various vehicles of communication that were discussed earlier.

After completing the Influence Structure Analysis for a given country, what one ends up with is a list of 500 to 5,000 or more persons (participants), depending upon the size and sophistication of the country involved. These are the people who hold the positions of greatest importance and influence in their society.

The flaw inherent in this attempt to identify the formal structure of a society through the Influence Structure Analysis is that the informal structure can be equally or perhaps even more important in moving and shaking that society than the formal structure. To make the Influence Structure Analysis as realistic as possible, the power brokers who may not be as visible as the editor of a leading newspaper, a high government official, or the owner of a television network must be included. There are also those in less exalted positions who nevertheless can get things done. To know who these people are requires an intimate knowledge and understanding of how a particular society or culture functions. For such understanding the public diplomat relies heavily on local sources and research documents available to him, and the local USIS staff.

The system being described here does not reflect an attempt to create a manipulative organization designed for nefarious purposes. It is an open, logical approach to identify the people in a society who are the ones whom public diplomats are most interested in, for obvious reasons. Most of them are also the ones who would tend to be most interested in receiving books and publications, invitations to meet visiting American counterparts, and invitations to participate in the educational and cultural exchange programs of the U.S. government. They are also writers, editors, and others who might be expected to find the kinds of informational and cultural materials distributed by USIA to be of value to them.

The DRS and its Influence Structure Analysis are, in short, tools of the trade which are used to determine the size and shape of the audiences U.S. public diplomats can realistically expect to reach in a given country. This system also provides a means whereby, through sophisticated word processors or computers, a visiting American economist, for example, who may not speak the local language, can quickly and easily be provided with a list of local English-speaking economists who can be invited to meet with him to exchange views. Other visiting American specialists under programs sponsored or facilitated by USIA can also be assured that the individuals most interested in their specialty, during what is usually a brief visit, can quickly be identified and contacted for reasons of mutual interest.

If USIA officials in Washington would be satisfied to simply allow their public diplomats abroad to use the system as originally intended, and let it go at that, there would be less concern by field officers about the considerable time and effort the DRS requires—time and effort which could otherwise be devoted to organizing and implementing programs. But when computers and sophisticated word processors are available, there are those who think they must be used for accountability purposes. Thus, though of highly questionable value, some USIS posts in the past were asked by Washington to keep records in order to determine the percentage of participants in the DRS with whom, in a given period, formal or informal contacts were initiated or maintained. If the percentages are high, this presumably indicates that the public diplomats at that particular post are really out there working hard for Uncle Sam!

It is difficult to see what relevance such statistics have, since the manner in which the system operates at some posts is to treat equally a two-hour, in-depth conversation with a top government official, the mailing of a magazine article to a participant, or attendance at a USIA-sponsored cultural event. This is mixing apples, oranges, and tangerines. Furthermore, even if such statistics, lumped together as they are, served some useful purpose beyond knowing that 80 percent (or whatever) of the DRS participants are being reached every two months (or whatever) in some way (through personal contact or mailings), the results are misleading. They are misleading because the number of public diplomats at any one post cannot possibly be expected to have the capability of knowing, let alone reaching, every one of a thousand or more participants. Many are contacts of other members of the U.S. Mission, from the ambassador on down, who seldom have kept, and seldom will keep, the kind of records the system, to be valid for accountability demands. When statistical data is so incomplete, of such questionable value, and a mixture of different techniques, it becomes a useless exercise to compile it.

Except for a small coterie of enthusiasts, most of whom are in Washington headquarters, the vast majority of public diplomats view this method of "accountability" as a time-consuming chore of little practical value. It should be either dropped completely or exchanged for a more meaningful system of program evaluation. Although the technology for extensive record keeping is available, this is insufficient reason for doing it. The real reason why a system designed initially and primarily to identify what used to be called "the target audience" has been called upon to emphasize accountability is that the sophistication of the technical equipment—the word processors and computers—enables accountability to be achieved. Today's whiz kids, as they might have been known in the era of the target audience, want to use that capability. Yet nowhere in USIA is the computer-age phrase, "garbage in, garbage out" more appropriate.

The attempt to measure success in public diplomacy—once called "evidence of effectiveness," has faced USIA for as long as it has been in business. The DRS, though rather successful in identifying and directing the resources of a USIS post to the most important audiences, cannot, no matter how much one would like it to, measure success. This can best be done, and possibly can only be done, by identifying actions or reactions which follow public diplomacy efforts. Even then the question arises—was it public diplomacy, traditional diplomacy, or something having no connection with either that brought into being an action (reaction) that public diplomats sought?

NOTES

1. Report of The United States Advisory Commission on Public Diplomacy, 1982, Wash. D.C., p. 22.

2. U.S. General Accounting Office. Report to the director, U.S. International Communication Agency, *U.S. International Communication Agency's Overseas Programs; Some More Useful Than Others*, Feb. 11, 1982, ID-82-1, p. iii.

3. *Ibid.*, p. 24.

4. *Ibid.*

5. Letter to USIA's public affairs officers throughout the world from Charles Z. Wick, director, and Ronald L. Trowbridge, associate director for Educational and Cultural Affairs, dated June 11, 1982 with Library Policy Statement as enclosure.

6. *Ibid.*

7. Two differing views on who should comprise USIA audiences have been argued within the agency for as long as anyone can remember. One view holds that because of the limited resources of USIA, public diplomats can only be effective if they concentrate these limited resources on the elites in host countries—otherwise the resources are spread too thin to be effective. The other view holds that American society is egalitarian and, therefore, U.S. public diplomacy efforts, particularly in relation to such things as libraries, should be available to all who are interested in the United States.

This long-standing argument came to a head during the reign of John Reinhardt as director of ICA. The emphasis initially was to utilize the agency's limited resources on reaching the people who "count," i.e., the decision makers and opinion moulders. The tendency in the early 1980s seems to be a return to the more liberal view—that while the "elites" are most important, since they influence decisions affecting U.S.-host country relations, those individuals who are genuinely interested in the United States and future generations of leaders should not be excluded from USIS programming. The statement that "No patron with serious interest in the United States should be denied access to the library" is a reflection of the latter view, as is the emphasis Director Charles Wick has given to the "successor generation" in such programs as the "Youth Exchange Council," initiated in 1982.

8. USICA Library Policy, issued June 11, 1982.

9. This and much of the material in the preceding paragraphs were developed by the ICA Book Committee and presented in various memoranda between February and June, 1981.

10. Report by the President's Commission on Foreign Languages and International Studies.

11. U.S. General Accounting Office, op. cit., p. 26.

12. *Ibid.*, p. 30.

13. Report of the U.S. Advisory Commission on Public Diplomacy, op. cit. p. 24.

14. *Ibid.*, p. 27.

15. *Ibid.*

16. *Ibid.*, p. 23.

17. *Ibid.*, pp. 21-23.

18. Greider, William, "The Education of David Stockman," *The Atlantic*, December, 1981, p. 47.

19. The Advisory Commission report, op. cit., states that NCIV includes some 725,000 individuals across the United States who are active in more than 90 nonprofit, privately supported organizations that seek to improve the quality of the experience of short-term visitors to the United States, p. 26.

20. *Ibid.*, p. 23.

21. *Ibid.*, p. 27.

22. *Ibid.*, p. 28.

11

WHAT OTHER NATIONS ARE DOING

When the U.S. Embassy in Islamabad was attacked and burned by raging mobs in November of 1979, the cause of the attack was said to be retaliation for the alleged invasion of the Great Mosque of Mecca by Americans, an allegation that was as ridiculous as it was false. The wild band of terrorists involved in that strange incident in far-off Mecca were disenchanted Moslems from the Middle East, but radio reports which reached Pakistan, presumably from India, attributed the attack on Islam's holiest shrine to the United States. This was enough, with a little organization, for raging mobs to destroy the U.S. Embassy in Islamabad and the American cultural centers in Rawalpindi and Lahore.

To the author's knowledge there was never any proof that it was the Soviet Union that planted those false reports, but since USIA began focussing on Soviet "disinformation" tactics a few years ago, there is far greater public knowledge of the extent to which the Russians will go to discredit the United States. This being so, it is not difficult to believe that the false reports which caused four deaths when the U.S. Embassy burned, and might have been much more tragic had the 70 or so people holed up in the embassy vault not survived, was yet another instance of Soviet machinations in the field of public diplomacy—public diplomacy of a type far different from that practiced by the Western democracies.

A typical Soviet ploy is to plant a story in a Communist or leftist newspaper or magazine in a third world country, then replay the story through Radio Moscow or other Soviet international information organs, quoting the third country source as if it were an independent third party. In early 1983, for example, the *Patriot* of Bombay, a Communist newspaper, was the first to "expose" an alleged plot to "destabilize" India, "master-minded" by the U.S. Ambassador in the U.N., Jeane Kirkpatrick. The story was complete with a photo of a forged U.S. government document, and was timed to coincide with the forthcoming meeting of the nonaligned nations in New Delhi. While not very successful because the idea was so ludicrous, because the forged communication was so amateurish that it was fairly easy to disown, and because it generated an immediate response from the U.S. government, with USIA concentrating on exposing the "exposé," other Soviet disinformation efforts have been more subtle and sometimes much more successful.

Malaria, one of the scourges of mankind which has not yet been defeated by the miracles of modern medicine, has for more than a decade been the subject of intensive research by a joint U.S.-Pakistani teams of scientists in the city of Lahore in eastern Pakistan. Yet in 1981, a Soviet-inspired propaganda campaign was launched which, again, first planted in India, alleged that the Lahore center, where the search for more efficient means to combat malaria had been conducted for many years, was experimenting with mosquitoes to be used "in germ warfare." This accusation, carried by Radio Moscow and other public information vehicles available to or at the service of the Soviets, originated at a time when more and more evidence was accumulating about the introduction of chemical warfare by Soviet troops in Afghanistan and Soviet-supported Vietnamese troops in Kampuchea.

Estimates of the amount of funds spent on information and cultural activities by the USSR total billions of dollars annually. In an address to the Los Angeles World Affairs Council, March 5, 1982, Charles Wick, then director of ICA, said that the Soviets spend 3,500 million dollars a year on "misinformation and propaganda."[1] In a report to the U.S. Congress in 1980, the CIA claims that the Soviet Union spends $3.3 billion annually for covert actions, which include what some describe as "the forgery offensive."[2] As difficult as it is to measure the total information efforts of the Soviets, it is clear that these efforts are the most extensive and costliest of any nation in the world. And despite the fact that the Soviet Union and the United States have no contiguous frontiers that might generate border disputes and similar concerns that are so common to so many areas of the world, a large share of Soviet information efforts are either directed against the United States and its policies, or designed to counter U.S. interests and activities.

Among other countries that recognize the importance of public diplomacy in world affairs today, and that Americans consider as "friendly competitors" in this as in most fields, are France, Germany, Great Britain, and Japan. How important the German government, for example, views public diplomacy can be seen in a remark attributed to Helmut Schmidt. He has said that the "three pillars of German policy are politics, commerce, and public diplomacy." The French government, which, a few years ago, reorganized its information and cultural programs along the lines of USIA's reorganization of 1978 (when ICA was born), has asserted that "cultural relations are as important as politics and trade, and perhaps more important" to key French interests.

The federal governments of Germany and France commit nearly 1 percent of their national budgets for information and cultural programs, as compared with the U.S. government's 0.1 percent. In recent years while America's public diplomacy efforts have had to make do with reduced budgets (in real terms), both France and Germany have increased their budgets for information and cultural activities abroad. In 1979, both France and Germany each spent more on public diplomacy than the United States.

France has for a number of years maintained one of the largest public diplomacy operations in the non-Communist world. A French government report of its public diplomacy activities described them as "essential instrumentalities of our foreign policy," which contributes "directly to the power of our country" in foreign affairs. It is interesting to note that according to a 1977 report, 70 percent of the budget of the French Press Agency (AFP) was underwritten by the French government. Next to the French, the external information and cultural programs of the Federal Republic of Germany are the largest among the non-Communist countries.

In 1980, France earmarked $1 billion for information and cultural activities, up from $604 million in 1976. In that same year, West Germany had a budget of $894 million while ICA operations, plus Radio Free Europe and Radio Liberty, worked with a total

budget of about $521 million. Next among non-Communist coun-
tries in total expenditures were Britain ($480 million) and Japan
with $237 million on the 1980-81 period.[3]

The primary targets of Great Britain's public diplomacy efforts
include about a dozen countries of Western Europe, the Middle
East, sub-Saharan Africa, plus North America and, to a lesser extent,
Japan and Australia. Their main emphasis is on promoting commercial exports and in attracting investment. The British government
published an extensive study by the Central Policy Review Staff in
1977 entitled "Review of Overseas Representation." It began with
the observation that "the UK's ability to influence events in the
world has declined and there is very little that diplomatic activity
and international public relations can do to disguise this fact."

The cultural and information programs of Japan emphasize
general image building to promote Japanese economic relationships, particularly with countries which provide export markets
for Japanese products and raw materials for Japanese industry.
Even though Japan was fifth among the non-Communist countries
in the early 1980s in terms of expenditures for public diplomacy,
since 1972 Japan has increased such expenditures threefold.

As can be seen from the above figures and statements, the
Western European democracies and Japan not only consider public
diplomacy to be important in the conduct of foreign relations in
the modern world, but have, in recent years, invested more in their
public diplomacy efforts than ever before. And they have done so
at a time when the U.S. government, despite a growing realization
of just how important the public diplomat's role has become, reduced its information, cultural, and educational exchange programs,
primarily for budgetary reasons. An examination in some greater
detail of the information and cultural activities of these countries
is instructive. These details came, for the most part, from studies
made by USIA's Office of Research.[4]

FRANCE

When France spent $1.06 billion on its overseas information
and cultural programs in 1980, this represented a 9 percent increase
over its 1979 budget for these activities, and a 76 percent increase
over the amount expended in 1976. In terms of 1976 dollars, however, the 1979 expenditure was about equal to the amount spent in

1976. Nevertheless, the 1980 budget represented a real increase of 12 percent over 1976. This increase was considerably larger in real terms than that of any other non-Communist country from 1979 to 1980.

As a proportion of the French annual budget, the amount expended each year for information and cultural programs rose from 0.7 percent in 1977 to 0.87 percent in 1978 and 1979 and to 0.89 percent in 1980. This was partly the result of increased proportions of the Ministry of Cooperation budget being earmarked for these activities (from 66.7 percent in 1977 to 69.2 percent in 1980).

Some $635 million, or about 60 percent of the 1980 budget went to the Ministry of Cooperation. This is the ministry that handles French activities in Francophone Africa. The remainder ($430 million) goes to the Ministry of Foreign Affairs, whose General Directorate for Cultural, Scientific and Technological Relations (DGRCST) is responsible for programs elsewhere. A large portion of the budget, particularly in Africa, is devoted to educational aid and assistance to French schools and Alliance Française centers.

The French emphasize cultural programs, thus the greater part of their budget is for cultural affairs and exchanges. Their information activities received a smaller part of their total budget, but this is somewhat misleading since book distribution and films are designated as "cultural programs." The budget for cultural programs also includes subsidies for para-governmental organizations like the Alliance Française. Radio France International also receives funds from the government for its operations.

The budget for DGRCST in the Ministry of Foreign Affairs supports a large cultural program that includes about 5,000 overseas teachers, 2,000 artistic events annually, 7,600 scholarships, 5,200 training grants, and 164 cultural institutes and centers in 86 countries.

In 1979, an independent study group known as the Rigaud Commission undertook a major review of the French overseas cultural program. When the commission issued its report at the end of that year, it was endorsed by President Giscard d'Estaing. It affirmed that cultural relations are just as important to French foreign policy as political and economic relations. It also emphasized that there is a vital link between cultural activities and the economic expansion of France.

The Rigaud report rejected the motion of "diffusion" of French culture overseas and substituted the idea of "partnership," with emphasis on the mutual exchange of ideas as well as reciprocity and cooperation. It noted that French cultural centers abroad, rather than being "bastions" of French culture should be places to exchange ideas and dialog with host country nationals. While continuing support for French-language training, the report indicated that language training per se should not be the raison d'être of any French cultural mission. (Similar views have been discussed within USIA over the years about English-language teaching.) The report also underscored the universality of the cultural mission of France and stated that a "minimum cultural presence" should exist in every country throughout the world.

The budget breakdown for French public diplomacy programs 1977 through 1980 is as follows (in millions of U.S. dollars):

	Foreign Affairs Ministry		Cooperation Ministry		Totals	
	1977	1980	1977	1980	1977	1980
Cultural Relations	$159.4	$264.0	$195.5	$383.9	$354.9	$647.9
Academic Exchange & Educa. Assistance	103.1	154.3	152.1	250.5	255.2	404.8
Press & Information	8.3	11.6	.1	.1	8.4	11.7
Totals:	$270.8	$429.9	$347.7	$634.5	$618.5	$1,064.4

Note: Although amounts intended for French scientific relations and technical cooperation programs abroad are listed in the cultural budgets of the two ministries, they are *not* included in the above figures.

THE FEDERAL REPUBLIC OF GERMANY

West German information and cultural programs cost $894 million in 1980, up from an estimated $415 million in 1976. This represents a 28 percent increase over 1976 in terms of 1976 dollars, though this estimate may be high since the 1976 base used lacked precise figures for bilateral cultural exchanges. Nevertheless, in 1980 West Germany was second only to France among Western European nations in terms of the cost of its foreign information and cultural activities.

West Germany's information and cultural programs are administered by at least ten ministries, including the Foreign Office. In addition, the chancellor's office and a number of semiofficial foundations are involved. The proportion of the West German federal budget devoted to these programs rose from 0.6 percent in 1977 to 0.76 in 1980. As an example of the budget increases, the following table depicts amounts spent for four selected activities (in millions of U.S. dollars at the prevailing rate of exchange each year):

Activity	1977	1979	1980
Federal contribution to Deutsche Welle and Deutschlandfunk	$93.7	$133.1	$141.7
German schools	n.a.	112.1	119.0
Exhibits, participation in fairs	10.2	16.4	18.5
France-German youth exchange	5.7	7.8	8.6

Among its fairly recent cultural initiatives, Bonn opened a cultural institute in Bucharest, Romania in 1979, signed a protocol for expanded cultural exchanges with Bulgaria, and launched a new Russian-language magazine for the USSR, all in support of its "Ostpolitik." Entitled *Guten Tag*, the 40-page magazine attempts to give Soviet readers an objective portrayal of everyday life in the Federal Republic. Its initial edition of 30,000 copies was to be increased to 60,000 within three years.

THE UNITED KINGDOM

Great Britain, like her French and German colleagues, has seen fit in recent years to steadily increase its budget for information and cultural programming, though not as markedly as her major European neighbors. Some $186 million was budgeted by the United

Kingdom for these programs in fiscal 1976/77. By 1979/80, the amount had risen to $357 million and about $480 million was budgeted for 1980/81. In the terms of 1976 dollars, however, the 1979/80 budget was only slightly larger than the budget three years earlier. In recent years, the total amount spent on these activities each year has remained about 0.2 percent of the annual U.K. national budget.

The semigovernmental British Council, the BBC external broadcasting services, the Central Office of Information (COI), the British Information Services (BIS) and the Foreign and Commonwealth Office (FCO) are all involved in varying degrees in carrying out British information and cultural programs.

The following table shows a breakdown of their budgets (in millions of U.S. dollars at the prevailing exchange rate for each fiscal year):

	1976/77	1977/78	1978/79	1979/80	1980/81
British Council	$117.7	$150.0	$182.5	$247.2	$296.9
UK grant to BBC External Services	47.1	64.2	74.7	98.2	132.5
COI	15.0	16.9	18.0	20.1	25.1
BIS (Provided by FCO)	1.6	1.5	1.7	2.2	1.8
FCO (capital & current expenditures for FCO-operated relay stations)	4.2	4.6	4.7	6.3	19.1
Other				1.3	5.0
	$185.6	$237.2	$281.6	$375.3	$480.4

(1 pound sterling = $2.4099)

Primary responsibiliity for British cultural activities overseas is assigned to the British Council. Its major programs include English-language teaching, cultural exchanges and presentations, and libraries. According to the Council's Annual Report of 1978-79, the Council in that period helped 142,000 students in the study of English; assisted nearly 30,000 persons from 160 countries in visiting Great Britain; and sponsored more than 200 cultural presentations and exhibits abroad. Because of the mutuality of interest between the British Council and USIA in the teaching of English as a second language, the two organizations have cooperated in various parts of the world in English-teaching seminars and workshops.

In recent years the British Council established new offices in Burma, China, Ecuador, and the Philippines, while closing their offices in Iran and Malta. They also opened new English-teaching institutes in Singapore, Spain, Venezuela, and West Germany. A new council library opened in Ahmedabad, India, making it the twelfth such library in that country, all of which, apparently, are heavily used. Among the major cultural events they have sponsored in recent years have been an Age of Shakespeare exhibit, shown in several countries; the first modern British dance company to visit Egypt; an exhibit of British art books in four Soviet cities; a British Industrial Exhibition in Mexico; and the London Festival Ballet Company tour in the United States.

In October 1979, it was announced that the 1980/81 budget for the BBC external language services would be cut for budgetary reasons. Demands by some members of Parliament as well as by the public enabled the BBC to announce on February 28, 1980 that the projected cuts would not be made. However, shortly there-after cuts in the number of BBC overseas correspondents were being discussed as one means of saving money. At the same time it was reported that increases were projected for BBC relay stations and transmitters in order to increase the strength of the BBC signal to the USSR and other Communist countries.

In some countries, particularly former British colonies, the BBC is frequently quoted in the local press and used by local radio and television stations as an authoritative source for world news. The BBC is generally regarded as one of the most accurate and reliable news sources in the world, though during the 1982 Falkland Islands crisis with Argentina it was accused of tendentious reporting.

JAPAN

The Japanese external information and cultural programs show, in terms of 1976 dollars, nearly 80 percent growth between 1976 and 1979. This is the largest growth of any of the major non-Communist nations which we have been discussing. In fiscal 1976/77 the Japanese budget for information/cultural programs was $87 million. In 1979/80 it rose to $244 million (or $156 million in "1976" dollars). Nevertheless, this amounts to only about 0.1 percent of the annual Japanese national budget.

The information and cultural activities of Japan are conducted by three government ministries, the prime minister's office, and the Science and Technology Agency. Funds are used mainly to finance educational exchanges and other exchanges of persons. These expenditures are shown in the following table (in millions of U.S. dollars at the prevailing exchange rates for each fiscal year):

	1977/78	1978/79	1979/80	1980/81
Prime Minister's Office	$ 5.1	$ 6.1	$ 5.3	$ 5.1
Ministry of Education	56.0	122.1	134.0	157.2
Ministry of Foreign Affairs	64.3	81.7	83.0	57.2
Ministry of Posts & Telecommunications	2.3	3.6	3.7	4.1
Science & Technology Agency	2.5	3.5	3.0	3.3
Radio Japan*	11.1	15.4	15.0	15.3
Totals:	$141.3	$232.4	$244.0	$242.2(est.)

*Radio Japan's budget is derived primarily from revenues of the Japanese Broadcasting Corporation (NHK), a public entity which reports to the Cabinet through the Ministry of Posts and Telecommunications.)

As can be seen from the above, most funds go to the Ministries of Education and Foreign Affairs. The Ministry of Foreign Affairs subsidizes the quasi-private Japan Foundation which promotes scholarly exchanges and basic Japanese studies as well as a variety of other information and cultural activities.

The information and cultural programs we have been discussing briefly all foster the political, economic, and cultural objectives of their respective countries. However, each appears to have a particular focus. For the French, it is the French élan; for the West Germans, it is to show that the new Germany has distanced itself completely from that of the Germany of World War II; for Great Britain, aside from expounding the great British heritage and the English language, the focus is on promoting British exports and attracting investors; and for Japan it is to emphasize a generally favorable image of post-war Japan with a view of promoting its economic relationships. But what all of these Western democracies and Japan have in common in their information and cultural programs is a generally straightforward, overt approach that reflects the ideals and mores of their respective cultures. Their public diplomacy activities, though emphasizing different themes, are essentially on a par with those of U.S. public diplomacy. Credibility, reliability and openness are paramount. This commonality in their public diplomacy activities, when viewed against the public diplomacy activities of Communist societies, is all the more striking. It is with this in mind that we turn to a discussion of public diplomacy as practiced by the Kremlin.

THE SOVIET UNION'S "PUBLIC DIPLOMACY"

The Soviet Union's public diplomacy efforts, while sometimes outwardly similar to those of the non-Communist countries, are not bound by the rules that guide most Western nations. "Public diplomacy," a Department of State report points out, "includes providing press releases and other information to journalists, open public broadcasting and a wide variety of official, academic and cultural exchange programs." By contrast, the report continues, Soviet propaganda activities are "frequently undertaken secretly, sometimes violate the laws of other nations and often involve threats, blackmail, bribes and exploitation of individuals and groups.[5]

Following one of Lenin's dictums, that "ideas are weapons," the Kremlin conducts its war of ideas as it conducts its society—the end is what counts. That one of the Western world's most basic tenets—that the means is as important as the end—is ignored by Communist propagandists is hardly surprising. Radio Moscow, for example, like the Voice of America, is a reflection of the society that produces it. This has led at least one wit to comment, "Can Communism really be as dull as they paint it on Radio Moscow?"

Different from Western nations also is the ability of the Soviet Union to spend whatever amount its leaders want to spend with no controls from either a parliament or the citizenry. This system is what has allowed them to spend so heavily on military hardware. It has also made them the world's largest spender in the "war of ideas."

In 1978, a CIA report on "Soviet Use of the Media," quoted during congressional hearings, mentioned about 2 billion dollars annually as the amount the Soviets were estimated to be spending on informational and cultural programs at that time. The report added that "our rough estimate of two billion dollars per year might be on the conservative side."[6] By 1980, as noted earlier, the CIA estimated these costs to be about $3.3 billion annually. On January 11, 1982, *U.S. News and World Report* stated that "The U.S.S.R. devotes an estimated 3 billion dollars a year to propaganda—far more than any other country." Charles Wick's estimate of $3.5 billion in March of 1982 was also cited earlier. Though all of these estimates may be open to question, since it is difficult to verify them, there is little doubt but that the Soviet Union, with its powerful radio stations, global press and publication operations, support to indigenous Communist and front groups, exchange programs, its "active measures" techniques and its "disinformation" campaigns, puts far more resources into trying to convince the rest of the world that Soviet intentions and actions are honorable than does any other nation. If the roughly $3 billion annual figure for these activities is anywhere near being accurate, and it probably is, that means that the Soviet Union spends at least four times as much on propaganda as the United States, its chief competitor.[7]

Best known and most open of the Soviet Union's public diplomacy operations is Radio Moscow. The world's leading international radio broadcaster, Radio Moscow and its regional stations in the Soviet Republics, as well as Radio Peace and Progress, were on the air about 2,100 hours weekly in 82 languages as of the end of 1982. This compares with about 1,900 hours broadcast weekly by VOA, Radio Free Europe, and Radio Liberty combined, in 45 languages. The yearly budget for Radio Moscow is an estimated $700 million compared with about $197 million for VOA, RFE, and RL combined.[8] With more than 285 transmitters, it reaches virtually every country in the world.[9] Another interesting comparison—in testimony before a Senate committee March 2, 1983, Charles Wick noted that "Radio Moscow has 37 state-of-the-art 500 KW (Superpower) transmitters, while the Voice of America has six, each made by coupling two 250 KW's into a 500 KW transmitter. Radio Free Europe and Radio Liberty have none."[10]

As noted earlier, the geographic location of the Soviet Union gives it a tremendous advantage over its competitors in reaching the far corners of the globe without the necessity, as in the case of the VOA, of creating a large network of relay stations on foreign soil. Nevertheless, for transmissions to the Americas, relay transmitters of Radio Moscow are located in Sofia and Plovdiv in Bulgaria, and in Havana, Cuba. In East Germany, a transmitter is used for transmissions to Western Europe. In addition, a number of programs are transmitted over the home service facilities of various countries. Radio Moscow World Service and separate English-language broadcasts to certain areas are beamed to Europe, Africa, the Near and Middle East, Asia and the Far East, North America, Australia, and New Zealand.[11] Radio Moscow's powerful transmissions are also heard in South America where, in addition to broadcasting in Spanish and Portuguese, the two leading languages of that area, as of the end of 1981 a half-hour, twice-weekly broadcast in Quechua, which is spoken only by the indigenous Indians in Bolivia and Peru, was still being made. One can only speculate as to why, of all the languages endemic to Latin America, the Russians have honed in on Quechua. Interestingly enough, when Che Guevara and Regis Debray (who later became a Minister of Culture in the French government) were captured by the Bolivian armed forces in the Bolivian jungles in 1967, Guevara, before meeting his death, was leading a "war of national liberation" in a Quechua-speaking region of that country.

In addition to Radio Moscow, the Soviet Union's answer to Radio Free Europe and Radio Liberty is a radio station known as Peace and Progress. It is described as a semiofficial broadcast service, but given the monolithic style of government in the Soviet Union, it is difficult to see how any organization operating in the USSR can be semiofficial.

Radio Peace and Progress broadcasts to Europe, Asia, Africa, the Near and Middle East, and Latin America. Its address is Moscow.

All of its broadcasts are carried on frequencies used at other times by Radio Moscow to the same target areas. Listeners to this station, whose frequencies are seldom announced or published, can identify it when they hear, "This is Radio Station 'Peace and Progress,' the Voice of Soviet Public Opinion." Radio Peace and Progress provides, apparently, the only known expression of "Soviet public opinion" available to the outside world. In addition to English, it broadcasts in French, Portuguese, and Spanish, as well as Creole to Haiti and Guarani to Paraguay.

Radio Moscow and Radio Peace and Progress are not the only international radio activities conducted by the Soviet Union. Two clandestine stations broadcast from Soviet territory: Radio Ba Yi, established in early 1979, beams Mandarin-language programs to China while the National Voice of Iran (NVOI), established in 1959, broadcasts in Persian and Azeri to Iran from transmitters located in Baku, U.S.S.R. Technical observations indicate that the transmitter for Radio Ba Yi is located in the Soviet Far East.

Radio Ba Yi takes its name from the Chinese words "Eight One," or August First, the traditional date of the founding of the Chinese Red Army in 1927. Radio Ba Yi claims to reflect the perspective of "our army" or "our country's representatives" and strives to identify with the Chinese cadre point of view.[12]

The National Voice of Iran (NVOI) presents itself as Iranian, speaking as the voice of "our" people and "our" country and frequently praising the attitude of "our friendly northern neighbor," the Soviet Union. In 1979 and 1980, NVOI consistently urged that the hostages held at the American Embassy in Teheran *not* be released, although Soviet official statements supported the hostages' claim to diplomatic immunity. Representing themselves as authentic local "progressive" forces, the Soviet Union has never publicly acknowledged that it sponsors these two stations.[13]

As an example of the type of programming broadcast by the National Voice of Iran, on March 9, 1982, an unattributed commentary in Persian was transmitted that, in English translation, stated:

> Dear compatriots. Imperialism, led by world-devouring America, and the Zionists have become concerned over the prospects of a resolution of the battle clash between our homeland and Iraq. Evidence is at hand to the effect that the U.S. Central Intelligence Agency and

Israel's Mossad are exerting all their efforts to prevent the arrival of the special delegation assigned by the Islamic Conference to resolve these disputes.

As we are aware, this war was imposed on our nation by U.S. imperialism and Zionism, and the enemies of the Islamic nations, and of our nation's glorious revolution in the Near and Middle East, are interested in prolonging this war. . . . The war imposed on our nation and its prolongation is part of the strategic plan of U.S. imperialism in connection with our nation's glorious revolution and all liberation and anti-imperialist movements in the region.

The above venom is typical of NVOI. Of course, the special delegation of Islamic leaders referred to above arrived as scheduled.

Radio is without doubt one of the most important and most widely used tools of Soviet information efforts. How it is used in special situations can be gleaned from a report issued by the Office of Research of ICA on December 22, 1981. Following the Soviet invasion of Afghanistan in December 1979, there was a substantial increase in overall Communist broadcasting to South Asia, i.e., external radio broadcasting of all Communist countries, not the Soviet Union alone. In 1980, over-all Communist radio broadcasts to South Asia rose to 564 program hours per week, an increase of 11 percent (58 hours) over 1979. This includes 370 hours per week by the USSR and 105 hours per week by the Peoples Republic of China. By comparison, the VOA was broadcasting at that time 94 and a half hours per week to South Asia, including a new three-and-a-half hour service in Dari.[14] The ICA report notes:

—Radio Moscow doubled its output in the two principal Afghan languages, Dari and Pushto, to 21 hours each per week (42 hours), alternating the two language programs every 30 minutes for six hours of programming each day.

—Radio Dushanbe, located at the capital of the Tadzhik S.S.R. about 500 miles north of Kabul, continued to broadcast 17 and a half hours of weekly programs in Dari to Afghanistan.

—Moscow stepped up its output in Urdu to Pakistan by three and a half hours to a new total of 28 hours per week.

—In addition, the Radio Moscow World Service in English expanded its programming to South Asia by 35 hours a week for a new total of 112 hours.

In addition to expanding its international radio broadcasting in recent years, the Soviet Union has increased its jamming of the radio broadcasts of other nations. Shortly prior to the closing of the 39th session of the UN Human Rights Commission meeting in Geneva in March 1983, the U.S. government urged that the next session of the commission take up the matter of Soviet jamming as a human rights issue. In a document presented by the U.S. delegation, the United States argued that "jamming is not an issue of exclusive concern to Western nations. Radio frequencies are scarce, and jamming seriously pollutes the international radio spectrum, wasting this precious international resource. At a time of spiraling demand for access to high frequency (shortwave) bands by all nations, jamming penalizes the developing nations and threatens the viability of the international radio regulatory regime." The U.S. document also estimates that the Soviet Union "invested three times as much on jamming as the United States has invested in broadcasting"; that for the first time, Soviet jamming now extends to broadcasts intended for third countries—specifically Poland and Afghanistan; and that jamming of international broadcasting is a serious violation of human rights that should be of concern to all nations, violating as it does the Universal Declaration of Human Rights as well as being incompatible with other international agreements such as the Final Act of the Conference on Security and Cooperation in Europe (the Helsinki Accords).[15]

The Soviet Union's press operations are nearly as far-flung as its global radio activities. The official news agency of the USSR is TASS, which maintains bureaus and correspondents in about 100 countries. The Novosti Press Agency (*Agentstvo Pechati Novosti*), identified as APN, was established in 1961. It is to TASS what Radio Peace and Progress is to Radio Moscow. Billed as a nongovernmental Soviet news agency, controlled by its founders, *Novosti* takes an even harder line than TASS.

In addition to TASS and *Novosti*, Moscow sends correspondents abroad to cover events that are reported in *New Times* and other publications. Cover is the right word. In 1979 a *Novosti* "correspondent" was declared persona non grata by the Japanese government when it was determined that he was a KGB agent. This was only one, publicly identified case. In Bolivia in 1970-72 the Press Attaché of the Soviet embassy was a personable young man named Smirnoff. He was forced to leave La Paz abruptly with the exodus of 60 or more other Russians attached to the embassy when a new, non-Communist regime threw out a pro-Communist one in a coup d'état, a fairly common occurrence in that country. About five years later this same Soviet official showed up in Peru as a correspondent for *New Times*, allegedly no longer a Soviet foreign service officer. After he left Lima, Peru, rumors circulated among foreign correspondents in that city that he had been reassigned to Moscow but that while painting his apartment, died of a heart attack. As a relatively young man who had not yet turned 40, this was a tragic turn of events, if true.

Perhaps to find accuracy and objectivity in Soviet international broadcasting and reporting is expecting too much since Soviet citizens themselves cannot expect anything better. The senior correspondent in Washington for the Soviet Newspaper *Izvestia*, Melor Sturua, when interviewed by Lewis H. Lapham, noted that, "For propaganda to succeed, the fact itself must be true. If the fact is true, then it is possible to believe the interpretation." It is in the interpretation, Lapham suggests, that Soviet reporters in the United States depict the "crazy America" they write about where "criminals roam the streets; unemployed workers stand in breadlines; pimps and pornographers work in broad daylight; and the nation's youth squanders its life in an orgy of drugs." By rearranging the news, and playing up statistics like 9 million unemployed, 2 million illegal guns in New York City, etc., they draw portraits far from reality. Lapham quotes Robert G. Kaiser, formerly chief Moscow correspondent for the *Washington Post*, as saying, "You must remember that the Soviets think of journalism as a weapon in the ideological struggle. To compare Russian and American journalism would be to compare apples and oranges."[16]

Exchanges are used by the Soviet Union, like other countries, to bring young people and leaders to their cultural, educational, and political centers. Students and other visitors from third world countries are particularly sought by the Soviets. This is in line with the belief that while the main struggle in the world today is between the two superpowers, the real battles are occurring in the third world. As for exchanges of performing artists, for a while in late 1970s so many travelling Russian ballet dancers from the Bolshoi were deciding not to return to Russia upon completion of their tours, opting instead for freedom in the West, that this aspect of Soviet public diplomacy was sharply curtailed.

These occurrences were hardly the kind of propaganda the Soviets were seeking.

In recent years, it has been contended that some of these exchanges involve training in terrorist tactics. The attempted assassination of Pope John Paul II in 1981 led many people to believe that these allegations are indeed plausible. Media reports suggested a link with the Soviets in the attempted assassination because the individual charged with the crime spent considerable time in Communist countries prior to the attempted murder. This type of activity, however, goes beyond the public diplomacy theme of this volume. Suffice it to say that some U.S. public diplomats occasionally comment, only half in jest, that the best way to convince young people of the failures of communism is to encourage them to accept grants to study in the USSR. The batting average of those who go as students to the Soviet Union and become converted to Communist ways is probably no greater than those who abhor Communism after their experience in Moscow.

Although the tactics of terrorism is not a subject being addressed in this volume, the black side of Soviet information efforts that has come to light is another matter. The Soviet Union, as part of its foreign policy, uses what has come to be known as "disinformation," as well as forgeries, blackmail, and other secret efforts to discredit and weaken the United States.

In the Department of State's Special Report No. 88, it notes that among the approaches used by Moscow are "control of the press in foreign countries; use of rumors, insinuations, altered facts and lies; use of international and local front organizations; clandestine operation of radio stations; (and) exploitation of a nation's academic, political, economic and media figures as collaborators to influence the policies of a nation." The Soviets look upon these activities as "active measures" (*aktivnyye meroprivatiya*). While the United States remains the primary target of such activities, the report notes, the Soviet Union is devoting increasing resources in these measures against the governments of other industrialized nations and third world countries.[17]

"Moscow seeks to disrupt relations between states, discredit opponents of the USSR and undermine foreign leaders, institutions and values," the study states, adding that "Soviet tactics adjust to changes in international situations but continue, and in some cases intensify, during periods of reduced tensions."

Among the activities cited by the State Department report were:

—Agents of the Soviet Union spread a false rumor in 1979 that the United States was responsible for the seizure of the Grand Mosque of Mecca.

—The Soviet News Agency Tass alleged in August 1981 that the United States was behind the death of Panamanian leader Omar Torrijos.

—The Soviets used Moscow-controlled front groups in Western Europe to campaign against NATO's Theater Nuclear Force modernization program and the U.S. decision to build enhanced radiation weapons. The report also noted that "of course, not all opposition" on these issues was Soviet inspired.

—To sway public opinion to support the leftist insurgency in El Salvador and discredit U.S. assistance to the Salvadorean Government, the Soviets have used forgeries, disinformation, front groups, and attempted manipulations of the press.

—The Soviets produced a series of forged letters, documents, and cables in an effort to weaken U.S.-Egyptian ties and undermine the Camp David Middle East peace accords.

The insertion of falsely attributed press material into the media of a foreign country is one technique the Soviets use. More than two dozen local journalists were used to plant media items favorable to the USSR in one developing country. The Soviets have also used the Indian news weekly *Blitz* to publish forgeries, falsely accuse Americans of being CIA personnel, and to disseminate Soviet-inspired documents, according to the report. When Radio Moscow in early 1982 charged that the Pakistan government and the U.S. government were planning to invade Iran, quoting a source in India, this was a typical Soviet effort at disinformation. The charge was immediately and correctly denied by the Pakistan government. In the West, the accusation was considered so ridiculous that it received no attention.

An example of Soviet use of forgeries occurred when Soviet agents, seeking to disrupt NATO theater nuclear force modernization, circulated a forged "top secret" letter from Secretary of State Cyrus Vance to another Western foreign minister. A few other examples of documents forged by Soviet agents as part of their "active measures" against the United States indicate how extensive this practice has been. These also are taken from the State Department report mentioned earlier.

—A purported speech by a member of the U.S. Administration that insulted Egyptians and called for "a total change of the government and the governmental system in Egypt."

—A forged document, allegedly prepared by the secretary of state, or one of his close associates, for the president, which used language insulting and offensive to President Sadat and other Egyptians and also to other Arab leaders, including King Khalid of Saudi Arabia.

—A series of forged letters and U.S. Government documents which criticized Sadat's "lack of leadership" and called for a "change of government" in Egypt.

—A forged despatch, allegedly prepared by the U.S. Embassy in Tehran, which suggested that the United States had acquiesced in plans by Iran and Saudi Arabia to overthrow Sadat.

—A forged CIA report that criticized Islamic groups as a barrier to U.S. goals in the Middle East and suggested tactics to suppress, divide, and eliminate these groups.

—A forged letter from U.S. Ambassador to Egypt Herman F. Eilts, which declared that, because Sadat was not prepared to serve U.S. interests, "we must repudiate him and get rid of him without hesitation."

What do the Soviets hope to gain with their many activities that go far beyond the bounds of public diplomacy as practices by the Western democracies? According to another ICA study, Soviet external propaganda has two main purposes:

1. To represent the Soviet Union as dedicated to peace and détènte.
2. To show the Soviet Union as a just, fair, progressive society, worthy of admiration if not emulation.[18]

To achieve these purposes, they follow several basic principles, the first of which is "a systematic denigration of the U.S., its culture, political system, and belief structures." At the same time the Soviet Union presents itself as "the only alternative to the U.S. as a system of social organization. It portrays itself as the near-perfect society."

Another key feature of Soviet propaganda is the argument that while the United States and the West are doomed in historical terms, "the U.S. is all the more dangerous because it will defend its way of life to the end." By contrast, "the Soviet Union arms only to defend itself and its allies." From these premises flow the whole litany of Soviet propaganda and, in fact, its foreign policy:

—Support for "national liberation" movements is justified in terms of putting them on the road to the higher plane of existence enjoyed by the Soviet Union.

—The foreign and domestic policies of Western countries are criticized because they are dedicated to the preseration of the status quo and are opposed to progressive change.

—Western military measures are portrayed as inherently aggressive because they are directed against the Soviet Union and the progressive principles for which it stands.

—Anti-imperialism (anti-Americanism) is claimed to be good because it represents a movement against the *ancien regime* and toward historical progress. The methods used in the anti-imperialist struggle are sometimes harsh but are justified by the ends.

—The Soviet Union is the natural ally of Third World countries and all others who have freed themselves from imperialism (i.e., Eastern Europe).[19]

Soviet propagandists are not restrained by truth, honesty, and morality, since they are guided by "a new morality," defined by Lenin as that which serves the good of the Party. Their ideology rationalizes the use of falsehood and deception by promising that the end—the perfect society—justifies the means. Thus they can use selective information, half-truths, distortions and innuendo, as well as outright lies. What we are witnessing today is nothing new for a Communist state. It is just more sophisticated in keeping with the times.

Some of the themes used in Soviet information efforts are instructive. As compiled in October 1981 by ICA's Office of Research, they include the following:

—The U.S. is escalating the arms race, provoking conflict, and trying to counter every aspect of Soviet influence in the world in its efforts to regain the military-strategic superiority it once possessed.

—The USSR, on the other hand, continues to be dedicated to the struggle for peace.

—The U.S. is not seriously interested in arms control negotiations.

—The U.S. is introducing sinister new weapons such as the neutron weapon, the Pershing II, the MX, chemical and biological weapons.

—The U.S. is forcing its allies to accept its weapons and to increase their own arms expenditures.

—The U.S. seeks to forge an anti-Soviet alliance with such countries as China, Japan, Pakistan, and Turkey.

—The U.S. engages in psychological warfare against the Soviet Union. It spreads untruths about the USSR through its propaganda activities—especially radio, and foments anti-Soviet hysteria and war mentality.

—The U.S. wages economic warfare against the USSR.

—The U.S. grossly interferes in the internal affairs of other countries.

—The U.S. faces vast resistence to its aggressive plans.

—The U.S. and allies are responsible for international terrorism.

—The CIA is behind much of the unrest in the world.

—The neocolonialist U.S. and its allies are not friends of the Third World, while the Soviet Union is the natural ally of Third World nations.

—The U.S. is an insecure, unstable, inhumane society in a permanent state of crisis.

—The U.S. violates fundamental human rights while accusing others of doing so.

—Soviets who fall prey to Western propaganda tend to be unsuccessful and miserable when they emigrate.

—With respect to the Polish crisis, outsiders are to blame, especially the West and particularly the U.S., for interfering in internal Polish affairs, stirring up trouble through its radio propaganda, and supporting antisocial elements.

—As for Afghanistan, major emphasis is on the humanitarian, economic, and otherwise peaceful aid rendered by the Soviet Union to Afghanistan. Outsiders, especially the U.S. together with the Peoples Republic of China and Pakistan are charged with interfering in Afghan affairs.

—The U.S. is propping up an oppressive, unpopular regime in El Salvador.

—South Africa, a racist, renegade state, suppresses its national liberation movement with the support if not the assistance of the U.S.

The above are, of course, only a smattering of the types of themes expounded by the Soviets in their information, and disinformation, programs. As the United States began in recent years to expose Soviet "active measures," it has become increasingly clear that the Soviets are using major resources to conduct their campaigns of vilification of the United States. They also have become sensitive to having their campaigns exposed. An example of this is a new Soviet pocketbook entitled "Information Abused: Critical Essays," translated and published by Progress Publishers, Moscow, in 1981, and which appeared in India early in 1983. Arthur Vladimir Artemov claims that the publication is an "exposé of anti-Soviet propaganda methods" used by the West. The author attacks Western radio stations, particularly the VOA, which, he charges, "does all it can to erase the objective image of the USSR among the better informed in its audiences."

As for USIA, Soviet media have depicted America's public diplomacy agency as a powerful and "far-flung" propaganda apparatus which leads U.S. "anti-Soviet and antisocialist" propaganda operations. USIA is charged with having close ties to the CIA. Some Soviet commentaries, such as a November 5, 1981 TASS item, characterized ICA (prior to its becoming USIA again) as "nothing more than a branch of the CIA." The VOA is the USIA component most often singled out for attack. Soviet media have accused USIA and the VOA of, among other things, spreading fabrications which glorify the West and "blacken socialism," and interfering in the internal affairs of other countries, especially Poland, for the purpose of instability and subversion.

What are the results of this plethora of charges against the West, particularly the United States? William L. Chaze and Harold Kennedy, who wrote "The Great Propaganda War" for *U.S. News & World Report*, summed it up as "Big Effort, Small Results." They wrote:

In Italy, the Soviets are waging a vast, well-coordinated and costly propaganda campaign. . . . Yet Russia has seen few returns on its investment. Italians are still among the staunchest pro-Americans in Western Europe. . . . The Russians also are mounting a more active propaganda campaign in France, but with similar poor results.

They conclude: "Over all, the Soviets these days appear to be living up to their reputation as master propagandists in only a few parts of the world. "The verdict from many experts," they say, "is that Russian propaganda is more pervasive than ever—but often ignored."[20]

So much for "public diplomacy" as practiced by the Soviet Union. It may not be quite the way it is depicted in the bestselling novel, The Spike, by Arnaud de Borchgrave and Robert Moss, where everything from sex to drugs to violence is mentioned, but it is certainly different from the manner in which public diplomacy is practiced by the United States and many others.

NOTES

1. In saying that the Soviets spend 3,500 million dollars a year on "misinformation and propaganda," USIA Director Wick was including estimates for cultural exchanges and scholarships for foreign students not generally included in CIA estimates of the cost of Soviet propaganda activities.

2. Soviet Covert Action (The Forgery Offensive), Hearings before the Subcommittee on Oversight of the Permanent Select Committee on Intelligence, U.S. House of Representatives (Wash. DC:GPO, 1980), Appendix, p. 60.

3. The British and Japanese fiscal years run from April 1 to March 31 while the French and West German fiscal years coincide with the calendar year.

4. Much of the information in this chapter is drawn from Foreign Cultural and Information Budgets Climb but U.S. Programs Lag in Real Growth, a briefing paper of ICA's Office of Research dated August 8, 1980 and other USIA/ICA research reports.

5. Soviet "Active Measures," Forgery, Disinformation, Political Operations. U.S. Dept. of State, Bureau of Public Affairs, Wash. DC. Special Report No. 88, Oct. 1981.

6. CIA "Report on Soviet Use of the Media," cited in The CIA and the Media, Subcommittee on Oversight of the Permanent Select Committee on Intelligence, U.S. House of Representatives, Wash. DC:GPO, 1978, Appendix R, p. 535.

7. William L. Chaze and Harold Kennedy, writing in an article entitled The Great Propaganda War, (U.S. News & World Report, Jan. 11, 1982, p. 29) estimate that the Soviets spend six times as much as the U.S. on informational and cultural programs.

8. The USIA budget request for Fiscal Year 1984 was for a total of $711.4 million.

9. Comptroller General's Report to the Congress, July 23, 1979.

10. Testimony of USIA Director Charles Z. Wick before the Senate Foreign Relations Committee, March 2, 1983, in presenting the authorization request

for USIA for fiscal year 1984 as well as the supplemental request for fiscal year 1983.

11. *World Radio TV Handbook*, 36th Edition, pp. 134-44.

12. Foreign Affairs Note, *Communist Clandestine Broadcasting*, U.S. Dept. of State, Wash. DC, December 1982.

13. *Soviet "Active Measures," Forgery, Disinformation, Political Operations*, op. cit.

14. Communist International Broadcasting to South Asia in 1980, Office of Research, USICA, Dec. 22, 1981.

15. *U.S. Charges Radio Jamming Penalizes Developing Nations*, USIA NESA-204, wireless file article, March 15, 1983.

16. Lewis H. Lapham, The Propaganda Man, *PARADE*, July 4, 1982.

17. *Soviet "Active Measures," etc.* op. cit.

18. *Soviet Propaganda Alert*, No. 1, October 15, 1981, Office of Research, ICA, Wash. DC.

19. *Ibid.*

20. William L. Chaze and Harold Kennedy, *The Great Propaganda War*, op. cit.

12

COMMUNICATIONS TECHNOLOGY
ONWARD AND UPWARD

About 20 years ago on a visit to the island of Trinidad in the Caribbean, I met the owner and manager of an estate where citrus, coffee, and cocoa were grown under somewhat primitive conditions. He told me that he was interested in expanding his cocoa production and had been experimenting with various techniques that he laboriously created and nurtured, based on his years of experience as a gentleman farmer in that part of the world. However, he lamented the fact that while his trial and error methods had shown some promising results, unavailable to him was information about the experiences of others in increasing cocoa production elsewhere in the world. Such information would have been invaluable, he said, but he lived in the wrong age.

Through my access to the library facilities of USIS Port of Spain and other sources, I was able to obtain the names and addresses for him of such places as the Cocoa Institute in London and the tropical fruit experimental station in Costa Rica that USAID and others supported. Much later these institutions were able to send him some written materials which were of great interest to him. But when they finally arrived by mail some months later, it was too late to be really beneficial, at least for that year's crop. Due to a variety of factors his farm ceased to flourish and was eventually sold. Had the above conversation taken place today, and if the USIS library or other facility in Trinidad's capital city had access to one of many data banks that now exist with the kind of information he sought, it could have provided a highly useful service.

The technology to quickly and efficiently gather and transmit all kinds of useful information to almost any place in the world now exists. That such information is not yet readily obtainable in most developing nations, despite its existence elsewhere and the technology to transmit it quickly and efficiently, will be discussed in the next chapter. But first let us examine briefly the state of communications technology today. By the time this is printed, however, what is said here will probably be somewhat outdated, for the technology of communications is moving so rapidly!

According to the Organization for Economic Cooperation and Development (OECD), it is estimated that in the fields of science and technology alone some 2 million scientific writings were issued each year during the early 1970s—in effect, 6 thousand to 7 thousand articles, reports, research papers, etc., per working day. There is no reason to believe that the number of scientific writings being produced annually in the 1980s has diminished. If anything, the number has probably increased, and not only because modern word processors make writing and editing less of a chore than it was a decade or so ago. Another estimate claims that the number of technical journals published throughout the world in the early 1980s is more than 100,000. Furthermore, notes the OECD, the stock of technical information already accumulated has been calculated at 10 trillion (10^{13}) alphanumerical characters representing the quantity of scientific and technical knowledge recorded in all forms from the birth of science to the mid-1960s.[1]

The amount of information now available in almost any field of human endeavor is staggering. Were it not for the invention of the computer, this inundation of ever-increasing amounts of information would be so overwhelming as to be useless to most of us. The invention of the computer, however, and later, its marriage to satellites, has provided the capability for utilizing information as it develops for political, economic, and social growth on a global scale. Computers have also, of course, sparked the avalanche of information. The society or nation that ignores the importance of information in the modern world, or fails to appreciate the technological advances that make information available to almost everyone for the asking, condemns itself to perpetual obsolescence. There may be some traditional societies which prefer that, but the clamor made by most of the developing countries of the world for a larger share of the economic and social benefits that the more developed nations enjoy indicates that economic and social progress is what the majority wants. Progress today comes only to those who have access to the information needed for progress.

The steady growth and development of human society has always been marked by significant inventions or events that periodically appear as watersheds of human activity. In communications and its related phenomenon, transportation, man's progress was markedly advanced with such inventions as the printing press, the steam engine, and the automobile, followed rather rapidly by radio, motion pictures, and, eventually television. In the last half of this century we have seen jet engines, stereophonic sound, transister radios, videotapes, satellites, and computers change the communication/ transportation environment throughout most of the world.

We are today witnessing a new spurt forward in the technological growth of global communications. Science fiction author Isaac Asimov has given such importance to communication satellites, for example, that more than a decade ago he called them "the fourth revolution in human communication." For him the first was the development of speech, the second the development of writing, and the third the invention of the printing press. The growth in the variety of uses and sheer numbers of satellite communications in recent years, and particularly the satellite-computer marriage, has opened communications vistas undreamed of by most of us as recently as a decade ago.

Douglas Cater, director of the Aspen Institute's program on communications and society, has noted, "It is a significant fact that, since the Second World War, the most dynamic growth activity in America has been among those entrepreneurs who search out, organize, package and transmit information." Put another way, Professor Anthony Oettinger, chairman of Harvard University's program on information resources policy, noted in testimony before a Senate committee, "The world is beginning to rely on information as a basic source. . . . Like energy and materials, information is a fundamental resource on which is based the well-being of every individual in every nation." And, according to an analysis made by two Stanford University professors, "1975 represented a significant passage point at which, after a quarter of a century of rapid growth, the enterprise known as information processing was engaging approximately half of the labor force of the U.S." In testimony March 23, 1983, before the Subcommittee on Telecommunications, Consumer Protection and Finance, U.S. Secretary of Commerce Malcolm Baldrige noted that international telecommunications services are increasingly important to the U.S. economy. He told the House of Representatives subcommittee that telecommunications and data processing services are major growth industries that have had an enormous impact on the U.S. balance of trade. In the past decade, he said, the telecommunications and electronic components sectors have experienced real growth of 8 and 10 percent, respectively, while the computer industry has grown at an 18 percent annual rate. By contrast, U.S. manufacturing as a whole inched along at an annual growth rate of about 1.2 percent. "In the United States, services (service industries) now represent 67 percent of economic output and 72 percent of employment, and in most developed countries account for more than half of gross domestic product," he said.[2]

Sociologist Daniel Bell has noted that just as steam and electrical energy enabled agrarian societies to industrialize, information today is the transforming resource of a new age. Nor need one go as far as the renowned scientist and writer, Arthur Clarke, who once expounded the idea that man can exist longer without food and water than without information, to conclude that information has indeed become a major symbol of the 1980s. And interestingly enough, while most products in today's world continue to rise in cost, communication costs have tumbled. Just as dramatic as the rise in the number of global messages relayed around the world in recent years has been the drop in cost to send these messages.

Lewis M. Branscomb, vice president and chief scientist of International Business Machines Corporation, speaking at the General Electric 100th Anniversary Symposium, also noted that information is as much a basic resource as food and energy. But whereas "food and energy challenge us because they are in short supply in major areas of the world. . . information is quite different. It is in quantitative surplus." Furthermore, he notes, "Information does not disintegrate when it is used: in fact, consumption generally increases its value. . . . The more you have, the more you want, and the easier it is to get." But since so many people in the world are information-poor, an important question arises: "How do you use the surplus of information in society to overcome the scarcity of information available to individuals?" The answer, he states, is the computer, "which is not only an information machine, but also a communication device."[3]

Information in machine-readable form can be both processed and communicated. This is what makes the computer both an information machine and a communication device. When it is utilized in connection with earth satellites, it is accessible to any place in the world where a ground station is located. At present the international satellite system Intelsat includes more than 200 earth stations, which provide a wide variety of telecommunications services, including data transmission, to more than 130 countries, territories and possessions.

Intelsat and Intersputnik, the two big international satellite systems, were initiated in 1965 and 1971, respectively. The first domestic synchronous orbit satellite system for telecommunication purposes and television, using low-cost earth stations and low-powered transmitters, was inaugurated in 1973 in Canada. In 1974, the United States launched WESTAR, with a capability of relaying 8 million words per second and capacity for voice, video, facsimile and data transmission. Three years later a new kind of satellite network was developed that could carry voice, facsimile, and data directly to the end user, bypassing commercial telephone lines.[4] In the meantime, advancements and experiments in more efficient communications go on apace.

A gallium arsenide laser that may enable numerous television programs to be transmitted along a fiber no thicker than a human hair was tested in 1970. Optical fiber cables for telephone traffic and television signals have been tested and are being developed. These new technologies open new paths of communication. Since a single glass fiber (the diameter of a human hair) can carry 800 voice conversations, tens of thousands of data messages, or 50 million bits per second (equal to 40,000 books if sent from one place to another in one hour), hundreds of these fibers in one packaged cable has enormous capacity. Taking full advantage of the bandwidth, Lewis Branscomb believes that eventually the traffic-carrying capacity of the visible light laser will be realized—about 600 trillion hertz, or 100 million times the capacity of today's optical fiber systems. Instead of 40,000 books per hour, that is 1 billion books per second on each optical channel! Beyond this phenomenal rise in communication capability is a device that sends out and receives invisible infrared light pulses that are deflected off the walls, thus permitting terminals and hand-held devices to communicate with other devices in a room without using wires.[5]

The merging of computing and telecommunications, that is, the interlinking of computers by telecommunication, is known as teleprocessing or *telematics*. This merging of computer technology with telecommunications technology is also known as *informatics*. When microcomputers enter the picture, *microinformatics* was born. Informatics has immensely increased the amount of information that is now available to those who have access to the new technologies. Computers and data banks can collate, store, and transmit millions of items of information. With the invention of the silicon chip, which allows a tiny electronic computer to be engraved on it, the space required for today's computers has been reduced to minute proportions since these silicon chips are only 5 millimeters in diameter. The number of components that a chip can carry has increased from 10 to 64,000 in recent years. A rise to a million components per chip by the mid 1980s has been predicted.

In the early 1960s, when the IBM Model 30 mainframe was introduced, for example, it required an air-conditioned room about 18 feet square that housed the central processing unit (CPU), the control console, a printer, and the desk for a key punch operator. The CPU alone, which is the brain of the machine, was five feet high and six feet wide and had to be water-cooled to prevent overheating. The CPU of IBM's current desktop personal computer is inscribed on a silicon chip. It can do 700,000 additions a second compared to the 360 Model 30's 33,000 additions per second at full speed. The old model cost $280,000 compared to less than $5,000 for the personal computer.[6]

While computer networks have become integral parts of communication systems, three basic functions constantly recur: storage (memory), arithmetical and logical operational units (processing), and peripheral input/output units (access), which is what makes communication between the user and the computer system possible. Improvements continue to be made in cost, performance, reliability, and, as noted above, the size of computer hardware. They are now capable of performing 1 billion operations a second, or a million times more than the pioneer computer of 1944. Processing and storage units have shrunk by a factor of about 10,000. The processing speed of computers has increased by approximately 50,000.

The speed of transmission from a computer or data bank to a terminal has likewise increased. The analog system (the use of signals in a form analogous to the relevant information) is translated into numerical form via the digital binary system (so-called because it uses two symbols instead of the usual ten numbers). Information in words is transmitted in binary form and decoded at the terminal, almost instantaneously.[7]

Two terms which are frequently used when talking about computers are "data bases" and "data banks." They should not be confused. Data bases are magnetic memories capable of representing billions of words, each of which is accessible in a computer system. These pieces of information are termed "data bases" in the case of bibliographical references concerning actual documents located elsewhere which, after being identified, must be retreived and read in order to obtain the information sought. "Data bank" tends to be used when referring to direct information through immediate reading of computerized "data." Once access to the computer system is gained it is possible to instantly obtain the terminal numerical values, statistical series, descriptive attributes, etc.[8]

Since the development of the digital computer, few human activities are not in some way connected with electronic data processing. Given the explosive rate of computer development, the trend is toward ever more extensive use of computers in the daily lives of more and more people. In the United States the production of personal home computers has become a multibillion-dollar industry. In early 1982, *Newsweek* reported that Apple Computer, which specializes in personal computers, had become a $600 million company, and since then it has gone beyond that. "Industry leader Tandy Corp. has sold 400,000 of its popular Radio Shack TRS-80 computers," *Newsweek* noted, and giant IBM, which brought out its personal computer in August 1981, "cannot turn them out fast enough to meet the demand." It was estimated at that time that almost 3 million personal computers would be sold in 1982, while Jack Tramiel, vice chairman of Commodore International, was quoted as saying, "I believe we'll sell 50 million worldwide by 1985."[9] Freshmen entering Drexel University in Philadelphia are now required to buy computers to be used for classroom work, the first college in the United States to require computers. although Clarkson College of Technology in Potsdam, New York announced in October 1982 that each of the 1,000 freshmen entering that school in 1983 would be lent a microcomputer to be used for regular class work.[10] While this is another indication of the extent of computer technology in *developed* countries, most *developing* countries still lag far behind in computer technology as in other fields. Yet it is this technology, as an information vehicle, which holds the greatest promise for accelerating political, economic, and social growth.

A major concern of computer engineers is how information gets into the computer, as well as how the needed results get out. Most computers today are limited in receiving new information by the speed of a pushbutton, a typewriter key, or a punch card. Computers that respond to speech are being developed. When fully developed, the technical distinctions between information technologies, typewriters, television, movies, telephones, and even radio, records and tapes, according to Lewis Branscomb, will become interrelated and interchangeable.[11]

Japanese companies are working on a "super computer" that will receive information faster than it can be received by pushbuttons, a typewriter key, or a punched card. These new computers, which are expected to appear by the end of this decade and have been coined "fifth generation" computers, will be able to accept voice commands in different languages. They will be designed to read Japanese and Chinese characters, something that until now has not been possible and which has resulted in the Japanese banking system still counting its yen without the help of computers. The reason they will be called fifth generation computers is that the first computers used tubes, the second generation used semi-conducters, the third, integrated circuits, and the fourth, large-scale integrated circuits.[12] But it is the international satellite systems which provide the capability of links between telephones, home and office terminals, and television receivers in networks which cover the globe.

SATELLITES

As noted earlier, there are currently two major international satellite systems, Intelsat and Intersputnik. Intelsat owns the satellites in the Intelsat system while the earth stations tied into the system are owned by the telecommunications entities in the countries where they are located. In 1980, Intelsat had about a dozen satellites in synchronous orbit at an altitude of approximately 22,240 miles. By utilizing Intelsat IV and IV-A satellites over the Atlantic and Indian Ocean regions and Intelsat IV satellites over the Pacific Ocean region, global service is provided. An Intelsat IV satellite has a nominal capacity of 4,000 voice circuits plus two television channels, while an Intelsat IV-A has a nominal capacity of 6,000 voice circuits and two television channels. There are more than 200 earth stations in the system which, in addition to being used for voice circuits and television, provides data transmission and other telecommunication services. The new Intelsat V satellite has a nominal capacity of 12,000 simultaneous two-way telephone circuits and the two television channels. The increased capacity evident in these figures was achieved in part by increased employment of frequency reuse techniques and the use of a new frequency band.[13]

Intersputnik was established in 1971 by a group of Socialist countries—Bulgaria, Hungary, the GDR, the Republic of Cuba, Mongolia, Poland, Rumania, the Soviet Union, and Czechoslovakia. The government of the Socialist Republic of Vietnam joined in 1979. The satellites are the property of the organization or are leased to its members while the earth stations belong to the states which built them or the organizations that operate them. Intersputnik's international operations began in 1973 with information exchanges between the Soviet Union and the Republic of Cuba. Earth stations were then built in Czechoslovakia and Poland (1974), Hungary and Bulgaria (1976), and in Algeria (1979). Vietnam, Laos, and Afghanistan joined later, and stations were planned for Angola, Ethiopia, Iraq, the People's Democratic Republic of Yemen, and a number of other countries.

The first functioning satellites of Intersputnik were "Molnia-2" and "Molnia-3," which were placed in an elliptical orbit. Since 1979, new satellites "Statsionar," in a geostationary orbit, have been used. Located over the Atlantic and Indian Oceans, each Statsionar satellite has six general-purpose radio-frequency broadband channels for telephone and telegraph communications as well as radio and television programming.[14]

Since the ATS-1 was launched by the United States in 1966, experimental satellites have provided pilot programs in a number of different educational, health, and rural and social development programs. Canada, the European Space Agency (ESA), Germany,

France, Italy, and Japan have also conducted experiments. Among these were the Appalachian Regional Commission Project, the Memorial University Telemedicine Project in Canada, and the Indian Site Project. Since 1975, the research objectives of earlier experimental satellite projects have changed to practical objectives such as the establishment of telecommunications systems for education and socioeconomic development. By 1980, domestic satellite systems were operating in the United States (RCA, WESTAR, COMSTAR, SBS), Canada (CTS and Anik series), Indonesia (PALAPA), France and Germany's joint venture (Symphonie 1 and 2) and systems were being constructed in India (INSAT), France (Telecom I), Germany (TV-Sat) and the regional European system (ECS). The European Space Agency, a consortium of 17 member countries, has its own experimental satellite, the Orbital Test Satellite (OTS) with 6,000 voice channels. The European Communications Satellite (ECS) is designed for digital communications and Eurovision. Some of the other regional and domestic satellite projects under discussion in the early 1980s were Project CONDOR (Andean region), Project SATCOL (Columbia) and the Brazilian satellite system, all in South America; the Arabsat system; AFROSAT for Africa; NORDSAT in Scandinavia; TDF in France, and H-Sat for the European Space Agency. More than a dozen countries also lease capacity on Intelsat for domestic communication needs.[15]

While the international Intelsat and Intersputnik systems continue to expand, so do regional and domestic satellite systems.[16] Satellites are also, of course increasingly utilized by the military and some systems are designed for maritime and aeronautical purposes. As satellite technology has improved, it has become possible to increase the power of satellites while decreasing the power and antenna size of the earth stations that receive the signals. This has led to what has become known as direct satellite broadcasting, i.e., transmission of broadcast signals from high-powered satellites that allow television and radio reception by small antennas on earth. The Communications Satellite Corporation (COMSAT) is considering a proposal to offer subscription service to millions of U.S. homes using rooftop antennas if it can get FCC approval. Western European nations are also planning direct-to-home television and radio broadcast services.[17] The era of direct satellite telecasts is already upon us, though the political problem of crossing national frontiers with direct satellite telecasting is yet to be resolved.

While technological changes involving computers and satellites scurry along at incredible speeds, efficient, large television screens have been developed on the one hand, and on the other, miniaturization has been achieved. Japan's Sony Corporation unveiled in early 1982 the world's first truly pocket-size TV. Using the conventional cathode-ray tube technology, the two-inch screen uses a new method of bouncing the electron beam so it strikes the screen from the side, allowing a sharp reduction in the depth of the set. The Flat TV is only 1.4 inches thick, eight inches long, and 3 1/2 inches wide.[18]

The lack of standardization in the television field has led to difficulties in exchanging programs between countries and regions, though equipment now exists to overcome these difficulties.

There are three television systems in common use today: NTSC developed in the United States and adopted by the Japanese as well—525 lines; the PAL system, developed by the Germans—625 lines; and SECAM, developed by the French. In addition to these three television systems, there are three basic types of videotape machines in common use, all of which employ cassettes. These are the 3/4″ U-Matic, the 1/2″ Betamax, and the 1/2″ VHS, which is similar to Betamax but made by a different manufacturer. Although conversion from one standard to another is no longer a problem, it is costly and the results are not always of the same quality as the original production. To add to the complexity of converting from one system to another, the Betamax and VHS formats come in three separate models, each with different capstan speeds: BETA I (FAST), BETA II (MEDIUM), BETA III (SLOW) and VHS II (FAST), VHS IV (MEDIUM), and VHS VI (SLOW). However, the latest machines for converting one system to another have variable speed controls.

Standardization, when it comes, as it probably will, will bring another spurt forward to the booming business of videotaping. Videotape cameras, like playback equipment, are also becoming more compact and portable. It was the communication demands of the Space Age, with its race to the moon and the development of the Space Shuttle and earlier space vehicles, which, along with the computer, greatly advanced communications technology.

Videotapes have today become not only an important element of television programming and home entertainment, but also an important tool of public diplomacy. Though originally not used as wisely by USIA as, perhaps, they should have been, since field posts were flooded with the "talking heads" type of programming mentioned earlier, today they provide U.S. public diplomats with a highly flexible, effective communication medium. The Sony 3/4″ cassette, which most USIA posts use because of its compatibility with local television stations in many parts of the world, still requires a rather heavy, somewhat awkward VTR machine which is inconvenient to move from place to place. While it is a great advance over the half-inch reel-to-reel equipment first used, an accelerated move to smaller, more portable systems can be expected. It remains to be seen how successfully videodiscs, a relatively new item in the home entertainment field, will be able to compete with videotape systems.

Cable television is another aspect of the communications revolution of the 1970s and 1980s. Cable TV employs coaxial cable and other sophisticated electronic equipment to deliver a wide range of programming to various receivers. Rudimentary systems were operating in the late 1940s but only in recent years has the cable industry expanded in an explosive fashion. In the United States in the early 1980s there were already nearly 4,000 cable systems serving 14 million subscribers and expansion into noncable areas was continuing at a rapid pace. Cable television's wide-band, multichannel capacity (30 to 40 channels or more) and potential for two-way communications are among its technological assets. The United Kingdom, the Netherlands, Canada, Belgium and Japan are among major countries where cable TV is increasingly popular.[19]

The multiple uses of television, including cable TV, have led to electronic newspapers, library services, and mail and banking services, to name just a few. And finally, word processing systems have changed the nature and appearance of modern offices. Sitting at the workstation of a word processor, one is able, even in a relatively small office information system, to almost instantly recall desired material selected from up to 835 megabytes of information (approximately 334,000 pages of text) in the more advanced models. Writing, erasing, and editing by the use of the cathode ray has become so easy that it is fun, while high-speed printers can be used to turn out 18 pages of copy per minute. These are among the new office″ procedures that are becoming increasingly common.

But while the information explosion brought on by modern communications technology has so drastically affected the personal, business and professional lives of almost everyone in the developed countries, the developing world has, for the most part, been left far behind. While it might be argued that information *per se* is not necessarily beneficial to a society, there is general agreement that a modern, complex nation cannot survive without information, nor can any country progress without meeting certain information needs that make progress possible.

There is little doubt but that the communications revolution taking place in the developed world today will continue onward and upward. It is in the interest of global peace and stability that the developing nations also have access to the new communications technology, so vital to their economic, political, and social development. A possible way for U.S. public diplomats to contribute to this worthy purpose is the subject of the next chapter.

NOTES

1. MacBride, Sean, et al., *Many Voices, One World*, Report by the International Commission for the Study of Communication Problems, Kogan Page, London/Unipub, N.Y./Unesco, Paris, 1980, citing OECD as the source, p. 94.

2. USIA NESA Wireless file of March 24, 1983.

3. Branscomb, Lewis M., *Information: The Ultimate Frontier, Science*, Vol. 203, 12 Jan. 1979, p. 143.

4. MacBride, Sean, et. al, op. cit., p. 11.

5. Branscomb, Lewis M., op. cit.

6. "To Each His Own Computer," *Newsweek*, Feb. 22, 1982, p. 42.

7. MacBride, Sean, et. al, op. cit. p. 65.

8. *Ibid*. pp. 73-74.

9. "To Each His Own Computer," op. cit. p. 40.

10. "No More Pencils, No More Books, Just Bring a Personal Computer," *International Herald Tribune*, Nov. 3, 1982, p. 2.

11. Branscomb, Lewis M., op. cit. p. 145.

12. Reuters news despatch, dateline Tokyo, Oct. 27, 1981.

13. MacBride, Sean, et. al, op. cit. p. 288.

14. *Ibid*. p. 289.

15. Casey-Stahmer, Anna, "The Era of Experimental Satellites: Where to Go from Here," *Journal of Communication*, Annenberg School of Communication, Autumn, 1979.

16. Communications Satellite Corp. has announced plans to build a $50 million earth station complex in central Pennsylvania in conjunction with four other major telecommunication companies. Traffic between the United States and the Atlantic Ocean region made up almost 85 percent of all satellite traffic in 1981, but there were only two earth station sites on the east coast of the United States to handle these signals, located at Andover, Mass. and Etam, West

Virginia. The new facility with three satellite dishes is expected to handle the telephone calls, television, facsimile and data services which, according to Comsat, are expected to double by 1985.

17. Wigand, Rolf T., "The Direct Satellite Connection: Definitions and Prospects," *Journal of Communication*, Spring 1980.

18. "Sony's Pocket-Size Television," *Newsweek*, Feb. 8, 1982.

19. MacBride, Sean, op. cit. p. 81. The French cabinet on Nov. 3, 1982, approved plans to connect most French homes over the next 20 years with a cable network that would carry television and telephone signals and could provide home banking, shopping, and information services. The plan, which puts heavy emphasis on fiber optics, calls for connecting 1.4 million households in this network by 1985. (*The International Herald Tribune*, Nov. 5, 1982, p. 11.)

13

ARE WE READY FOR A BOLD NEW STEP?

What is required is a bold new initiative which transcends the limits of past thinking about propaganda and considers the opportunity that the United States has to use its resources of information and technology in assisting the human race to ascend into the future as more free people—free of poverty, free of violence, free of ignorance, and free to become.[1]

The communications revolution of the last half of the twentieth century has given U.S. public diplomats an historic opportunity to de-emphasize their roles as propagandists and become truly modern pioneers in an endeavor which would serve not only U.S. interests, but the interests of all who seek political, economic, and social development.

In a world beset with frictions, often resulting in physical violence, where all of us live in the shadow of a nuclear holocaust, where ever-increasing amounts are devoted to armaments, and where our globe is divided East from West and North from South— the gaps in living standards and in understanding continue to widen rather than diminish. This is occurring despite the dramatic and continuing shrinkage of the world in terms of transportation and communication, exemplified by the U.S. space shuttle as it circles the globe in 90 minutes, and expanding global communications networks capable of relaying information instantly to almost any place on earth.

The "drawing and quartering" of the world, East from West and North from South, is no less a barbaric custom today than it was in the past when men themselves were drawn and quartered. It is time to put our modern technology and skills to better use in closing the widening gaps of living standards and understanding. If information is the key element for the political, economic, and social development of modern societies, as many now believe it is, then an organization which is as knowledgeable about, and experienced with, modern communications technology and methodology as USIA is is in an excellent position to transmit to developing nations the kinds of information they need for their development goals.

For more than a quarter of a century USIA has been communicating on a global scale under the varied conditions and within the various cultures found in the more than 100 countries in which USIA offices are located. The communications knowledge and experience thus gained, if used for the transfer of technology and other information needed by developing countries for their political, economic, and social growth, could have a highly positive impact not only on the development goals of individual countries, but also on the U.S. goal of a more peaceful and stable world. What is needed is for U.S. government leaders to have the wisdom, the intelligence, the vision, and the courage to enable U.S. public diplomats to share in pursuing U.S. development assistance goals that are now carried out solely by AID and international agencies and generally kept in a conventional mold that, while successful in some instances, has been notably unsuccessful in others. To do this U.S. public diplomats would have to initiate a bold, new step—one which would be applauded by those who, no less than ourselves, would gain by such a step.

While some still question the value of U.S. aid programs as an instrument of U.S. foreign policy, designed as they are to accelerate economic and social growth in developing societies, such programs have been conducted by every U.S. administration since the end of World War II. Beginning with the well-known and highly successful Marshall Plan for post-war Europe, and continuing through the period of the Alliance for Progress and beyond, development assistance has now been an integral part of U.S. foreign policy for nearly 40 years.

AID administrators were directed in the 1970s to focus their programs on "the poorest of the poor," both as regards the relative position of one nation to another, and the relative position of one group to another within a recipient country. They were also directed to concentrate on basic human needs. In recent years, however, this "poorest of the poor" philosophy has met with increased criticism. In this respect economics is no different, perhaps, from public diplomacy—each has many schools of thought.

The "poorest of the poor" approach is no longer considered decisive since AID administrators now seem to believe that the poorest of the poor can be helped in many ways, including doing things that do not include them as the chief or only target group. But strategy and tactics aside, there is nearly universal agreement that economically healthy societies serve U.S. interests far better than a world of growing poverty and dissatisfaction. Thus, whatever the United States can do to foster healthy economic growth in developing societies, assuming that what we do is practical, reasonably cost-effective, and that the countries we are aiding are not basically antagonistic toward us, is in our interest. These interests are economic, political, and humanitarian. Above all, however, the contribution economically healthy nations can make to world and regional peace and stability is paramount. The greatest threats to world peace and stability since the end of World War II have occurred *not* in the developed world, though the developed world has almost invariably become involved, but in the developing countries, and mostly in those countries that suffer severe economic difficulties. It is also in such countries where the ideological differences of the two superpowers so often become rallying points for opposed indigenous groups.

The importance of communications for development has been increasingly stressed in recent years in the writings of academics, in many United Nations forums at both the political and technical levels, and especially at UNESCO meetings, from the General Conference to numerous experts' meetings. Despite this recognition of the importance of communications for development, there has been no significant increase in communications development projects. Aid for development of communications is still not regarded, apparently, as a priority matter. Such projects are largely outside the priorities of organizations like the UNDP, the World Bank, the regional development banks, and the many institutions which supply bilateral assistance. A OECD document on the world aid flow and its applications to telecommunications, for example, mentions that out of a total of $13 billion in public aid to development granted by member states of that organization in 1975, the total aid programs devoted to communications amounted to only $175 million.[2] Nor have U.S. economic assistance programs moved much beyond the demonstrations with the ATS-6 satellite that the Agency for International Development conducted in the summer of 1976 for 30 developing countries in Asia, Africa, and Latin America. AID's emphasis continues to be in agriculture and rural development, public administration, health programs, and family planning. There are no indications that U.S. aid administrators are planning to include communications technology as a priority program for development needs now or in the future.

The UNESCO Report by the International Commission for the Study of Communication Problems, which was first published in 1980, recommended that:

1. Communication be no longer regarded merely as an incidental service and its development left to chance. Recognition of its potential warrants the formulation by all nations, and particularly developing countries, of comprehensive communication policies linked to over-all social, cultural, economic, and political goals.[3]

In supporting this recommendation, the UNESCO report notes that "National governments as much as the international community should recognize the urgency of according communications higher priority in planning and funding," and adds, "Communication is not only a system of public information, but also an integral part of education and development."[4] As the first recommendation under the rubric "Basic Needs," the report states:

11. The Communication component in all development projects should receive adequate financing. So-called "development support communications" are essential for mobilizing initiatives and providing information required for action in all fields of development—agriculture, health and family planning, education, religion, industry, and so on.[5]

While the hue and cry in the Western democracies in general, and in the United States in particular, has been against those aspects of the "new world information order" that threaten freedom of information within and across national boundaries, other aspects of the UNESCO deliberations are worth much more attention than they have received, particularly the relationship of communication to development. This relationship is highlighted throughout the report. For example, the report argues, "There is no longer any room for uncertainty either about the role that communication should play in economic planning, nor about its place in development strategy, nor about the need for the resources that should be devoted to it by every nation and the international community."[6] And more specifically, it states: "As distance becomes an increasingly irrelevant factor in transmission costs (in particular in the case of transmission by satellite, but also in broadband digital transmission by microwave light conducters and cables), the inequalities between developed and developing countries can diminish."[7]

In discussing the integration of communication into development as a prelude to making a specific recommendation regarding this subject, the authors of the UNESCO report state:

> Development strategies should incorporate communication policies as an integral part in the diagnosis of needs and in the design and implementation of selected priorities. In this respect communication should be considered a major development resource, a vehicle to ensure real political participation in decision making, a central information base for defining policy options, and an instrument for creating awareness of national priorities.[8]

In commenting on the necessity of technical information for development purposes, they then note:

> The flow of technical information within nations and across national boundaries is a major resource for development. Access to such information, which countries need for technical decision making at all levels, is as crucial as access to news sources. This type of information is generally not easily available and is most often concentrated in large techno-structures. *Developed countries are not providing adequate information of this type to developing countries.*[9] (Italics my own.)

Based on the above rationalization, the UNESCO authors make the following recommendation on the subject under discussion:

> 34. Developing countries should pay particular attention to (a) the correlation between education, scientific and communication policies, because their practical application frequently overlaps; (b) the creation

in each country of one or several centers for the collection and utilization of technical information and data, both from within the country
and from abroad; (c) to secure the basic equipment necessary for
essential data processing activities; (d) the development of skills and
facilities for computer processing and analysis of data obtained from
remote sensing.[10]

Of the 82 recommendations cited in the UNESCO report, a number
of others touch upon the role of communication in political, economic, and social development, but the few quoted above make it
clear that the authors of the report believe that role to be an extremely important one.

If, as appears to be the case, information is vital for economic
life; if, given modern communications capabilities, this vital information is not as accessible to developing countries as it could be; and if
the United States continues to believe, as evidenced by its economic
assistance and other programs and actions, that in its own self-
interest the development efforts of developing countries merit our
full support, is it not time to seriously consider utilizing the global
resources and the communications knowledge and experience of
USIA in the development effort? As Wilbur Blume has noted in
his perceptive essay on this subject, "The promise of technology is
that if our resources of information are properly used, the developing
world will not repeat our evolution through the industrial age but
will leap over it into the post-industrial society of increased
affluence."[11]

The idea which is being proposed here and which Wilbur Blume
and others have advocated is to establish, in a number of USIA
libraries in developing countries, computer terminals which have
access to numerous data banks in the United States. This is not
necessarily a new idea. Such computer terminals have been established in some USIA libraries in Western European countries but that
is not where they are most needed. There are already innumerable
sources of information available to the developed societies of
Western Europe. It is in the developing world where the greatest
need exists for technology transfer and where USIA could be instru-
mental in providing, initially, a ready source of information needed
for social, economic, and political development and a means for
government, business, educational leaders, and others to be introduced to the wonders of the Computer Age. Although databank
access is becoming available to some parts of the developing world,

the pace at which this is occurring is by no means as rapid as the pace of communication developments and changes in the developed world. For the most part "databanks" and "information retrieval systems" remain elusive and mysterious terms in most of the third world. Some third world countries, like Colombia, Argentina, Mexico, and Brazil have begun to plug in daily by telephone to computers in the United States that are run by companies providing information packets on medicine, business, news, engineering, and many other subjects, but the number of users remains extremely small compared to the potential numbers who would benefit if greater knowledge of these systems and how to access them existed.

Placement of computer terminals in USIA's overseas libraries in developing countries that can provide access to numerous data banks in the United States is an idea whose time has come. To do so will require a degree of boldness, vision, wisdom, and courage on the part of the leaders of U.S. public diplomacy and a willingness to shift America's information effort, not completely but in part, to the goal of political, economic, and social development in developing countries. U.S. public diplomats would continue to expound U.S. foreign policy, provide information about the United States, and expose communist "disinformation" campaigns much as they do today. However, this new dimension to U.S. public diplomacy would not only be highly beneficial to developing countries where this new service is provided, and thus, presumably, would be welcomed enthusiastically by its citizens, but would once again demonstrate the values, interests, and ideals on which the American nation was founded and which the American people have espoused throughout our history—the belief in the free flow of information and the creation of opportunities for all men to develop to their fullest capacity.

As with any new project or system, its initial development should be undertaken as a pilot project in only one or a few countries. Furthermore, when and if initiated, this service should not be cost-free. There are several reasons for this. After the initial cost of installing the system, which would be borne by the U.S. government, the fees for accessing data banks in the United States, while relatively inexpensive and well within the means of most government and private organizations in even the poorest countries, could be costly in the aggregate. Furthermore, when other priorities of U.S. public diplomats continue to require attention and funding, it would not be realistic to advocate a bold, new step that would have little chance of being financed. Even if sufficient funds were available, costs should be shared by end-users both because what one pays for is almost always more worthwhile than what one receives gratis, and because a minimal fee for the type of information that can be provided by accessing a variety of U.S. data banks would help assure the seriousness of information requests.

The installation of a computer terminal in a USIA library, in addition to immediately providing substantive information of value to the development needs of the host country, can serve the equally important purpose of demonstrating modern communications technology. Communications technology has grown so rapidly in recent years, as noted earlier, that part of the problem of adopting the new technology to developing countries is the fact that few people in such countries have first-hand knowledge of the dramatic changes that have taken place in the communications field. It would be quite natural, and would also serve U.S. interests, for interested nationals of the host country to visit USIA libraries where computer terminals are installed to learn more about modern communications technology and methodology. Eventually, USIA libraries might phase out their computer terminals as more and more host country individuals and organizations become familiar with the new technology, develop their own systems, and install their own terminals. In short, the demonstration effect of USIA computer terminals provides an incentive for their establishment in other institutions. And as the United States leads the world in computer hardware and software, the eventual trade that may be expected to develop in this field, while not a primary goal, can be expected to redound favorably for U.S. manufacturers. An example of this on a very small scale can be seen in Pakistan, where USIA ordered an American-made word processor for its operations in Islamabad. After it was installed in early 1983, the local representative was able to show potential clients the word processor in operation at USIS Islamabad. As it was one of the first of iis kind in that country and represented the latest technology of word processors at the time of its installation, it was used by the local dealer as a demonstration model that could be expected to create a demand among other potential users.

In September 1976, the Resource and Operations Analysis Staff of USIA completed a study entitled *European Libraries and*

Data Banks. While this study provides a great deal of useful basic information as to how data banks can be used in U.S. public diplomacy efforts, it is unfortunate that Western Europe, which is an integral part of the developed world, was the venue for this study. As the report itself notes, "Because of reductions in computer processing costs and telecommunications costs, data banks are attracting increasingly more users. OECD, for example, predicts more than 2 million European users by 1985. Already several dozen American data banks are commercially available throughout most of Western Europe."[12] The report also notes that the Scandinavians and Germans have each established their own documentation service in Washington, D.C. in order to procure U.S. government documents. Thus the information-rich Western European area is not the place for USIA to initiate data bank services. Even in Western Europe, however, the report notes that "most of the likely demand (e.g., science and medicine)" for U.S. government documents "is outside of conventional USIS interests."[13] If data banks were to become accessible through USIS libraries in developing countries, however, scientific and medical information, along with technology, economics, and many other fields, should be made available. If one agrees with Professor Blume that it is in the long-range interests of the United States to help to address the more compelling issues of developing countries, and that "the simple understanding of American culture, ideas, and policies is somewhat irrelevant to most of the world's people," then it becomes more important (in developing countries) to meet the needs associated with technology transfer than to solely push U.S. policy explanations, American Studies, and similar traditional pursuits.[14]

The USIA study of European libraries and data banks lists three options under "data bank recommendations." The report notes that the simplest and fastest way to provide on-line services at major West European posts is by accessing data banks that already exist, many of which are available through two large American data bank brokers—Lockheed and System Development Corporation (SDC Search Service). "But because the services of these and other data bank suppliers are already widely available in Europe and will become far more so during the next ten years with the development of the commercial market and of subsidized mechanisms of supply and distribution such as EURONET," the report notes, providing such services "does not warrant serious consideration by the Agency, except as an ancillary service on a much reduced scale."[15] It makes infinite sense not to duplicate services that are already available. The situation in developing countries, however, is completely different from that encountered in Western Europe.

The second option the report mentions is the development by the agency of a foreign affairs data bank, based initially on the European wireless file. But it concludes that the major value of that option would simply be "to educate ourselves in implementing and managing a computer-based information service in Washington." That is hardly a sufficiently compelling reason to initiate such a project, especially since the same experience could be gained by establishing a pilot project, not in Washington, but at one of USIA's overseas libraries in a developing country.

The third option mentioned was the development of an American Studies data bank, but, the report concluded, European posts were doing just as well or better with their noncomputerized "table of contents" service.[16]

The 35 recommendations which are made at the conclusion of the study include the suggestion that some experimentation with data bank usage be undertaken in Europe. What would have been much more useful, but which can still be done, would be to experiment with data bank usage in one or more of the developing countries.

One source of funding for such a bold new step of U.S. public diplomacy in developing countries might be to close or further reduce USIA's library operations in Europe (excluding the information-starved Communist countries). In fiscal year 1976, libraries were the single most expensive activity of USIS posts in Europe, as seen from the following table:

Percentage of Program Funds to Library Operations: FY 76

Country	%	Country	%
Austria	23	Ireland	22
Belgium	37	Italy	19
Bulgaria	20	Malta	28
Canada*	28	Netherlands	20
Cyprus	23	Norway	30
Czechoslovakia	19	Poland	20
Denmark	25	Portugal	29

Country	%	Country	%
Federal Republic of Germany	23	Rumania	37
Finland	26	Sweden	28
France	8	Switzerland	10
German Democratic Republic	_	Turkey	21
Greece	27	United Kingdom	13
Hungary	44	U.S.S.R.	8
Iceland	37	Yugoslavia	38

*Canada is serviced by USIA's European Area Office.

As can be seen from the above, the average percentage of program funds being used for library programs was about 25 percent. One reason for this, aside from inflation, which affects everyone, and the fact that library operations require a high number of skilled personnel, is the dramatic rise in the cost of books. As the report notes, "the average cost of books in 1960 was $5.24. By 1975 it had increased to $16.95."[18] While the cost of information in the form of books more than tripled in the 15 years prior to 1975, the cost of computerized information is now steadily dropping.

Another factor which further brings USIA's library operations in Western Europe into question is the observation made in the library report under discussion that "USIS Officers and staff do not share a common view of what our libraries are nor whom they should serve."[19] In fact, not only are USIS libraries "dwarfed in size practically everywhere in Europe," the report notes, but "many of the materials are duplicated tenfold or hundredfold in libraries and bookstores. . . . Without specialization," it concludes, "USIS libraries risk becoming increasingly marginal in the communities in which they operate."[20]

When data banks first came into use and USIA explored the possibility of utilizing them for servicing overseas reference questions "off-line" by having posts cable Washington with their requests, the results were not completely satisfactory. One reason for this is that interactive searches are a kind of dialogue with the computer in which the subject or theme is gradually narrowed down to the most important and relevant issues. A large number of citations tend to be irrelevant (perhaps as high as 90 percent) and, furthermore, the list of citations is incomplete. Thus, when USIA made use of the *New York Times* data bank, for example, in handling cabled requests from overseas via the terminal to the NYT data bank, which is located in the USIA library in Washington, the results were often disappointing. This is another reason why, to be effective, terminals should be located in the agency's overseas libraries in countries selected for this service.

Data banks are essentially files of specialized information stored in one or more computers. Usually bibliographic in nature, this information serves to refer the user to documents that may be of interest to him and may contain only citations with standard document descriptors assigned from a thesaurus or selected automatically from free text. The Social Science Citation Index (SOCIAL SCI-SEARCH) produced by the Institute for Scientific Information is of this type, as are the "cataloging" data banks produced by Information Dynamics Corporation on the Library of Congress collections (IDC/LIBCON) and by the Ohio College Library Center (OCLC).

Some data banks store the full text of documents. Examples are the LEXIS data bank (which contains the U.S. Code in full, as well as Supreme Court decisions and the decisions of the U.S. Circuit and District Courts), and the Associated Press and UPI wire services. The 1976 library report noted that even then, according to the Electronic Systems Division of the U.S. Air Force, "this kind of full-text data bank will become cost-effective in the next several years."[21]

Another type of data bank or data base contains "raw" numerical or nonnumerical information rather than bibliographical information. Users are guided to "facts" rather than to documents. A number of such raw data banks are produced by Predicasts Corporation including one on worldwide statistical abstracts, historical data, and time series for international economic, demographic, industrial, and product data (PATS INTERNATIONAL STATISTICS). The LEGISLATIVE ISSUES DATA BASE of the Congressional Research Service is another example.

Although by the mid-1970s data banks were providing access in developed countries to much of the world's primary scientific and technical literature, emphasis was shifting to nonscientific fields of interest. A sample of data bases in the social sciences available in Europe even in 1975 is revealing:

Sample of Data Banks in the Social Sciences[22]

Name	Coverage
ABI/INFORM	Management
ASI	Government Statistical Publications
Bibliographic Data Base	Congressional Documents, Relevant Series
CIS	Congressional Hearings, Reports, Prints
Dissertations	Ph. D. Dissertations since 1861
ERIC	Educational Information and Research
IDC/LIBCON	Catalog of Library of Congress Collections
JURIS	U.S. Code, Briefs of U.S. Courts
Legislative Information	Status of U.S. Legislation
MATRIX (1)	Materials on Urban Affairs—Policy and Plans
MATRIX (2)	Materials on Environment—Policy and Plans
MATRIX (3)	World Developments in Communications
New York Times	News items from 67 Non-technical Journals
Psychological Abstracts	Psychology and Related Disciplines
Sociological Abstracts	Journals of Sociology
SOCIAL SCISEARCH	1,400 plus Social Science Journals
SSIE	Research in Progress (Smithsonian)

An informal survey of selected European USIS posts conducted by the authors of the European library report of 1976 concluded that there was little perceived need for the following data banks:

a. NTIS (National Technical Information Service, Dept. of Commerce);

b. ERIC (Educational Resources Information Center, HEW);

c. ERDA (Solar Energy Information Data Bank);

d. INFORM (Business and management journals) Numerous other technical and scientific data banks.[23]

What makes the above observation interesting is that the data banks *of least interest to European users* are among those one would expect to be *of most interest to developing nations*, where technical and scientific information is sorely needed, yet so difficult to obtain.

Access to data banks is obtained by a series of instructions called "software." Though bibliographic software packages differ considerably in their mode of operation, all perform essentially the same functions. RECON, a fairly sophisticated package, is used by a number of U.S. government agencies such as NASA and the EPA, as well as the European Space Agency. Lockheed, one of the largest commercial data bank suppliers in the United States, uses a software package called DIALOG. Its competitor, the System Development Corporation, uses a system known as ORBIT II.

Communications networks connect users to computers. Local and long distance telephone lines, via satellites if need be, connect one end of the computer with the terminal attached at the other end of the communications chain. An ordinary telephone and a device (an acoustic coupler or a modem) designed to convert digital computer signals into analog telephone signals and vice versa can be used. If the volume of traffic between the data bank and the user is not more than a few hours per day, and assuming that the connection is static-free (which is a necessary condition), the normal dial system can be used to transmit messages (citations, etc.). A greater volume of traffic may make leased lines less costly.

In addition to commercial telephone systems, there are commercial networks specialized in data communications, such as TELENET and DATRAN, which use their own communications facilities that are linked to local telephone lines. TYMET, operated by Tymshare Inc., leases long-distance lines from Bell Telephone, adds data communication services, and resells the lines to the public. Some of these "value-added-networks" (VANs) also provide service internationally over cables and satellite circuits leased from RCA, ITT, and other international carriers.

The cost of transmission using regular telephone facilities is the cost of a telephone call. Tymshare was charging $11.00 per hour to California from any telephone in the United States and $22.00 per hour from the major European capitals when the European library study was made.[24]

The terminal device operated by the user is the fourth and final link in the chain of access to data banks. This is generally a typewriter terminal that produces hard copy, and a video unit on which messages are displayed. The user establishes a direct connection with the computer and enters search terms singly or in combination via the terminal. In the "online" system, which is what USIA libraries should have, initial results will be printed on the terminal within two to five seconds and the search can be refined by qualifiers to pinpoint specific aspects of a subject or to limit the search to certain authors, journals, years of publication, etc. Finally, when the user is satisfied with the results, the full citations and abstracts can be printed on the terminal, or they can be printed at the computer site and mailed to the user.[25]

When one compares what is being advocated here—a service which can be highly beneficial to many individuals, organizations, and societies, with the type of "public diplomacy" practiced by the Soviet Union, as described in Chapter 11, the differences in objectives are as great as the differences in the two competing political and economic systems that the United States and the Soviet Union represent. The United States, an open society, has traditionally been willing to share its scientific and technological information with other nations. The Soviet Union, on the other hand, by the nature of its closed society, has been generally unwilling to share information with others, while its disinformation efforts are something else again. Yet, as we have seen, information is today more vital than ever before if the widening gap between the developed and the developing worlds is ever to be reversed, or, at the least, slowed down.

The type of data bank service we have been discussing, if initiated, should only be provided to those developing countries where the local government would welcome such a service. While inconceivable that such a fantastic resource would not be welcomed, political motivations have historically been markedly successful in preventing actions or activities which, while practical and beneficial in themselves, are sometimes perceived as being "imperialistic" or worse. Much has been said and written, for example, about the "one-way flow" of information. This "one-way flow" may be accelerated by computer terminals that bring information from abroad into the host country. But just as the communications revolution cannot be detained, neither can the "one-way flow."

It is the unequal control and distribution of information in the world today that has brought forth cries for "a new world information order." While access to U.S. data banks increase the "one-way flow," it also makes available, quickly and easily, information of vital importance to the recipient. This particular "flow" will occur only when specific information is requested by the person or institution that seeks information. By having access in developing countries to the data banks which are available in the developed nations, the inequalities among both are diminished.

Because the "new world information order" has been the subject of so much discussion for more than a decade, and because the development of computer terminals in developing countries should help meet some of the concerns of those who seek a "new world information order," this is a fitting subject for some commentary here. But before doing so, one further important consideration in initiating data bank services as a bold, new feature of U.S. public diplomacy should be noted. This would not be at the expense of other traditional USIA programs and purposes. Support for U.S. foreign policy, cultural programs involving American Studies, the teaching of English, presentation of U.S. performing artists, and most other functions of USIA would continue. The data bank service would enhance some of them. It would most certainly increase attendance and usage of those USIA libraries where computer terminals are installed.

THE NEW WORLD INFORMATION ORDER

In 1970, at the sixteenth session of the General Conference of UNESCO, the delegations of several developing countries raised the issue of unequal distribution of information, particularly by the mass media. They expressed their concerns about international news exchange systems, the degree and type of news that flows to and from the developed to the developing world, and they stressed that the cultural identity of developing countries was in danger because of the control by developed nations of most of the world's sources of news and news distribution systems.

There followed several drafts, which were successively presented at meetings of experts as well as at governmental levels, and were all heatedly discussed and debated. At the nineteenth session of the General Conference of UNESCO, held in Nairobi in 1976, it was decided that no decisions could possibly be made and that the study of the problem would continue.

By July 1976, the first UNESCO-sponsored Conference on Communication Policies was held in San Jose, Costa Rica. It unanimously recommended the formulation of new national and international communication policies and urged that national communication councils be set up, scientific research in this field be developed, and national and regional news agencies be established.

The twentieth session of the General Conference of UNESCO, held in Paris in 1978, adopted, by consensus, the text of the "Declaration on Fundamental Principles Concerning the Contribution of the Mass Media to Strengthening Peace and International Understanding, to the Promotion of Human Rights and to Countering Racialism, Apartheid and Incitement to War." While many conceded UNESCO's good faith, others are of the opinion that the declaration is harmful in that it may be used to legitimize interference with freedom of the press.

In February 1979, a conference similar to the one held in 1976 in San Jose, Costa Rica, was held in Kuala Lumpur, to study all aspects of communication policy, though in the context of Asia and Oceania. This conference stressed that "communication, considered both as a means of affirming a nation's collective identity and an instrument of social integration, has a decisive role to play in the democratization of social relations insofar as it permits the multidirectional flow of both horizontal and vertical messages."[26]

The "new world information order" is shorthand for "a new, more just and more efficient world information and communication order," which was the term adopted at the 1978 General Conference of UNESCO and the General Assembly of the United Nations. The declaration, referred to above, was heavily criticized and strongly opposed by many professionals, especially journalists, in many Western countries. Concern was expressed that some governments, ostensibly trying to correct imbalances, might enforce measures whose real purpose was to control press freedom. Objections were also voiced that mention in the declaration of journalists' "responsibilities" could be used to arbitrarily label some journalists as being "irresponsible," with consequent results. Other criticisms of the declaration included its failure to mention human rights; its lack of recognition of the need to have access to various and diverse sources of news; and its lack of mention of the desirability of a multiplicity of news outlets. There was also strong objection to the role assumed by UNESCO in making such a declaration, since this role was interpreted by some as being designed to control the flow of news.[27]

Advocates of the "new world information order" argue that a small number of developed countries provide most of the world's news coverage, entertainment, and advertising, and that much of the news coverage is controlled by only a few multinational news agencies. They find this unacceptable because, they say, these agencies devote too little attention to the domestic affairs of the developing countries and foster a negative image of those countries by focusing on sensational and disastrous events while ignoring positive ones, particularly those involving development issues. Furthermore, they view commericial advertising as fostering biases in favor of the industrialized world and multinational corporations, and as a threat to their cultural heritage.[28]

To test the view that the four leading Western news agencies reflect the biases of the developed world to the detriment of the third world and its development goals, Professors Wilbur Schramm of the East-West Center in Honolulu and Erwin Atwood of Southern Illinois University analyzed 18 Asian dailies and the Asian news wires of United Press International (UPI), the Associated Press (AP), Reuters, and Agence France Presse (AFP). As described in their book *Circulation of News in the Third World—A Study of Asia,* they found, for example, that far from ignoring third world news, the Asian wires devoted about half of their space to such stories in the study week which was used (December 4-10, 1977).[29] Despite the availability of this amount of third world stories, the 18 Asian dailies in ten nations surveyed during the same period used only a small percentage of these stories. And while it is true that only a few items fit the classification of "development news," a subject which critics say Western news agencies ignore, nevertheless only a small fraction of what the 18 subscribers received was printed. This and similar studies may not be very convincing to those who advocate a "new world information order" as a means of correcting what they see as an imbalance in the world's news flows, but the Schramm-Atwood study does indicate that the problem of such flows is as complex as it is difficult to resolve.

The more radical advocates of "the new order" contend that the remedy is to restrict the free international flow of information, particularly by curbing the power of the multinational news agencies. They would do this by requiring journalists to be licensed, by imposing international codes of journalistic ethics, by inhibiting advertising, and by extending government control over the press. Thus they would hope to limit outside influences and more effectively control the information coming in and out of their countries. The

Soviet Union is particularly enthusiastic in supporting any proposal designed to restrict press freedom.

It would be unfair to say that all developing countries see the "new world information order" in the same light as the more radical advocates. Many view the gaps in information and communications capacity as genuine imbalances which need to be corrected and can be alleviated if the developed nations will cooperate with them through economic assistance programs and by other means. One of these means could be the placement of computer terminals in USIA overseas libraries in developing countries.

The official U.S. government position with respect to the "new world information order" is that, while agreeing that an information and communications imbalance exists between the developed and the developing worlds, this problem can best be met through practical approaches. As the result of a U.S. initiative in late 1980, UNESCO established the International Program for the Development of Communications (IDPC). It is the hope of the United States, according to the U.S. Department of State, that the IDPC "will bring a greater degree of coordination to international development efforts and that it will raise the priority assigned to communications by national and international experts."[30] The State Department also points out that the United States has a fundamental commitment to the First Amendment of the U.S. Constitution as well as a free market economic philosophy, which causes the United States to reject any efforts designed to restrict the free flow of information, such as those advocated by some proponents of a "new world information order."

The United States backs up its position on this issue by referring to the Universal Declaration of Human Rights and UNESCO's own constitution, both of which protect the free flow of information. Article 19 of the universal declaration states: "Everyone has the right to freedom of opinion and expression; this right includes the freedom to hold opinions without interference and to seek, receive and impart information and ideas through any media and regardless of frontiers."

Finally, the United States supports the views expressed in the May 1981 Talloires Declaration made in France by 62 members of the private media from 21 developed and developing countries. Among other things the declaration rejects censorship and other press restrictions as a violation of an individual's right to be informed;

it sees the licensing of journalists as being inconsistent with a free press; and in a world of differing views and communications policies, it notes that an international code of ethics would be damaging to press freedom as well as impractical.

The U.S. position, therefore, is to work constructively with others to take advantage of the rapid technological changes which are occurring in the communications field, but not to do so in a way that restricts in any way the free flow of information. For example, because scientific and technological expertise is one of the most sought-after things that the United States can offer the developing world, the U.S. Agency for International Development is placing new emphasis on scientific and technological transfers in its foreign assistance programs. It has established a new Bureau for Science and Technology for this purpose.

At the January 1982 meeting of the International Program for Development of Communication (IDPC) at Acapulco, Mexico, the U.S. delegation urged that the program be used "to strengthen a pluralistic communication system in the world" encompassing both public and privately owned media. U.S. Representative William G. Harley stressed the importance of the private sector in communications. He noted that "in countries such as the U.S., they (private donors) are a source of greater communications resources and expertise than the government, so their potential for contributions should not be neglected."

IDPC's terms of reference call for projects to concentrate on infrastructure, equipment, and training. As Harley noted, "IDPC is intended to accord full attention to the whole range of information flows, channels and techniques of transmission, processing and presentation. Linking computers to satellites offers truly revolutionary opportunities, and there are other possibilities as well. These new technologies can create an abundance of new channels for more and diversified messages and broader participation in the communication process." He said that U.S. telecommunications companies are willing to help develop the communications capability of the third world, and that the U.S. government is working on ways to use their expertise in a coordinated international effort.

While the communications expertise of private industry will unquestionably be helpful—in fact, absolutely necessary—it is clear that despite the recognized growing importance of communications in development efforts, government funding of communications projects under AID to date has been relatively small when compared with other fields. The United States pledged $650,000 in the Acapulco IDPC meeting to be available during the two following years for the improvement of communications in developing countries. This, unfortunately, will not go very far to meet the communication development needs of the developing countries. And while $36 million worth of communications assistance has gone to developing countries in such fields as communication of educational, nutritional, and health information and rural telecommunications under AID programs in the post-World War II period, this must be measured against the billions of dollars of assistance provided in other fields. Of course, it has always been a basic tenet of U.S. economic assistance programs that the U.S. government alone can only provide an impetus for economic development. The contribution of private investment is essential for genuine economic development to take place. While more can and should be done by governments in communications development, the importance of the private sector is no less here than in other development fields.

The IDPDC Acapulco meeting approved 27 regional and intra-regional project proposals, of which only 14 received funding for 1982 from the IPDC's special fund. Among them were two regional news networks—the Pan-African News Agency, which received $100,000, and the Asia-Pacific News Network, which received a grant of $80,000. Decisions on other projects were scheduled for the IPDC meeting in Paris later that year.

The U.S. representative to the Acapulco IPDC meeting, while stressing that the primary governmental relationship of the United States with the development work of the IPDC would be through USAID programs, also noted that other U.S. agencies, "such as the International Communication Agency (now USIA) would also be involved." One way to do this is, of course, by installing computer terminals in USIA libraries in developing countries. Another way is to emphasize the training of third world journalists and other media personnel in the USIA Educational Exchanges, American Participant, and other traditional public diplomacy programs. Workshops and seminars with visiting U.S. communications specialists could receive a higher priority than they now do. To coordinate all of the activities involved in assuring that U.S. public diplomats make the fullest possible contribution to the goals we have been discussing, USIA established in its Associate Directorate for Programs a unit known as the International Communication Policy Staff, which is specifically concerned with all matters related to international communication policy. This unit performs coordination and liaison functions with governmental and private bodies concerned with these matters. Presumably this unit, along with USIA's Office of Systems Technology (including its Automatic Data Processing Division and the Planning and Development Staff), and the Office of Cultural Centers and Resources (with its Library Program Division) would be among those offices of USIA which would seem to have special interest in the proposal under discussion.

U.S. public diplomacy should move ahead with computer terminals in some of its overseas libraries out of our country's own self-interest, in the interest of the developing countries where they would be installed, and as a contribution to the genuine concerns of those who understandably decry the current imbalance of information and communication resources in the world today. The only question is, are we ready to take this bold new step?

NOTES

1. Blume, Wilbur T., *A Policy Position Proposal for International Audiovisual Communication* entitled "Beyond Persuasion: In Pursuit of Public Diplomacy," Appendix 19, Public Diplomacy and the Future, Hearings before Subcommittee on International Operations, Committee on International Operations, House of Representatives, June 8-24, 1977.

2. MacBride, Sean, ed., *Many Voices, One World*, Report by the International Commission for the Study of Communication Problems, Kogan Page, London/Unipub, N.Y. UNESCO, Paris. 1980. p. 219-21.

3. *Ibid.*, p. 254.

4. *Ibid.*, p. 256.

5. *Ibid.*

6. *Ibid.*, p 25.

7. *Ibid.*, p. 32.

8. *Ibid.* p. 258.

9. *Ibid.*, p 260.

10. *Ibid.*, p 261.

11. Blume, Wilbur T., op. cit., p. 663.

12. *European Libraries and Data Banks*, a study by the Resource and Operations Analysis Staff, U.S. Information Agency, Wash. D.C., Sept. 1976, p. iv.

13. *Ibid.*, p. 31.

14. Blume, Wilbur T., op. cit., p. 663

15. European Libraries & Data Banks, op. cit., pp. 61-64.

16. *Ibid.*, pp. 64-69.

17. *Ibid.*, p. 9.

18. *Ibid.*, p. 11.

19. *Ibid.*, p. 15.

20. *Ibid.*, p. 36.

21. From a publication by Gordon Pratt (ed.), *Data Bases in Europe*, London: Aslib, 1975 and a report by the Committee on House Administration, *Computer-Based Information Resources* for the United States House of Representatives, GPO, Washington, 1975.

22. *European Libraries and Data Banks*, op. cit. p. 14.

23. *Ibid.*, p. 45.

24. *Ibid.*, p 46.

25. MacBride, Sean, et. al, op. cit. p. 41.

26. *Ibid.*, p. 42

27. GIST, "New World Information Order," Bureau of Public Affairs, Dept. of State, Wash. D.C., Oct. 1981.

28. Wilbur Schramm and Erwin Atwood, *Circulation of News in the Third World—A Study of Asia*, The Chinese University Press, Hong Kong, 1981.

29. GIST, op. cit.

14

POSTSCRIPT

As the writing of this volume neared completion, I happened to mention to the cultural attaché of a European embassy in Islamabad, Pakistan, where he and I were serving our respective governments at the time, that the subject of my book was "public diplomacy." Although this, in American terms, is the profession in which he himself is engaged, he remarked, "Why, that sounds interesting, but what is public diplomacy?"

The above incident was a fitting reminder of how relatively new the term "public diplomacy," not to mention its practice, is. The growth of public diplomacy has coincided, more or less, with the communications revolution of the last half of the twentieth century. Though this phenomenon has now become an integral part of every modern nation state, the United States leads the world in its development.

Although all modern societies now practice public diplomacy, whether or not they call it that, public diplomacy is still at a pioneering stage. The varied views concerning it, the experimentation that nations conduct in seeking public diplomacy objectives, and the general lack of agreement as to what public diplomacy is or should be, all make the pioneering label a seemingly appropriate one. And while the U.S. government's efforts in public diplomacy have now gone on for decades (the coinage of the phrase "public diplomacy" being, of course, of more recent vintage), what U.S. public diplomats should be doing, how they should be doing it, and why, remain good subjects for sometimes heated discussions. What has been presented in the foregoing pages have been one public diplomat's personal views, based on a career of nearly 30 years of practicing, learning, and experimenting with public diplomacy.

The time if propitious for a thorough analysis of U.S. public diplomacy. No such analysis has been made, except in the context of congressional hearings or governmental reports, for more than a decade.[1] Thomas C. Sorensen's book, *The WORD WAR, The Story of American Propaganda*, published in 1968, was the last major attempt by a single authoritative individual to examine USIA in depth. And never has anyone with more than 25 years of experience in this field, and one who has shared in its development during those years, attempted as thorough an analysis as I have tried to present herewith, simply because the field is so relatively new.

It is my hope that this book will provide timely information on USIA and ICA that has not been available in any single convenient form in recent years; that it will serve to interest students and scholars as well as the general American public, in the work of America's public diplomacy agency; that it will bring to the attention of U.S. government leaders not directly involved in public diplomacy its importance in achieving U.S. foreign policy objectives, as well as its strengths and some of its weaknesses and limitations; that it will merit the attention of USIA's current leaders who are in a position to remedy some of the administrative and program defects that the author believes need remedying; and, finally, that it may encourage the implementation of the "bold new step" the author and others envisage as being capable of making a major contribution, in the mutual interest of the United States and the third world, to the social, economic, and political growth of developing nations.

It is my view that while not everyone agrees on how the term "public diplomacy" should be defined, there is general agreement that it involves information programs which support, in the case of USIA, U.S. foreign policy, and educational and cultural exchange programs designed to help foreigners better understand the United States and its people, hopefully leading to empathy, if not sympathy, with our policies. Thus U.S. public diplomats are "propagandists" in the original meaning of "propaganda," i.e., advocates of a cause—and as such they are "pioneers" in a relatively new profession.

Since shortly after the end of World War II, America's public diplomacy goals have been discussed and debated innumerable times, as have the means to carry out those goals and the manner. I have left for others a detailed presentation of the history of those debates, choosing to discuss, instead, the inner workings of USIA and how, in my view, its effectiveness can be sharpened. The directions America's public diplomacy efforts should take to best serve current and projected U.S. interests abroad have also been discussed, culminating in the presentation of arguments as to how and why greater utilization by USIA of modern communications technology, particularly the linking of computers with satellites, could contribute importantly to U.S. foreign policy objectives.

Having depicted support of U.S. foreign policy as the primary goal of U.S. public diplomacy, we have examined the importance of organizing USIA's global operations along geographic lines; the need for clear and succinct individual country objectives or Country Plans; and the desirability of providing greater attention to the special needs and importance of the developing world than has been practiced by USIA's leaders in the past, while being equally aware of the need for different approaches to the developed world and to Communist societies.

In examining the nitty-gritty of USIA's internal administration, we have discussed how the agency's personnel system works—and, sometimes, doesn't seem to work very well. In any event, no one can deny the importance of the men and women who carry out U.S. public diplomacy at home and abroad. Its successes, and its failures, rest with them. For this reason the role of labor-management relations within USIA was also examined, as was the position of women and minority employees, a subject which has always been of great concern in American thought and actions, though particularly in recent decades.

Good administrative practices in American society have always had much in common with democratic political concepts. In those organizations where the individual is held in highest regard, a basic tenet of all truly democratic societies, happier, more effective, and generally more efficient results can be expected. Yet large organizations, whether private corporations or government entities, and regardless of their goals, often tend to emphasize their "mission" at the expense, sometimes, of the individual. The establishment of unions and employee groups, the former recognized generally as a positive force by the U.S. Congress (in the U.S. Foreign Service Act of 1980, for example), helps offset this tendency, but unions are of limited power and influence. This view underlines my call for better internal administration of USIA in a number of varied aspects, all of which directly affect individual public diplomats, their families, and the support staff.

All human endeavors can be improved, but administrative and personnel practices in particular, because they so directly affect individuals, should be subject to constant review. When found wanting, administrative and personnel practices should be corrected as soon as possible. Among a number of USIA administrative and personnel services in need of special attention, the need for improving such mundane things as the handling of travel vouchers and the shipment of personal and household effects of foreign service personnel transferring from one post to another was discussed, as well as major changes and innovations such as the advantages of consolidating the headquarters of USIA in as few buildings as possible. However, no two factors in any organization, regardless of size, are as vital to the successful accomplishment of its overall mission as administrative and personnel matters. Within USIA, the need to upgrade the quality of these services clearly exists.

In the chapters on "the tools of the trade," we examined the traditional tools or vehicles used by public diplomats in pursuing their objectives. The wireless file is seen as one of the most useful tools of U.S. public diplomats. The agency's various magazine and other publications are described, as are the roles of radio, film television and videotape programs. The various educational and cultural exchange activities of USIA, including traditional libraries and reading rooms, the Fulbright Program, book programs of various types, and the presentation of U.S. performing artists are all reviewed. Some of these activities are questioned, such as the Latin American Book Translation Program, which began in a different era when books were much more difficult to obtain in Latin America than they are today. The question is raised as to whether such programs continue to be useful in the Age of Information. Funds now expended on outdated or outmoded programs could be used to initiate programs utilizing more modern communication vehicles—television programs and computer terminals are two examples. Also, a hard practical look at the Distribution and Record System (DRS) leads to the conclusion that while the system is useful, and in fact, essential in some form in order to focus USIA's limited resources on the most important audiences, past attempts to provide accountability through DRS was a useless, time-consuming exercise that should have been abolished long ago as it lacks both purpose and validity.

The Voice of America, the radio section of USIA, is unique in many ways, as was pointed out in the chapter on the VOA. It is older and much better known than its parent agency, is the most expensive single public diplomacy activity of USIA, and has the highest number of employees of all of the agency's varied activities. Putting VOA in perspective, although it has been replete with problems of various kinds in the past—many being, of course, administrative and personnel problems—it has a well-earned reputation for reliability and credibility. It is like a brother to the BBC, and so feared by the Soviet Union that the Russians spend more in jamming the Voice, along with the BBC, than is spent by the VOA in broadcasting its programs to the Soviet Union and Eastern European countries. The necessity of doing nothing that would lessen VOA's credibility, which USIA Director Charles Wick says is "of paramount importance," is the main thrust of my comments on the VOA.

The growing importance of public diplomacy in the modern world is evidenced by the growing budgets the Western democracies and Japan devote to their public diplomacy efforts. However, the most striking fact to emerge from even a brief review of what other nations are doing is the lengths to which the Soviet Union has apparently gone, and is still going, in its campaigns of misinformation, "disinformation," and other "active measures." Whereas Western democratic thought contends that the means is as important as the end, such is not the case for the Soviet Union. The Russians operate their "public diplomacy" by using any and all means, including forgeries, lies, half-truths, and bribery, so long as Soviet information objectives are advanced. This places Soviet information efforts in a framework totally alien to that of the United States and its Western allies.

Finally, in our examination of public diplomacy as practiced in the Computer Age in which we now live, sparked by a revolution in communications technology that has been equated by some as being as significant as the introduction of writing, we can only conclude that we are, indeed, in a new age, the ramifications of which we are only now beginning to understand and that have not yet been clearly defined—as miniaturization proceeds apace, and as the transit time for information to go from one part of the globe to another diminishes at phenomenal rates. What appears at this time to be certain, however, is that the information gap between the *developed* and the *developing* world is increasing, just as the economic gap continues to increase. Furthermore, it is becoming increasingly clear that information is today a key element for economic and social progress. The opportunity exists for U.S. public diplomats to make a major contribution to the social and economic growth of developing countries by placing, in USIA overseas libraries in such countries, computer terminals linked by satellite to U.S. data banks. This would provide a means for USIA to serve the interests of developing nations while serving our own national interests. For those who seek social, economic, and political development and want to utilize social, scientific, economic, and technological information that exists in abundance in the United States, an effective, practical means to transfer such information from the developed to the developing world would thus be made available. How different this mutually-beneficial purpose is from the motives that lead the Soviet Union and its vassal states, like Cuba, to pursue their version of "public diplomacy" is clear. Tuning in on Radio Moscow, Radio Havana, "Radio Peace and Progress," or the Soviet Union's "National Voice of Iran" is all that is necessary to understand the motives and methods of Soviet Communism.

Providing a linkage between information needs of developing countries and the rapid and efficient accessibility of information stored in U.S. data banks would find ready acceptance in most of the countries that would benefit from this service. At the same time, the increase in substantive knowledge about the United States and its policies, which would also occur, coincides with traditional public diplomacy objectives. Eventually, the display of U.S. technological capabilities in the communication field could be expected to stimulate the growth of similar communication ties between the developing countries and the United States, since USIA's example, sooner or later, would surely be followed by other host country entities, to the mutual benefit of both nations.

One of the amazing things about this innovation is that it would not necessitate any great increase in finances or manpower, only the redirection of some of USIA's current resources with, perhaps, small budget and personnel increases. To initiate a new emphasis within USIA on how communications technology and methodology can stimulate political and economic growth, to the advantage of U.S. global objectives, it is only necessary for this idea to be accepted and implemented by USIA leaders.

When one considers the extent of our foreign aid programs, U.S. private and public humanitarian efforts overseas, and our investment in the Peace Corps—among other indicators of U.S. interest in, and concern with, problems affecting the third world— it is indeed surprising that America's public diplomacy organization has virtually been ignored as an important resource for U.S. assistance to third world economic development objectives. Of course, USIA's ongoing informational, educational, and cultural activities have contributed somewhat to social, economic, and political development in many developing countries. But, for a variety of reasons, earlier USIA administrations have not seen fit to engage the agency's resources in furthering specific economic development goals. Most have taken the view that economic development is "AID's responsibility."

Concern was once expressed by some USIA officials that AID was stepping on USIA's toes by getting into television. Later "educational TV" was found to be an acceptable pursuit for both AID and the Peace Corps, but *not* for USIA or ICA, and at one stage USIA emphasized the importance of "national development," but without consciously contributing to that development. None of this is similar to what I and a small but growing number of advocates argue, to wit, that communications is a key element of social/economic/political growth and USIA resources could be used to foster such growth. In so doing it would not only serve U.S. and third world interests in a highly acceptable way, but could provide a positive answer—a concrete contribution, to those who advocate a "new world information order" because of the current information imbalance between the developed and the developing countries.

SPORTS IN PUBLIC DIPLOMACY

Despite the detailed analyses of traditional public diplomacy activities presented earlier, the broad scope and complexities of these activities, and the varied purposes they seek to serve are such that there are, undoubtedly, some aspects of USIA that I glossed over or failed to mention. One of these is the role of sports in public diplomacy.

Sports, it has often been noted, is a "universal language." It enables individuals of different cultures to meet together in an activity common to both, and by so doing, to communicate with each other. Where USIA is in a position to provide grants or facilitative assistance for American coaches to train teams in developing countries, particularly in sports in which Americans generally excel, as in basketball, for example, considerable goodwill can be generated by such assistance. Often sports leaders and active sports enthusiasts are political or social leaders; thus communication and rapport established through a common interest in sports can be expanded to other fields.

Those who urge a greater role for sports in U.S. public diplomacy programs sometimes argue that by creating "goodwill," and by serving as an entrée to host country leaders in other fields, sports programming belongs in the tool kit of public diplomats. I do not disagree with the above observation, but practitioners of public diplomacy must ask themselves, when it comes to including sports among their activities, the same question which should be asked regarding every USIA activity to be undertaken at a specific time in a specific place. Does it further the objectives developed and crystalized in the Country Plan? "Goodwill" alone does not justify the use of limited resources that may be needed elsewhere and for other activities, unless, as happens on occasion, the local environment is such that seeking "goodwill" is a priority goal. As for gaining a communication entrée, if this too is a priority, sports could be high on the list of public diplomacy pursuits in a particular country. The generalization that "sports programming is good public diplomacy because it creates goodwill" is not sufficient reason to include sports programming in all countries at all times. Like any other public diplomacy effort or activity, unless it has a specific focus it is best left to others who do not have, as their primary mission, the support of U.S. foreign policy.

It is well recognized that the Soviet Union and Communist countries generally are especially active in using sports as a public diplomacy vehicle. Part of the reason for this is that, in most Western countries at least, this is one of the few public diplomacy options open to them.[2] Their ability to utilize press, radio, and television in open societies is extremely limited—their product simply doesn't sell very well as far as the major media in most non-Communist countries are concerned. In societies where U.S. public diplomats find the local information media unreceptive to USIS materials, they also turn more toward sports and such cultural activities as performing artists. In short, sports programming, like most other activities conducted by USIA, can be a valuable vehicle of public diplomacy at certain times in certain places. The "ping-pong diplomacy" which led to the normalization of diplomatic relations between the People's Republic of China and the United States was an example of a sports event serving a major political purpose at a unique moment in U.S.-Chinese relations. It is also a unique example of a sports event serving a major political purpose at a unique moment in U.S.-Chinese relations. It is also a unique example of the use of sports in public diplomacy.

THEMES CHOSEN FOR PUBLIC DIPLOMACY TREATMENT CAN SOMETIMES BE UNIQUE

Since public diplomacy, by its nature, covers so many fields, running the full gamut of political, economic, military, sociological, psychological, educational, etc. activities of a people—the American people in the case of U.S. public diplomacy—one must always make choices. Which of many possibilities is best suited to achieve a particular goal or purpose? Which article? Which book? Which exhibit? Which speaker? Which magazine? Which film? Which video-tape?

The theme, the audience, and the manner of delivery are the three major factors which must be considered in conducting public diplomacy. At times there will be a theme which, while considered important to foreign policy objectives, is so unique that it requires a special effort on the part of its advocates to convince both Washington bureaucrats, and public diplomats abroad, of the value and necessity of developing programs involving that theme. One such theme, first introduced about 20 years ago, was "family planning."

When President Lyndon B. Johnson first announced that U.S. economic assistance programs overseas would include family planning if requested by a recipient country, reluctance to engage public diplomacy efforts in this theme was shown by many USIA officials, both in Washington and abroad. Yet once this decision had been made by the highest U.S. government authority, the subject needed substantial public diplomacy treatment, particularly in view of its controversial nature. As official U.S. policy, it should have received the immediate, active support of the U.S. government's public diplomacy agency in appropriate ways. An example of an appropriate approach might be the distribution of feature articles concerning the social and economic problems caused by the "population explosion." On the other hand, USIA-sponsorship of a seminar on family planning in a country where this subject was extremely sensitive obviously would have been inappropriate. In any event, USIA lagged behind other agencies of the U.S. government in supporting this issue when it first arose, since attitudes among some key officials were slow to change even after the president enunciated the U.S. government's new population policy. Also contributing to a reluctance to move forward faster with the family planning theme was the lack of agreement within USIA as to what constituted appropriate programs in support of a subject which, at the time, was much more controversial than it is today.

Also meeting resistance within USIA in earlier days, as far as public diplomacy support was concerned, was the U.S. government's antinarcotics effort. In the late 1960s and early 1970s, as an epidemic of illicit drug use swept the United States and illegal drug trafficking not only became big business for criminal elements, but caused major social problems in hundreds of American towns and cities, the federal government created new organizations and institutions to combat the growing drug menace. The Drug Enforcement Agency (DEA) was established, a special office on drug abuse prevention was set up in the White House to demonstrate the federal government's interest and concern with this problem and to coordinate the complex prevention, enforcement, educational and rehabilitation activities required in dealing with illicit drug trafficking and use, and many other groups and institutions took up the battle cry against narcotics. Within USIA there were those, at the time, who argued that "illicit drug trafficking" was the concern of the DEA and, therefore, USIA should not become more than marginally involved. This kind of reasoning, unfortunately, ignored the fact that once antinarcotics efforts had become a priority policy of the U.S. government involving other nations, and thus a foreign policy issue, it should have received appropriate support by the government's public diplomacy agency. Any policy, be it political, economic, or special in nature (such as family planning, antinarcotics, or antiterrorism, for example), is more apt to be successful it it is supported by public diplomacy. However, the history of the public diplomacy role in support of the U.S. government's antinarcotics efforts is an example of how it sometimes can take nearly a decade to develop full public diplomacy backing when a nontraditional subject, important to U.S. foreign policy though it may be, does not receive priority attention from USIA's front office.

In 1972 Latin America had become one of the major routes for illicit drugs entering the United States. As USIA's policy officer for Latin America, I argued, with relatively few others among our colleagues, that we needed a greater public diplomacy role in combatting the international drug problem that was so adversely affecting U.S. society. Most Latin Americans, at the time, were convinced that the drug problem was primarily a problem for the United States, despite the fact that Latin America was a major source of drugs and a number of countries in that area had become major transit points for heroin and cocaine enroute to U.S. markets. However, as most of these nations learned to their regret, societies where illicit drug trafficking is conducted soon become drug-ridden themselves. The message that U.S. public diplomacy carried, though it could have carried it much more effectively if narcotics had received a higher priority within USIA than was the case, was that cooperation between the United States and Latin American governments in antinarcotics efforts was necessary if both were to rid themselves, or at least reduce the effects of, the scourge of illicit drug use.

Aside from printed materials that provided basic information about illicit drug use and trafficking, there was a great need for audio-visual materials covering both of these subjects as well as other dimensions of the narcotics problem such as prevention, education, and rehabilitation. Although some videotaped programs on this theme were developed, only one motion picture was produced by USIA on narcotics, following a bureaucratic struggle within the agency among those who wanted to produce a narcotics film and those who argued that there was no need to use agency resources for such an esoteric subject. *The Trip*, mentioned briefly in the chapter on information activities, was finally produced by USIA on location in Colombia in cooperation with the Colombian government. The Colombian government officials who supported this project deserve great credit for their interest, courage, and foresight in cooperating in such a venture. The film is a case study of illicit drug use and trafficking in one Latin American nation and of how the local government faced this problem. As noted earlier, it was widely used throughout Spanish-speaking Latin America, but at this writing, nearly a decade after *The Trip* was first produced, nothing comparable has been developed by USIA, although in early 1983 a new USIA film on this subject was under production. (The new film is expected to be ready for distribution late in 1984.)

Among those who recognize the importance of the public diplomacy role in combatting the international narcotics problem (a problem which, if anything, has grown in size and scope during the past decade), the comments made by USIA Director Charles Z. Wick on April 22, 1982, when speaking to the Foreign Affairs Committee of the U.S. House of Representatives, are highly welcomed. On that occasion he told members of the U.S. House Foreign Affairs Committee that USIA will cooperate with other U.S. agencies and departments in implementing "a long-range, coordinated effort to address the related problems of drug production, drug trafficking and drug use." He appeared with two other officials of the Reagan administration, Carlton Turner, director of the White House Drug Abuse Policy Office, and U.S. Associate Attorney General Rudolph Giuliani, all of whom testified at the final session of three days of hearings on international narcotics control held by the Foreign Affairs Committee.

Emphasizing that the international narcotics problem is "critically important to the United States" and that it "poses a complex and very sensitive issue in international relations, requiring creative planning and close coordination of all activities undertaken," Mr. Wick said that "information can only be a very small piece in the very complex puzzle the international narcotics problem creates." He concluded by noting that "The principal means for tackling the problem rests with eradication, interdiction and law enforcement. . . . Information serves as a support and an occasional catalyst." This public recognition of the role of public diplomacy in helping to combat illegal drug trafficking, as stated by the director of USIA, is an historic first that bodes well for the possibility of more effective antinarcotics programming by USIA than at any time in the recent past. In fact, encouraged by the priority given antinarcotics by President Reagan, USIA Director Wick has brought America's public diplomacy agency further along in pursuing this theme than at any time in the agency's history. With such support, narcotics has become a global theme for USIA planning in fiscal year 1984, and the first antinarcotics film in more than a decade is now under production, as noted above.

THE ROLE OF RESEARCH IN PUBLIC DIPLOMACY

One activity that was not covered in the preceding chapters, but which permeates all USIA activities and is of such import that it warrants more than just a passing reference, is that of USIA's Office of Research. Just as research and development is of cardinal importance to producers of technology, proper, timely social science research is of cardinal importance to the producers of public diplomacy programs. Since USIA operations take place in many different cultures, concern many different subjects, and utilize many different methods of transmission, the more public diplomats know about their audiences, the attitudes of these audiences, what messages are received by them and how, and similar information, the greater is the possibility that USIA programs will achieve what they are intended to achieve. Much of this type of information can be obtained by utilizing modern methods of social science research.

USIA's Office of Research is concerned primarily with two types of research: (1) surveys of foreign public opinion designed to indicate the attitudes and opinions of selected groups toward major U.S. policy questions and other issues of importance to the United States, and (2) studies that demonstrate whether or not agency programs are effective.

When ICA was first established in 1978, Director John Reinhardt, working with an austerity budget, decided to eliminate studies designed to determine program effectiveness. This was a decision that many regretted because, it was argued, if ICA did not check on the effectiveness of its own programs, who would? The answer, of course, is no-one, at least not anyone with the knowledge and interest held by the organization conducting these programs and activities. The one exception to the Reinhardt regime's rule that abolished research on program effectiveness was VOA listenership studies, which were continued.

The Office of Research, not unlike other units of USIA, has undergone a series of reorganizations in recent years. Most of these have entailed swings from emphasizing geographic areas to emphasizing functional areas. The latest swing has been a return to geographic area prominence. Thus there are four branches in the Office of Research, each headed by a branch chief who is generally a foreign service officer, as follows: (1) European Research (made up of a USSR and Eastern Europe unit and a West Europe/Canada unit); (2) East Asia and Pacific Research; (3) Africa, Near East, and South Asia Research; and (4) American Republics Research. The staff of each of these branches consists of professional social science researchers who conduct research programs using the latest social science research techniques available. Ideally, all of the members of the branch, but particularly the branch chief, have had first-hand experience in the geographic area involved. The branch chiefs report to the director of the Office of Research and his deputy. Senior research advisors and a technical support manager who supervises computer operations complete the staff.

Two units that are supervised by the director of the office of research but operate separately, are the agency library, a highly useful resource for Washington and overseas officials, and the media reaction staff. This latter unit is especially interesting, since it performs a very special function for USIA and other Foreign Service agencies in Washington.

Daily on working days, and sometimes more frequently when there is a major crisis in global affairs, the media reaction staff prepares analyses of how the media throughout the world treat major news stories and critical foreign policy issues of importance to the United States government. All major USIA posts overseas scan the local daily newspapers and the electronic media and report on how local editors and commentators view events and situations of foreign policy significance. These reports, cabled to Washington by USIS posts from throughout the world, are assimulated by the media reaction staff, at times along geographic lines, i.e., what Latin American concerns are that day, and at times by major themes, i.e., what the world's leading newspapers and commentators are saying with regard to nuclear proliferation, for example (or any other subject of interest to Washington at the time). Reduced and simplified, brief analyses are prepared and sent to the director and other top USIA officials, the White House, the Department of State, and a number of other interested government agencies, thus enabling U.S. policymakers to get a quick view of foreign perceptions on key issues of the day. This service has been praised by U.S. government users outside of USIA who need to know the public reactions of other nations toward major U.S. policies as quickly as possible. Though only one of many sources available to judge foreign opinion, USIA's Media Reaction Reports have, apparently, proven to be highly useful.

The United States Advisory Commission on Public Diplomacy, in its first report on ICA which was issued in 1980, cited the Office of Research, "with its focus on foreign public opinion," as being "critically important to all of the Agency's activities." The Commission's report recommended that because of its importance, the Office of Research "should be given independent organizational status, additional funds, and assigned the responsibility for evaluating program effectiveness." (At the time program effectiveness was not being evaluated.)[3] The report also observed that "Many Agency officers are not sufficiently aware of research as an indispensable policy and program guide. There are too many instances in which research is not utilized because of ignorance of social science capabilities."

An interesting sidelight with respect to the use of the term "public diplomacy" is that when the International Communication Agency was created on April 1, 1978, the U.S. Advisory Commission on International Communication, Cultural, and Educational Affairs was also established with a mandate to serve as a public trustee for the new agency. But in October 1979 the Congress changed the name of the commission to "The United States Advisory Commission on Public Diplomacy." In assessing the policies and programs of the agency, the commission reports to the president, the Congress, the secretary of state and (now) the director of USIA.

Finally, one does not have to go far to recognize the value of Office of Research products. Their reports were particularly useful in developing Chapter 11, "What Other Nations Are Doing." The recommendations made by the Advisory Commission in 1980 have not yet been fully implemented, due primarily, one suspects, to budgetary considerations. But evaluating the effectiveness of USIA programs is once again generally acknowledged as an important task of USIA's Office of Research. Much more could be done in this field if and when more funds were to become available for research activities.

THE GAO SEES SOME ICA (USIA) PROGRAMS "MORE USEFUL THAN OTHERS."

In February 1982, the U.S. General Accounting Office published a report to ICA's director which was entitled, *U.S. International*

Communication Agency's Overseas Programs: Some More Useful Than Others.[4] At the time that this is being written this report was the most recent of a long list of U.S. government analyses of U.S. public diplomacy efforts. Its conclusions, like those of earlier studies, point up once again that public diplomacy is not a science—what public diplomacy is, and how it should be conducted, is a matter of opinion.

The February 1982 report of the GAO questions the proposition that each country needs the same set of communications methods. To promote economy and efficiency of operations, the report recommends changes in the programming methods used in the overseas missions as well as improvements in the support provided to the missions by ICA (USIA) Washington headquarters. It also recommends greater attention to the running of libraries and cultural centers abroad.

Preliminary visits to posts in Mexico and Canada were made by the authors of the report, and selected visits to 18 other countries where Public Affairs Officers and others were interviewed. To assess the extent of Washington headquarters management of the overseas missions, they interviewed USICA officials in the geographic area offices and relevant Country desks, in the educational and cultural affairs directorate, and in the Office of Systems Technology. In addition they reviewed pertinent documents, including internal memoranda from the director, operations manuals, computer printouts of all USICA programming, staffing patterns, and cables to the field. They discussed the role of USICA overseas with the acting staff director of the U.S. Advisory Commission on Public Diplomacy, and, finally, they made onsite inspections of USICA libraries, reference centers, and binational cultural centers, and attended USICA-sponsored events.

I will not review here all of their recommendations, but it is obvious from the above that they became well-versed in the agency's programs and problems. And yet, once again there is room for discussion, perhaps even disagreement, as to what the U.S. government's public diplomacy organization should be doing, and how. For example, the report notes:

> Today, USICA has a role to serve in four specific areas: (1) explaining official U.S. Government policies to people overseas; (2) portraying American society as accurately and completely as possible to the

people of other nations; (3) advising and informing the President and the U.S. Government adequately as to foreign public opinion and foreign cultures; and (4) assisting to develop American understanding of other nations.

The above is the latest interpretation of USIA's role. It is one with which I do not fully concur, for it is my thesis that USIA must do more than simply "explain" official U.S. government policies, unless presenting the rationale for those policies and urging their acceptance, when feasible, is encompassed in the word "explain." I also have a problem with "(4) assisting to develop American understanding of other nations," if, by this, is meant the carrying out of former President Jimmy Carter's Second Mandate. This Second Mandate is to tell Americans about other countries and cultures. This was, for all practical purposes, dropped by the Reagan administration, an action applauded by many public diplomats, given the impossibility of effectively pursuing this objective with USIA's limited resources and its many other priorities. The GAO report itself questions this "mandate" and recommends that USIA should "establish a policy for the overseas mission concerning the role to be played, *if any*, in carrying out the 'Second Mandate.'" (Italics my own.)

Told at each post visited that "direct and substantive personal contact was the mission's most important activity," the authors of the report expressed the same doubts that I myself have voiced for many years about USIA's and ICA's almost overwhelming emphasis on this aspect of public diplomacy.

"In our view," they note, "personal contact activities need to be examined on a country-to-country basis to determine if the resource investment is worthwhile. We believe personal contact could serve as an important communication vehicle in some countries, less so in others. Unfortunately, it is expensive in all countries." In some of the countries they visited they found that the investment in personal contact "bore little resemblance to U.S. host country communication needs."

Once again, differences in views among those charged with carrying out U.S. public diplomacy was evidenced in the following observation:

"In our discussions with some 20 Public Affairs Officers and their American staffs in the overseas missions," they noted, "we sought an understanding of the role of personal contact. We asked, 'What is personal contact?' As one Public Affairs Officer observed, 'ask a dozen USICA officers this question, and you are apt to get a dozen (different) answers.' Needless to say we did receive an abundance of different responses."

On the subject of libraries, the report notes that between 1946 and 1979, libraries and/or reading rooms were set up in 426 foreign cities. Of these, 129 (119 American centers and ten reading rooms) were in operation in fiscal year 1981. The rest, about 68 percent, were discontinued for essentially budgetary reasons. In addition, the number of American professional librarians working for ICA (USIA) dropped from a high of 53 in the mid-1950s to 18 in 1979. Their recommendation: "Examine the usefulness of overseas libraries as they are currently maintained and eliminate those that are no longer useful." This is in line with my recommendation that a hard look should be made at libraries in *developed countries* in particular, where many other sources of information are available, whereas libraries in *developing countries* have the potential of becoming more important than ever if computer terminals are installed in them, as suggested in Chapter 13. As for libraries in Communist countries, their special role remains.

In discussing cultural programming, the GAO report points out that "some events are largely superfluous and duplicative of those already available in-country." They recommend elimination of such "redundant USICA cultural program efforts within a given host country."

Regarding binational centers, they state that USICA missions often have "an ambiguous relationship to these private, tax-exampt institutions which teach English and organize bilateral cultural activities." They note further that "binational cultural centers are suffering from what must be called 'benign neglect.' USICA does not have a stated Center policy for guiding the overseas missions." Their recommendation is that "the Director (should) develop a policy outlining the responsibilities of the overseas missions toward the Centers." This is something that many senior U.S. public diplomats have sought for years, particularly in those countries where binational cultural centers are located. Policy papers designed to clarify the relationship between USIA posts and the centers were drafted from time to time at Washington headquarters, but there was never, apparently, enough agreement among the top brass in recent years to issue a definitive policy statement on this subject.

In discussing the Distribution and Record System (DRS), the report notes that the DRS is "off to a poor start." This is an understatement. While observing that failure to meet delivery dates for computerized equipment contributes to the problem, the real difficulty with DRS, as I noted earlier, is that it is based on some false premises and it will never, as currently envisaged, obtain the full cooperation of other U.S. government officials, let alone all USIA officers. Thus the report's recommendation to "contact the Department of State and the Agency for International Development to solicit their cooperation in ensuring the recording of personal contacts in DRS" is unrealistic. It is whistling in the wind.

Finally, I note here, though it is listed as the first recommendation of the report, that ICA "reassess the need for each mission to have all of the various communication methods, and direct overseas missions to discontinue programming of those methods they believe irrelevant to their needs or even significantly less useful than others." Old ways die slowly. Some USIS posts must have been observed maintaining "across the board" activities although logic dictates that this recommendation should have been a part of standard operating procedure at all posts for many years. In fact, in the early 1960s—20 years ago—USIA instructed its overseas posts to review all of their ongoing programs with the same objective in mind and the same philosophical bent implied in the GAO's first conclusion, i.e., that not all types of programs should be undertaken in all countries, and that it is better to concentrate on a few program vehicles of proven effectiveness than to utilize all avenues and techniques simply because they may be available. One is reminded of the preacher who, when asked how he communicates with his congregation, remarked: "First I tells them what I want to tell them, then I tells them what I told them, and then I tells them again, and, sometimes, some of them gets the message." Twenty years later some posts in the U.S. government's "communications agency" may not have gotten the message.

By 1983, the Reagan administration had launched three new public diplomacy initiatives that initially created some confusion in the press and, therefore, in the public, regarding the purposes and manner in which these new initiatives were to be implemented. Despite this confusion, they clearly demonstrated the importance given public diplomacy by the Reagan administration, first, because, while not necessarily new ideas, their manner of implementation is innovative, and, secondly, because White House interest and control of these new initiatives was apparent.

The first initiative was the appointment by President Reagan of U.S. Ambassador to Ireland Peter Dailey to chair an interagency working group on strengthening U.S. communications with European publics on nuclear weapons and related issues. Creation of this working group was said to have been the result of a suggestion by U.S. Secretary of State George Schultz.

The second initiative, announced in February 1983, was the establishment by the president of a new Special Planning Group to plan, direct, coordinate, and monitor the U.S. government's policies and activities in the area of public diplomacy. This group is chaired by the assistant to the president for national security affairs and has as its members the secretary of state, the secretary of defense, the director of USIA and the administrator of the Agency for International Development (AID). Other U.S. government agencies participate on an ad hoc basis at the invitation of the chairman. At the same time four interagency standing committees were established who report to the Special Planning Group:

> The International Information Committee, chaired by a senior representative of USIA, is responsible for planning, coordinating and implementing international information activities.
>
> The International Political Committee is chaired by a senior representative of the Department of State and is responsible for planning, coordinating, and implementing international activities in support of U.S. policies and interests.
>
> The International Broadcasting Committee is chaired by the Deputy assistant to the president for national security affairs and is responsible for the planning and coordination of international broadcasting activities sponsored by the U.S. Government.
>
> The fourth committee is the Public Affairs Committee. Cochaired by the assistant to the president for communications and the deputy assistant to the president for national security affairs, this group is responsible for planning and coordinating activities relating to foreign policy and national security issues.[5]

The third public diplomacy initiative of the Reagan administration is possibly the most important and one which has drawn fire from the Soviet Union. Designed to increase support for democracy and democratic institutions, it was first mentioned in the president's June 1982 speech to the British Parliament in which he developed two principal themes: The United States should make a major effort to help "foster the infrastructure of democracy" around the world, and the United States should engage more vigorously in a peaceful "competition of ideas and values" with the Soviet Union. As explained later by the Department of State spokesman, "The President thus laid the groundwork of a long-term, positive program by the United States to advocate the principles of democracy, support those people and institutions committed to democratic development, build and reinforce bonds based on shared values between peoples and nations, and combat through the active interchange of ideas and vigorous democratic institutions the spread of totalitarianism."

The Reagan administration proposed a $65 million budget for Fiscal Year 1984 to carry out this program, and said it would focus on five areas: (1) leadership training, (2) education, (3) strengthening the institutions of democracy, (4) conveying ideas and information, and (5) development of personal and institutional ties.

Received with some skepticism by some members of Congress and others, the *New York Times* reported when the program was first announced that there was a bureaucratic struggle in Washington "to get a piece of the project" as well as concern that the CIA might become involved, though Robert C. McFarlane, deputy director of the National Security Council at the time was quoted as saying that participation of the CIA (which was, apparently, at first considered) was dropped from the program.[6] The program's biggest critic, however, was the Soviet Union. *Pravda*, for example, attacked it as being "psychopolitical warfare" and "ideological sabotage" against "real socialism." Other Soviet media and commentaries labelled the new program as "crude interference in the affairs of other countries" and called it "a serious threat to universal peace." Commenting on the Soviet Union's concern about "Project Democracy," Secretary of State George Schultz, in hearings before the House Foreign Affairs Subcommittee on International Operations February 23, 1983, remarked: "It has been attacked by Tass as one more link in what they call 'a chair of ideological subversive measures' that is being undertaken against the Socialist camp. Tass says that these activities flout 'the recognized norms of relations among nations.' Imagine the nerve of us, talking about democracy and human rights and things like that."

Democracy and human rights, and things like that, are what USIA has been talking about for decades, and will continue to talk about, with or without Project Democracy. However, since USIA is the key U.S. government agency in this new endeavor, perhaps we will now see a renewed emphasis on democratic principles in USIA programming. This should be welcomed if for no other reason than to offset what some consider to be an overemphasis recently on anti-Communist materials in USIA programming generally, and in VOA programs in particular. The concern expressed here is the danger of boredom, not disagreement with anti-Communist philosophy.

With these relatively brief comments on the latest analysis of America's public diplomacy efforts by the General Accounting Office and the latest public diplomacy initiatives, I bring my own analysis to a close. For those who have stayed the course, whether you see America's public diplomats as propagandists or pioneers, or a little bit of both, I think you will agree that what they do in the future, and how they do it, will remain debatable, with differing views prevailing at different times. For this reason, the profession of public diplomacy is always challenging, and seldom, if ever, dull.

NOTES

1. In 1970, *The Case for Reappraisal of U.S. Overseas Information Programs* was published by Praeger in its Special Studies in International Politics and Special Affairs. Edited by Edward L. Barnays and Burnet Hershey, it incorporated Congressman Dante Fascell's hearings report, "The Future of Public Diplomacy."

2 This also helps account for their heavy reliance on short-wave radio.

3. The 1982 report of The United States Advisory Commission on Public Diplomacy again recommended that the staff and budget of USIA's Office of Research be increased "to provide the research capability required for national security and foreign policy needs." In introducing the report, the Commission's Chairman, Leonard L. Silverstein, wrote: "We are pleased to note that Congress has approved additional funds for the Agency for FY 1981, and we hope that the Administration's request for FY 1983 will be approved. We regret, however, that the resources provided for research were not increased but instead have been reduced."

4. U.S. General Accounting Office, Report to the Director, U.S. International Communication Agency, *U.S. International Communication Agency's Overseas Programs; Some More Useful Than Others*, ID-82-1, Feb. 11, 1982.

5. U.S. Dept. of State statement released Feb. 7, 1983.

6. Gertha, Jeff, "Problems in Promoting Democracy," *New York Times*, Feb. 4, 1983.

SELECTED BIBLIOGRAPHY

Adelman, Kenneth L. 1981. Speaking of America; Public Diplomacy in Our Time. *Foreign Affairs*. Spring. Vol. 59, No. 4, p. 921.

Branscomb, Lewis M. 1979. "Information: The Ultimate Frontier," *Science*. Vol. 203. January 12. p. 143.

Browne, Donald R. 1982. *International Radio Broadcasting: The Limits of the Limitless Medium*. New York. Praeger.

Califano, Joseph A., Jr. 1981. "Getting Fired by Jimmy Carter," excerpts from his book, *Governing America: An Insider's Report from the White House and Cabinet*. *The Washington Post*. May 24. p. C-5.

Casey-Stahmer, Anna. 1979. "The Era of Experimental Satellites: Where to Go from Here," *Journal of Communication*. Autumn.

Chaze, William L. & Kennedy, Harold. 1982. "The Great Propaganda War," *U.S. News & World Report*. January 11. pp. 27-32.

Fenyvesi, Charles. 1981. "I Hear America Mumbling, Why the Voice of America Won't Win Any Emmys This Year," *The Washington Post Magazine*. July 19. p. 22.

Fenyvesi, Charles. 1981. "Voice of America Is Unhappy and Uncertain of Its Mission," *Current*. August 30. pp. 6-7.

Frost, J.M., Ed. 37th Edition. *World Radio/TV Handbook*. *Billboard*.

Gardner, Richard N. 1983. "Selling America in the Marketplace of Ideas," *The New York Times Magazine*. March 20.

Gertha, Jeff. 1983. "Problems in Promoting Democracy," *The New York Times*. February 4.

Greider, William. 1981. "The Education of David Stockman," *The Atlantic*. December. p. 47.

Hansen, Allen C. 1977. *Whither USIA? Exploring New Directions for USIA Policy*. Mimeo.

243

"Improving the Quality of America's Voice." 1983. *Nation's Business.* April. pp. 64-65.

Lapham, Lewis H. 1982. "The Propaganda Man," *Parade.* July 4.

MacBride, Sean, et al. 1980. *Many Voices, One World.* Report by the International Commission for the Study of Communication Problems. New York. Unpubl.

"No More Pencils, No More Books, Just Bring a Personal Computer." 1982. *International Herald Tribune.* November 3. p. 2.

Perzanowski, Christopher. 1983. "Russia's Radio Putch," *National Review.* April 15. pp. 439-40.

Pratt, Gordon, 1975. *Data Bases in Europe.* London, Aslib.

Pye, Lucian W., 1963. *Communication and Political Development.* Princeton Univ. Press.

Reid, T. R. 1981. "Affirmative Action Is Under a New Gun," *The Washington Post.* March 27.

Roth, Lois. 1981. *Public Diplomacy and the Past.* – Studies of U.S. Information and Cultural Programs. (1952-1975). U.S. Dept. of State, Foreign Service Institute.

Schramm, Wilbur & Atwood, Erwin. 1981. *Circulation of News in the Third World–A Study of Asia.* Hong Kong. The Chinese University Press.

"Sony's Pocket-Size Television." 1982. *Newsweek.* February 8.

Sweet, William. 1981. *America's Information Effort Abroad.* (Editorial Research Reports.) Vol. II, No. 10. September 11.

"To Each His Own Computer." 1982. *Newsweek.* February 22.

U.S. Advisory Commission on Public Diplomacy. 1982. *Report on the International Communication Agency.* Washington, D.C. Govt. Printing Office.

U.S. Advisory Commission on Public Diplomacy. 1980. *Report on the International Communication Agency.* Washington, D.C. Govt. Printing Office.

U.S. Department of State. Bureau of Public Affairs. 1976. *U.S. Development in an Interdependent World.* GIST Series. Washington, D.C. March.

U.S. Department of State. Bureau of Public Affairs. 1981. *Soviet Active Measures, Forgery, Disinformation, Political Operations.* Washington, D.C. Special Report No. 88, October.

U.S. Department of State. 1982. *Communist Clandestine Broadcasting.* Foreign Affairs Note. December.

U.S. Dept. of State. Bureau of Public Affairs. 1981. *U.S. Prosperity and the Developing Countries.* GIST Series. June.

U.S. General Accounting Office. 1982. *The Voice of America Should Address Existing Problems to Ensure High Performance.* Report to the Director, U.S. International Communication Agency. July 29. GAO/ID-82-37.

U.S. General Accounting Office. 1982. *U.S. International Communication Agency's Overseas Programs; Some More Useful Than Others.* Report to the Director, USICA. Feb. 11. ID-82-1.

U.S. General Accounting Office. Comptroller General. 1977. *Public Diplomacy in the Years Ahead—An Assessment of Proposals for Reorganization.* Report to the Congress. May 5.

U.S. General Accounting Office. Comptroller General. 1979. *Flexibility—Key to Administering Fulbright-Hays Exchange Program.* Report to the Congress. December 10.

U.S. House of Representatives. Subcommittee on Oversight of the Permanent Select Committee on Intelligence. 1980. *Soviet Covert Action (The Forgery Offensive.)* Hearings. Washington, D.C. Govt. Printing Office.

U.S. House of Representatives. Subcommittee on Oversight of the Permanent Select Committee on Intelligence. 1978. *The CIA and the Media.* Washington, D.C. Govt. Printing Office.

U.S. House of Representatives. Subcommittee on International Operations, Committee on International Operations. 1977. Hearings. *Public Diplomacy and the Future.* (June 8-24.) Washington, D.C. U.S. Govt. Printing Office.

U.S. House of Representatives, Committee on House Administration. 1975. *Computer-Based Information Resources.* Washington, D.C. Govt. Printing Office.

U.S. Information Agency Library. 1976. *A Bibliography*. 2nd Edition. Mimeo.

U.S. Information Agency. 1983. *U.S. Charges Radio Jamming Penalizes Developing Nations*. (Wireless File Article). NESA-204. March 15.

U.S. International Communication Agency. Office of Research. 1981. *Communist International Broadcasting in South Asia in 1980*. December 22.

U.S. International Communication Agency. Office of Research. 1980. *Foreign Cultural and Information Budgets Climb but U.S. Programs Lag in Real Growth*. (A briefing paper.) August 8.

U.S. Information Agency. 1976. *European Libraries & Data Banks*, a study by the Resource and Operations Analysis Staff. Washington, D.C. September.

Wigand, Rolf T. 1980. "The Direct Satellite Connection: Definitions and Prospects," *Journal of Communication*. Spring.

Wilson, James Q. 1981. "Equal Merit, Equal Opportunity," *The Washington Post*. March 4.

INDEX

ABOUT THE AUTHOR

ALLEN C. HANSEN is a 30-year veteran of public diplomacy, having joined the U.S. Information Agency as an officer trainee in 1954 shortly after USIA was established. He has held almost every conceivable position public diplomats fill abroad while serving in eight countries, most recently as Deputy Public Affairs Officer in Islamabad, Pakistan (1981-84). In addition to having been the director of USIA operations in Bolivia (1970-72) and Peru (1976-80), he has also practiced public diplomacy in Venezuela, Mexico, British Guiana (now Guyana), Uruguay, and Spain. His three Washington, D.C. assignments included Caribbean desk officer for USIA at the time of the Dominican crisis in the mid-1960s; USIA policy officer for Latin America (1972-76); and chief of the Latin American branch of USIA's Office of Research (1981).

After serving in the U.S. Navy in World War II and graduating from Syracuse University with a B.A. in political science, he was a newspaper reporter for the Perth Amboy Evening News, Perth Amboy, N.J. before being called back into the navy during the Korean War. In 1962 he received an M.A. degree in American Studies from the University of Pennsylvania. At various times in his career he has performed such diverse roles as textbook translation officer for USIS (Madrid) and as a technical advisor for a USIA film on narcotics trafficking in Latin America. While he has written numerous official communications, this is his first book.